THE COMPLETE ILLUSTRATED BOOK OF THE

ACOUSTIC
GUITAR

THE COMPLETE ILLUSTRATED BOOK OF THE
ACOUSTIC GUITAR

LEARNING TO PLAY • CHORDS • EXERCISES • TECHNIQUES
GUITAR HISTORY • FAMOUS PLAYERS • GREAT GUITARS

JAMES WESTBROOK AND TED FULLER

LORENZ BOOKS

This edition is published by Lorenz Books
an imprint of Anness Publishing Ltd
Blaby Road, Wigston
Leicestershire LE18 4SE
info@anness.com

www.lorenzbooks.com
www.annesspublishing.com

If you like the images in this book and would
like to investigate using them for publishing,
promotions or advertising, please visit our website
www.practicalpictures.com for more information.

Publisher: Joanna Lorenz
Senior Editor: Felicity Forster
Production Controller: Wendy Lawson

Designed and produced for Anness Publishing Ltd
    by Ivy Contract
Project Editors: Jonathan Bastable, Kim Davies,
    Judith Chamberlain-Webber
Editorial Assistant: Georgia Amson-Bradshaw
Art Director: Lisa McCormick
Designer: JC Lanaway

© Anness Publishing Ltd 2012

A CIP catalogue record for this book
is available from the British Library.

PUBLISHER'S NOTE
Although the advice and information in this book
are believed to be accurate and true at the time of
going to press, neither the authors nor the publisher
can accept any legal responsibility or liability for
any errors or omissions that may have been made
nor for any inaccuracies nor for any loss, harm or
injury that comes about from following instructions
or advice in this book.

Contents

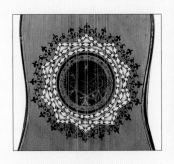

Chordfinder 120

History of the guitar 154

Directory of guitars 172

Introduction

The guitar has become established as an icon of 20th-century music and continues to be the instrument of choice for many popular artists. Though its design has evolved from earlier instruments, and many of its musical advantages are mirrored by the piano, the guitar has several unique features that influence the way its music is created and heard.

History

The ancestry of the modern guitar appears to trace back through many instruments and thousands of years to ancient central Asia. Guitar-like instruments appear in ancient carvings and statues recovered from towns in what is now Iran. There is also an ancient Hittite carving – dating back more than 3,000 years – that depicts an instrument bearing many of the same features as today's guitar.

In the last few hundred years, the guitar has evolved from guitar-like instruments such as the lute, the vihuela and the Baroque guitar into the guitar as we know it today. Its appeal has been so universal that virtually every society throughout history appears to have used a variation of the instrument.

How a guitar works

A member of the family of musical instruments called chordophones, the guitar produces its sound by the plucking of a series of strings running along the instrument's body. While the strings are plucked with one hand, they are simultaneously shortened and lengthened with the other hand against frets, which are metal strips placed on the instrument's neck. The sound that is made is then amplified through a hollow resonating body.

Types of guitar

An acoustic guitar is a guitar that uses only acoustic methods to project the sound produced by its strings, as opposed to electric guitars, which rely on electronic amplification to make their sound audible. There are two main categories of acoustic (non-electric) guitars, which are differentiated by the material used for the strings: gut or nylon-string and steel-string.

Gut or nylon-string guitars include the classical guitar (also called the 'Spanish guitar') as well as the flamenco guitar. The classical guitar is a six-stringed instrument and was established from the designs of the 19th-century Spanish luthier Antonio de Torres. Guitar terminology can be confusing, so the term modern classical guitar is sometimes used to distinguish the classical guitar from older forms of guitar. The sound of this guitar is much more mellow and rounded than a steel-string acoustic, and tends to sound better played with the fingernails.

A steel-string acoustic guitar is a modern form of guitar descended from the classical guitar, but strung with steel strings for a brighter, louder sound. It is often referred to simply as an acoustic guitar, although strictly speaking the nylon-string classical guitar is acoustic as well.

The most common type can be called a flat-top guitar to distinguish it from the more specialized archtop guitar and other variations. steel-string acoustic guitars are used more often in rock, country, blues and also in folk music, and generally are more suited to strumming or playing with a guitar pick than the nylon-string guitar.

LEFT: A woodcut from Luis Milan's Vihuela *book* El Maestro *from 1536, showing Orpheus taming wild beasts with his vihuela.*

ABOVE: An example of a modern-looking nylon-string classical guitar. This one is made by Hernandez y Aguado from Spain.

ABOVE: Plucking the strings of a guitar above the soundhole makes the distinctive sound that has made it such a popular instrument.

Construction of a guitar

Historical and modern acoustic guitars are extremely varied in their design and construction, to a far greater extent than electric guitars. The back and sides of the guitar's body are usually built with East Indian or Brazilian rosewood. Historically, Brazilian rosewood has been the choice of connoisseurs. However, in an attempt to preserve the wood's dwindling supply, the Brazilian government has placed restrictions on its export, thus raising the price and making East Indian rosewood the current wood of choice. Mahogany is sometimes used for steel-string guitars, and maple is nearly always found in archtop guitars.

The top (or soundboard) of the guitar is traditionally constructed of Alpine spruce, although American Sitka spruce has also become popular among manufacturers in the USA. Cedar and redwood are often substituted for spruce, although these woods are soft and can be easily damaged during the construction of a guitar.

The neck, which must resist distortion by the pull of the strings and changes in temperature and humidity, is usually constructed from mahogany or cedar, and joins the body either at the 12th or the 14th frets. Ideally, the fretboard is made of ebony, but rosewood is often used as a cheaper option.

Learning to play

The guitar has long been a popular choice for beginner musicians, partly because of its iconic position in popular culture, and partly because of its inherent virtues, which include portability, great versatility and the availability of reasonable instruments for comparatively little cost. The steel-string acoustic, classical guitar and electric guitar are all closely related (for example, the tuning is usually the same). This means that much of the knowledge that is related to one type of guitar can be of use when playing another, and can even to some extent be transferred to other fretted and stringed instruments such as the banjo or mandolin.

Famous acoustic guitar players

The success of the acoustic guitar has been sustained over the years by many great players, arrangers and composers.

Famous classical guitarists

- Francisco Tárrega (1852–1909)
- Agustín Barrios Mangoré (1888–1944)
- Andrés Segovia (1893–1987)
- Alirio Díaz (b.1923)
- Julian Bream (b.1933)
- John Williams (b.1941)

BELOW: One of the most successful blues/roots musicians of recent years, John Butler's style is gutsy and distinctive.

Famous steel-string guitar players

- John Butler – Roots/Rock
- Joni Mitchell – Folk
- James Taylor – Folk
- Tommy Emmanuel – Country

In this book

This book will guide you through all you need to know to play a guitar, from how to buy the right guitar for you up to mastering advanced blues. 'How to play the guitar' covers the basics of looking after your guitar, playing chords and scales, how to use the fingers and the basics of reading music and more advanced techniques used in blues and jazz. It also introduces the different genres of music played using the guitar. A useful 'Chordfinder' section is included, and a detailed description of the evolution of the guitar is featured in the 'History of the guitar'. Finally, a 'Directory of guitars' explores the many forms of guitar through history up to the modern day in more depth.

ABOVE: Learning the acoustic guitar is a gateway into a musical world of many genres, from blues and ragtime to funk.

Guitar music spans such a wide range of styles that learning to play opens up a whole world of musical possibilities, from rock and jazz through to classical.

How to play the guitar

This chapter will guide you through the basic steps and provides exercises to help you develop your skills. You will discover scales, tuning and chords to get you started in a variety of musical styles.

Buying your guitar

There are several types of acoustic guitar, and the price and quality of new instruments varies widely. Your choice will depend on the style of music you want to play, and on how much you are prepared to pay. The goal is to end up with a reasonably decent guitar that you can begin to learn on.

Choosing a guitar

Acoustic guitars can be broadly divided into two types: the classical (or Spanish) guitar, and the steel-string acoustic guitar. Naturally enough, the classical guitar is mainly associated with classical music and related styles originating from Spain or South America. The tone of a classical guitar is generally softer and gentler than that of a steel-string instrument – although a high-end classical guitar, played with correct technique, can be surprisingly loud.

Until recently, a classical guitar was widely regarded as the natural choice for a beginner, partly because the soft nylon strings are a little kinder to the left-hand fingertips than steel strings. But the idea that classical is best has lost ground. On a technical level, its wide, flat neck makes some chord shapes unnecessarily difficult for small hands (although smaller 'student' models are available).

Generally, most people who take up guitar are more interested in modern styles such as pop and rock than classical, and for this kind of music a steel-string guitar is the natural choice. Other contemporary styles such as country, folk and blues also sound best when played on a steel-string guitar. This kind of guitar is also the best starting point if you aspire to play electric guitar, since these, too, are steel-strung. Many respectable makers produce guitars at various prices, among them Yamaha, Washburn, Ibanez, Takemine, Taylor and Martin.

On the other hand, if you already feel drawn towards classical playing or related styles such as flamenco, a classical guitar may be the best choice for you.

RIGHT: *Classical and steel-string guitars look superficially similar. However, most steel-string acoustics have a larger, squarer body as well as a protective plastic scratchplate.*

Classical guitar

Steel-string guitar

New or used?

The quality of even the lowest-priced instruments available (which are usually produced in the Far East) has improved dramatically in recent years. Although there are always good guitars available on the second-hand market, there are also some very poor ones produced in the years when cheaper guitars were often very badly made. So buying new is usually a safer bet, unless you know what you are doing, or you have a friend who does.

Most reputable guitar shops will check that a new guitar is well 'set up' (meaning that playing action and neck curvature are adjusted for both sound and playing comfort). You should ask whether this has been done or can be done, and think twice about buying from a seller who refuses. Many new instruments will also need to be adjusted after a few months of use (see 'Guitar care'), so you may wish to establish whether this service can be included in the purchase price, or for a modest extra fee.

RIGHT: *Electro-acoustic guitars often feature a cutaway body design for improved access when playing the higher frets.*

FAR RIGHT: *The pre-amp is usually placed here for easy access in the playing position. Controls may include volume, tone shaping, the ability to blend the outputs of more than one pickup, and sometimes even a tuner.*

Electro-acoustic guitars

An electro-acoustic guitar is a steel-string that comes with a built-in pickup (or microphone). This enables the guitar to be directly connected to an amplifier, PA system or recording equipment – in the same way as an electric guitar. Unlike the solid-bodied electric guitar, however, an electro-acoustic is a fully functioning acoustic instrument. It does not require amplification in order to work, and it does not sound like an electric when it is amplified. If you already envisage performing live with your first guitar, or you have access to recording equipment (which can be a valuable practice aid), this choice makes perfect sense.

Accessories

Here is a list of guitar accessories, listed in order of importance:

- Plectrums
- Tuner
- Strap
- Guitar stand
- Case
- Capo

Clip-on tuner

Plectrums

Capos

Strap

Anatomy of the guitar

Guitar making involves a complicated combination of materials, where old-fashioned woodworking techniques meet modern mechanical engineering. Each part of the guitar has a specific function; centuries of accumulated knowledge have resulted in an essentially standardized design for each component. It is useful to understand how these parts work together, in both steel–string and classical guitars.

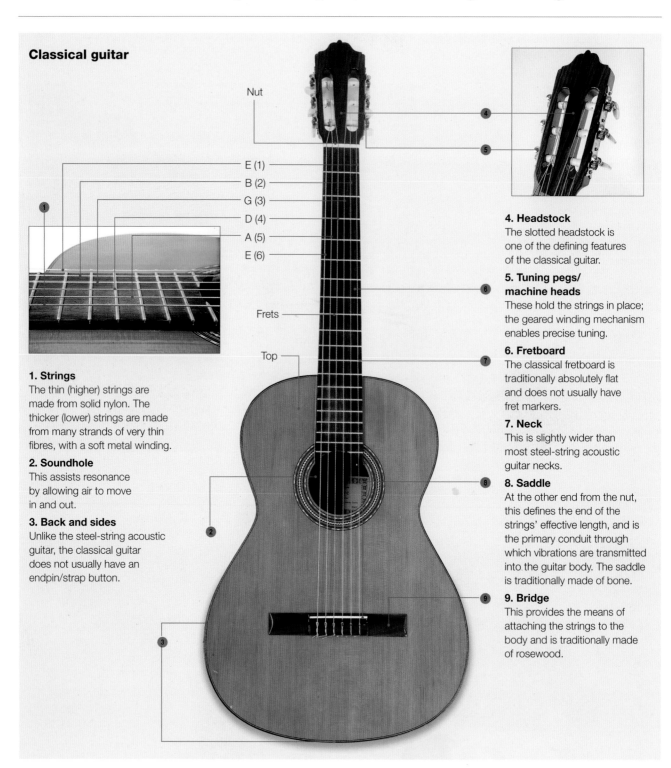

Classical guitar

Nut

E (1)
B (2)
G (3)
D (4)
A (5)
E (6)

Frets

Top

1. Strings
The thin (higher) strings are made from solid nylon. The thicker (lower) strings are made from many strands of very thin fibres, with a soft metal winding.

2. Soundhole
This assists resonance by allowing air to move in and out.

3. Back and sides
Unlike the steel-string acoustic guitar, the classical guitar does not usually have an endpin/strap button.

4. Headstock
The slotted headstock is one of the defining features of the classical guitar.

5. Tuning pegs/ machine heads
These hold the strings in place; the geared winding mechanism enables precise tuning.

6. Fretboard
The classical fretboard is traditionally absolutely flat and does not usually have fret markers.

7. Neck
This is slightly wider than most steel-string acoustic guitar necks.

8. Saddle
At the other end from the nut, this defines the end of the strings' effective length, and is the primary conduit through which vibrations are transmitted into the guitar body. The saddle is traditionally made of bone.

9. Bridge
This provides the means of attaching the strings to the body and is traditionally made of rosewood.

Steel-string acoustic guitar

Headstock

E (1)
A (2)
D (3)
G (4)
B (5)
E (6)

Neck

Saddle

Bridge

1. Strings
These are usually referred to by their sounding pitches ('A string', 'D string'…) and occasionally by number (first, second…). The thicker (lower-sounding) strings are made from a steel core with a winding usually made from another metal or alloy such as bronze. The higher-sounding (thinner) strings are made of plain steel wire.

2. Soundhole
This helps the top to move freely by allowing air to move in and out.

3. Scratchplate
A piece of very thin plastic placed to prevent accidental finger/plectrum contact from damaging the top.

4. Bridge pins
These hold the strings in place at the bridge and may be made of ebony, ivory, bone or plastic.

5. Endpin/strap button
When a strap is used, one end is attached here. On an electro-acoustic guitar (see 'Buying your guitar'), this usually doubles as a jack socket for connecting an audio cable.

6. Tuning pegs/ machine heads
These work exactly the same way as those found on the classical guitar.

7. Nut
A narrow strip of bone or plastic with slots cut for the strings to pass through. The nut holds the strings in place and defines their vibrating length.

8. Fretboard
The neck's playing surface. This area is usually made of a separate piece of dark hardwood such as rosewood. The surface is usually flat but may also be slightly curved.

9. Frets
Thin strips of metal, placed at precisely calculated positions, which govern the pitches of notes produced when the strings are pressed down towards the fretboard and lie on the frets.

10. Fret markers
These dots, usually made of mother-of-pearl or a similar material, allow easy navigation of the fretboard while playing and reduce the risk of accidentally pressing down at the wrong fret.

11. Truss-rod access
The truss-rod is a steel bar inside the neck, which may sometimes require adjustment if the strings buzz. This should only ever be carried out by a professional guitar technician.

12. Top
This is the most important sound-shaping part of the instrument, since it is responsible for translating vibrations from the strings into vibrations in the air (sound). The top is usually made from one or two pieces of thin, tight-grained wood (almost always either spruce or cedar), and is usually reinforced by a system of braces (thin strips of wood) on the inside.

13. Back and sides
These are usually made from the same type of wood. Many different woods are used, including rosewood, mahogany and various exotic African hardwoods such as bubinga and wengé.

Tuning the guitar

For the music you make to sound right, your instrument must be in tune. Guitars go out of tune in the course of being played, and tuning can also be affected by temperature, air pressure, humidity and other external factors. No amount of flashy technique can compensate for a badly tuned instrument; conversely, the simplest ringing chord can sound pleasing if it's perfectly in tune.

What is tuning?

On a guitar, the six strings are tuned, from lowest to highest, to the notes E, A, D, G, B and E. Their pitch is determined partly by the thickness of the string, but also by the degree of tension in the string. Tuning involves adjusting the tension of each string by turning the machine head, or tuning peg, to which it is attached, until the correct pitch is reached. The auditory reference for each string may come from a note on another string, a piano or keyboard, or an electronic tuner.

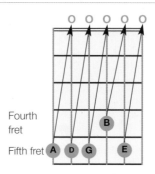

LEFT: *Relative tuning involves tuning each open string with reference to a fretted note on the next lowest string. For perfect results, the low E string still needs to be tuned to an external reference first.*

Relative tuning

To get the guitar in tune with itself, you need to use a process called relative tuning. This means that you can play alone and sing along, however, your guitar may not be in tune with someone else's instrument. Assuming that the bottom E string is in tune, or not far off, the next step is to tune the next string (A) relative to the E string. To do this, play the bottom E string but hold down the note at the fifth fret (see below).

Now play the next string – the open A string. The two notes produced should be the same pitch; the A string should be adjusted up or down until the two notes are the same. Listen for the distinct 'warbling' effect produced when two notes are very nearly, but not exactly, the same pitch. The speed of this warbling will slow down as the notes approach the same pitch, at which point it will disappear.

Now proceed to tune the next string (D) relative to the A string, using exactly the same method. This pattern is repeated until the top E (thinnest) string is in tune, with one exception: the B (second thinnest) string is tuned to the G string's fourth fret.

You may well find that the very act of tightening the higher strings puts the lower strings out of tune. If this happens, there is nothing for it but to begin the process over again, and perhaps again after that. Using this method, eventually you will reach a point where all six strings are simultaneously in tune with each other.

RIGHT: *The low E (6) string, fretted at the fifth fret, produces the note A, which is used as a reference note for tuning the A string.*

Tuning a string

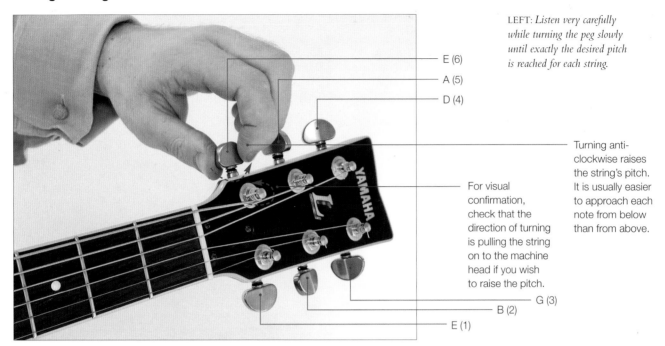

E (6)

A (5)

D (4)

LEFT: Listen very carefully while turning the peg slowly until exactly the desired pitch is reached for each string.

Turning anti-clockwise raises the string's pitch. It is usually easier to approach each note from below than from above.

For visual confirmation, check that the direction of turning is pulling the string on to the machine head if you wish to raise the pitch.

G (3)

B (2)

E (1)

Tuning to a piano or keyboard

If you tune your guitar to a keyboard, especially an electronic one that cannot itself go out of tune, then you are in a position to play with other musicians. As with relative tuning, you use your own ear to arrive at the correct pitch. This is not always easy, but it is good training, a form of musical calisthenics.

First locate bottom E on the keyboard (see diagram right). Play the note on the keyboard, and while it is ringing in the air, pluck your open E string and manipulate the machine head to find the same pitch. This will take several attempts. Once the E is pitched right, adjust each string very slowly, listening as you go, to avoid the possibility of tuning far too high and breaking a string.

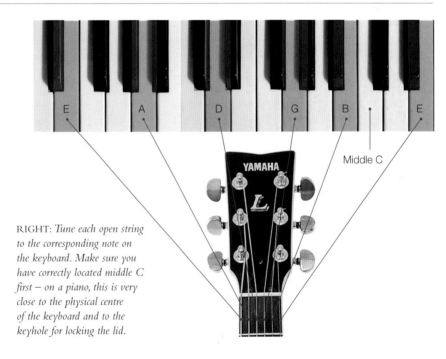

E A D G B E

Middle C

RIGHT: Tune each open string to the corresponding note on the keyboard. Make sure you have correctly located middle C first – on a piano, this is very close to the physical centre of the keyboard and to the keyhole for locking the lid.

RIGHT: This type of tuner is very popular and has an integrated microphone as well as an input socket, allowing an electro-acoustic to be connected directly. It can be very useful for tuning in noisy environments.

Using a tuner

You can take the effort out of tuning by investing in an electronic tuner. Some guitar tuners are restricted to tuning the open strings of a six-string guitar in standard tuning. Others, known as chromatic tuners, are far more useful in that they allow tuning to any note within a large part of the musical spectrum, giving guitarists access to alternative tunings (see 'Altered tunings'). Some chromatic tuners can also be switched to 'guitar mode'.

Changing strings

Guitar strings inevitably pick up moisture from the player's hands. This has a corrosive effect on the strings, which grow dirty over time. Dirt on the strings dulls the sound of the guitar, and makes them more likely to break. So sooner or later, you will have to change a single string and eventually you will need to change the whole set. Just like guitar playing, changing strings is a skill that requires practice.

Choosing strings

You should change your strings from time to time, as soon as you notice that they have become lacklustre. It is a tedious task, but worth the effort, because new strings sound bright and zingy, and feel great under your fingers.

It is important to get the right type of strings: nylon for classical guitars, steel otherwise. Do not under any circumstances try to fit steel strings to a classical guitar: they exert far too much pressure, and are then likely to damage the neck of your guitar.

Steel strings come in different thicknesses or 'gauges'. The gauge of the strings that came with your guitar can be looked up on the manufacturer's website. But there is nothing to stop you from trying a different gauge. Medium or heavy strings have a full sound with lots of volume. Light or extra-light strings are easier to press down, and so are not so punishing for the fingertips, but they sound both quieter and thinner.

ABOVE: *A new string stretches, and so goes flat after a few minutes' playing, so you may need re-tune* *repeatedly at first. But you can speed up the stretching process by tugging the string towards you a few times.*

Changing a classical guitar string

Pass the string through the bridge from the soundhole side, then loop the string around itself at the point of entry. Now wrap the end around the string two or three times on the top side of the bridge for extra friction (some players omit this step for the wound strings). Finally, tuck the end under the looped string behind the bridge and pull tight. Pass the other end of the string through the hole in the machine head roller, again twisting the string around itself to ensure that that it does not continually slip out of tune. Remember to leave the string slack enough to allow it to be wound around the roller several times, but try to avoid leaving so much that an ugly 'ball of wool' effect is created.

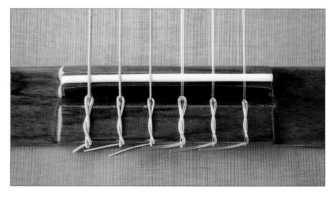

ABOVE: *Classical guitar strings secured at the bridge. There should* *be enough twists that the string is held in place by friction.*

A string winder

This useful gadget speeds up the laborious process of winding strings by hand. Most players favour a combination winder/cutter tool that can be used to trim the end of the string after it has been wound on to the machine head. The cutter also helps when removing strings.

LEFT: *This winder/cutter also has a third function: the small notch at the end of the winder is the perfect shape for removing bridge pins (right).*

Changing steel strings

Many players replace all six strings at once. This provides an excellent opportunity for you to clean and polish those parts of the guitar that are hard to reach with the strings in place.

As a beginner, you may, however, find it useful to replace one string at a time, using the old strings as a guide to help you get the new ones attached correctly.

1 The string is anchored to the bridge by means of an ivory or plastic pin. This must be removed in order to free the string. Some string trimmers incorporate a tool to do this; if not, you need to push the pin out from inside the guitar using a hard object such as a coin.

2 Fasten the new string to the bridge using the same bridge pin. One end of each string is attached to a steel ring, known as a ball end. Feed this end into the hole in the bridge, insert the pin and pull on the string until you feel that the ball end is anchored firmly.

3 Feed the other end through the hole in the machine head. Make a kink in the string on the far side of the hole, leaving enough slack to enable the string to be wound four or five times around the machine head before it is tight. This can be hard to estimate; if in doubt, leave more slack rather than less. Slowly wind the string anti-clockwise until it is tight enough to sound a note.

4 Trim the end of the string, leaving about 10mm/ ½in protruding from the headstock. Tuck this down-wards, but make sure the end doesn't make contact with the guitar headstock. Trimmed ends pointing upwards will tear the inside of a soft guitar case to shreds, while a string that touches the headstock may gouge a groove around the machine head.

Guitar care

Your guitar is a machine for making music, and like all machines it requires careful handling as well as a certain amount of maintenance. Look after your guitar properly, and you will be helping to keep it sounding like new as well as protecting your investment. Above all, take some basic steps to make sure that it does not get damaged beyond repair. Most tasks are fairly easy and require no specialist equipment.

Protection

If you are planning to take your guitar anywhere, some form of case is essential. The very cheapest soft cases offer little or no protection against knocks. A padded soft case, known as a 'gig bag', is a much better option if you want to protect your guitar by a sensible minimum. Gig bags usually have backpack straps as well as carrying handles, which makes them a good way of transporting your guitar on foot over short distances. A hard case is a more cumbersome solution but it is a safer choice – particularly for car travel.

Waterproof outer

External pockets

Back strap

Accessory compartment

LEFT: *A padded gig bag with backpack straps and useful external pockets.*

Neck support

Soft 'velvet' lining

All-round protection

Secure clasps

Hard exterior shell

ABOVE/LEFT: *Hard guitar cases may be heavier and more difficult to transport, but they will ensure that your instrument is properly protected.*

Guitar stands

Most damage to guitars occurs for want of one simple accessory: a guitar stand. If you do just one thing to look after your guitar, buy a stand. Countless instruments have been spoiled as a result of falling down while propped up against a wall or a chair. It stands to reason that you should keep your guitar in the house (not the garage or the shed), and that you should not expose it to direct sunlight if possible. Keep it in a shady room, and avoid playing outdoors too much (enjoyable as that is). While a stand is useful if you wish to pick the guitar up and put it down several times a day, putting it back in its case for longer periods will prevent it from gathering too much dust or getting accidentally damaged.

RIGHT/FAR RIGHT: This guitar stand holds the neck of the guitar in place and gives some support to the body.

Cleaning

It is important to keep your guitar clean. A good time for a spring clean is when you change the strings, because this presents an excellent opportunity to clean areas that are otherwise impossible to reach.

The area between the bridge and soundhole tends to gather dust, as does the headstock. This is best removed using a soft cloth. The mysterious gunk that builds up under the strings can also clog up the fretboard. This should not be scraped off directly, as fretboard damage may result, but gently wiped instead. Most music shops carry guitar polish, which will help with general cleaning without damaging the guitar's finish.

The useful life of your guitar strings can be extended by wiping them down after playing – especially underneath each string, where dirt tends to accumulate very easily.

RIGHT: Use a soft cloth that is thin enough to pass under the strings without getting stuck.

When to get help

Some maintenance tasks should be left to professional technicians. One clear sign that you should take your guitar to the mender's is a problem called fret buzz.

If one or more note on your guitar produces a nasty buzzing sound instead of a clean note, that is a symptom of a problem that needs technical help (see box on the right for more details).

The solution will probably involve adjusting the truss-rod, which is embedded inside the neck. It is important to note that attempting this yourself could make matters worse or even possibly lead to permanent damage if it is not tackled properly.

Fixing fret buzz

If a buzzing sound is produced, one of the following procedures may be required to correct it.

Truss-rod adjustment: The neck of a steel-string acoustic guitar is reinforced with a steel rod under the fretboard. The tension in the truss rod is adjusted in order to balance the tension in the strings to result in the correct curved neck shape. This is a skilled and delicate task, and incorrect adjustment can easily make things worse. Do not attempt it at home!

Fret dress: Guitar frets can become worn with use. This can often manifest as small dips or notches in the most frequently fingered frets. The procedure, known as 'fret dressing', involves removing these dips by filing all the frets on the fretboard so that they are once again uniformly smooth, while maintaining equal height. As with fixing the truss-rod, this is no job for the amateur.

Refret: After many fret dresses, the frets may eventually have to be removed and replaced.

Holding the guitar

Classical guitarists and teachers tend to follow exact rules for posture and hand positions, but most acoustic guitarists in other styles like to be a little more relaxed. The most important thing when you sit down with your guitar is to find a comfortable playing position – but make sure that you don't fall into any bad habits that might be hard to shake off later on.

Sitting and standing positions

While many guitarists perform standing up, you will probably want to practise the guitar sitting down at first. For a right-handed player, the guitar rests comfortably on the right thigh. Your legs should not be crossed. The whole length of the neck of the guitar is then within easy reach of the left hand.

The position of the guitar when you are in a comfortable sitting position serves as a rule of thumb for strap adjustment if you wish to play standing up. When standing, the strap should be adjusted so that sitting down has little effect on the tension of the strap. If the strap goes completely slack when you move from standing to sitting, it is definitely too low. Many rock guitarists wear the guitar very low when standing. For the purposes of learning to play, this pose should be avoided since as well as being uncomfortable, it is likely to cause injury to the back and the left wrist.

RIGHT: *A comfortable seated position for a right-handed player. Using a strap, even when sitting, may help to prevent the guitar from sliding off the thigh.*

ABOVE: *This position is about right for playing while standing. The guitar is held at the correct height, avoiding injury to the back and wrist.*

ABOVE: *Here, the guitar is worn too low. This makes good technique difficult for both hands, and can also result in back strain.*

ABOVE: *Wearing the guitar too high is equally inadvisable, for similar reasons to wearing it too low, and also looks rather silly.*

The position of the hands

If you are right-handed, you finger the strings with the left hand and pick or strum with the right. If you are left-handed, the roles of the hands are reversed. The right arm of a right-handed player rests lightly on the bulge of the guitar's body, so that the hand is poised over the soundhole. The left hand holds the neck of the guitar and frets the strings (we will be looking at the position of the left hand for right-handers in detail on the following pages).

For now, we will concentrate on playing with a pick or plectrum in the right hand (we will come to finger-style technique later). The plectrum is held in the right hand, usually between the thumb and index finger. The plectrum should protrude around 5mm (¼in) beyond the end of the index finger. It should not be so exposed that it flaps around noticeably when you are strumming. How tightly it is held is a matter of personal preference and style – but you should hold it firmly enough so that it does not fly out of your hand when you play a big chord.

ABOVE: *The plectrum in position, ready to play. For optimal control, try to avoid having any more of the plectrum protruding from between the fingers than shown here.*

1 Position the thumb and index finger in a 'T' shape.

2 Place the plectrum on the finger with the point facing downwards.

3 The angle of the plectrum depends on the shape of your hands.

Strumming

The strumming technique is the simplest of all right-hand movements. It involves playing several strings, often all six, in rapid succession using a fluid arm movement. This may come from the elbow or wrist, depending on the playing style. We will start by learning to strum from the elbow – just doing downward strokes for now.

Holding the plectrum as described above, bring the right forearm downwards across the strings in a fluid motion. The plectrum should make contact with all six strings in sequence. Reverse this motion, bringing the arm upwards towards its starting position but *without striking the strings*. Repeat this entire cycle – down and up – trying to keep your arm moving rhythmically and regularly.

ABOVE: *The plectrum should make contact with all six strings in rapid sequence in order to make a single sound rather than separate notes.*

ABOVE: *Reverse this motion, bringing the arm upwards towards its starting position but without striking the strings.*

EXERCISE STRUMMING

This exercise involves strumming continuously and – most importantly – in time. The simplest device available to help you learn how to strum properly is a metronome, which helps you to keep time by producing a clicking sound at evenly timed intervals.

If you have a metronome, set it to **60 beats per minute**. However, if you don't have one, you can keep an eye on the second hand of a watch or clock to perform the same function.

Now strum the guitar in time with the metronome or watch (once per click, or once per second).

Experiment with making some strums deliberately louder than others (usually each '1' strum should be a little louder, but try 1 and 3, and also 2 and 4 for slightly different effects).

Basic left-hand technique

The job of the left hand is to push the strings on to the fretboard so as to alter their pitch by shortening their active length. Generally, the thumb is anchored at the back of the guitar's neck in order to provide leverage to the pressure of the fingers at the front. These basics are fundamentally the same for all playing styles, although some styles require stricter 'rules' than others.

Thumb position

Classical guitar teachers insist that the thumb of the left hand never strays from an imaginary line down the very centre of the neck. In this, as in other matters of technique, classical players are the sticklers. As a matter of playing style, most rock and folk players allow the thumb to move upwards from the classical position, and even occasionally to wrap around in order to help form chords. The thumb should never be allowed to drift below the centre line, however, as this makes it harder to form chords, while providing no balancing pressure. Likewise, the thumb should be kept roughly perpendicular to the neck and not allowed to stray sideways.

ABOVE: *Classical thumb position – the thumb is positioned squarely at the centre of the neck, and does not stray from this position.*

ABOVE: *Rock thumb position – the thumb is allowed to move up around the back of the neck, and occasionally even over on to the fretboard.*

ABOVE: *Poor thumb position – the thumb position here is too low, resulting in loss of pressure and control.*

Finger position

When fretting a note, the finger presses the string down to make contact with a fret so that its vibrating length is reduced. Generally speaking, the finger should not be positioned directly above the fret, but rather just behind it. The further the finger is allowed to stray back from the active fret, the greater the finger pressure required. Sometimes there are two or even three fingers positioned on adjacent strings in the same fret, in which case one or more fingers has to be further back. Try to listen out for the buzzing of the string, which is the sound that may be produced if the finger is too far from the active fret.

ABOVE: *Good finger position – the finger is placed as close as possible to the active fret, but not actually on top of it, producing a clean note.*

ABOVE: *Poor finger position: here, the finger is too far away from the fret, which is likely to result in a buzz rather than a clean sound.*

Left-hand nails

The nails of the left hand should be cut as short as possible. This is one point on which it is unfortunately not possible to compromise: long nails will prevent you from fretting notes properly and can also damage the guitar's fretboard. Right-hand fingernails can be allowed to grow, however. Finger-style players and classical guitarists pay considerable attention to their right-hand fingernails.

Chords and chord boxes

When two or more notes are played together on the guitar (or any other instrument), the result is called a chord. Many songbooks use chord symbols (G, C, F7, C#13…) on the assumption that you will know how to play each named chord. Guitar books often provide additional help in the form of a chord box (or fret box) that tells you exactly where to place your fingers. This takes the form of a grid where six vertical lines represent the guitar's six strings; horizontal lines represent the frets. Dots represent the fingers. In this book and other beginners' books, the dots are numbered to tell you which finger to use: 1 is the index finger, 2 the middle finger, and so on. An 'X' placed above a string means this string is not played; 'O' tells us that the open string is played.

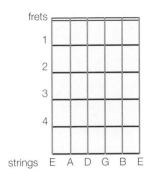

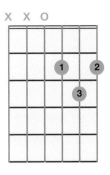

ABOVE: *This empty chord box is labelled to show the names of the strings along the bottom and the fret numbers up the left-hand side of the box, for reference.*

ABOVE: *On this chord box, the finger dots are added, which tell you exactly where to place the left-hand fingers. Finger numbering starts from the index finger.*

Forming the D major chord

Our first chord is the chord of D major, usually known simply as 'D'.

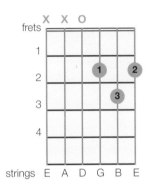

1 Study the chord box. All the information enabling you to form this chord is contained here.

2 Use the first finger (1) to fret the G string at the second fret.

3 Use the second finger (2) to fret the top E string at the second fret.

4 Use the third finger (3) to fret the B string at the third fret.

EXERCISE D CHORD

Try strumming the D chord, lifting the fingers and strumming the open strings, then making the D shape again as you continue to strum. The more frequently you have to form a chord shape, the more quickly and easily you will be able to do it. Later, you can add other chords while still maintaining this approach.

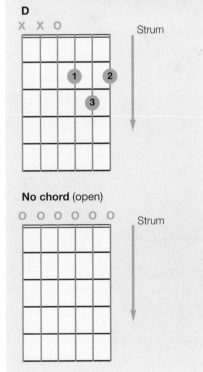

D

Strum

No chord (open)

Strum

Strumming with three chords

One of your first tasks as an aspiring guitarist is to build up a vocabulary of chords. The more chords you know, the more songs you will be able to play in various moods and keys. At the same time, a surprising number of pop, folk and country songs can be played with a repertoire of just three related chords, universally known as the 'three-chord trick'. These three shapes are easier in some musical keys than others.

Tackling the C, D and G chords

You already know D; the two chords that you are about to tackle are G and C. These three chords occur together in the key of G. Once you can play these three chords fluently, you will be in a position to unlock a vast treasure house of popular music – songs as diverse as "Twist and Shout", "Breakfast at Tiffany's", "This Land is Your Land", "Mr Tambourine Man", "Peggy Sue" and "Wild Thing" – and the addition of just a few more chords will give you access to an even greater variety.

C

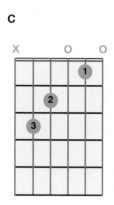

The C chord requires the use of three fingers, each at a different fret. This is a relatively easy shape, because the fingers are not crowded together. Remember, 'X' indicates that the low E string does not sound – in simple playing styles, this is achieved by starting each strum from the next string.

G

The G chord involves the full width of the fretboard: you have to fret both the top and the bottom string at once. This will probably present a challenge at first. If you find yourself really struggling to get your fingers into this shape, there is an easier version using just one finger (see Easy G below).

Easy G

As with the D chord, the bottom two strings are not played here. If you fall back on this shape at first, resist the temptation to use a different finger (the fourth finger does at least help towards the goal of perfecting the full shape), and do remember to practise the full G shape, as the easy version, while fine for strumming, will be less useful for more advanced playing styles.

Changing between chords

Almost all 'real' songs involve frequent chord changes, which you have to perform while maintaining a strict tempo. This will seem like an impossible feat at first, but the key is to start slowly. One way of getting used to making chord changes at speed is to practise moving between them in as many combinations as possible:

G	→	C	→	D
G	→	D	→	C
C	→	D	→	G
D	→	C	→	G

This will seem hard to start with, but don't worry if it takes a while before it becomes anywhere near fluent. The key is to do it very slowly at first and build up the tempo as you get faster at the changes. Aim for minimal movement of the fingers, for example, when moving the first and second fingers between the G and C shapes.

EXERCISE **FIRST THREE-CHORD PIECE**

Now you can attempt chord changes at a real-life tempo, in time with your strumming. The diagram below is a simple strumming instruction. The downward arrows indicate downward strums (there are other symbols that we will come to later). The vertical lines indicate the beginning and end of a bar. In this piece, as in a large proportion of Western music, there are four beats in each bar, as indicated by the $\frac{4}{4}$ symbol (this is called the time signature).

Set your metronome to 60 beats per minute. Strum down with each beat, trying to change to the chords as shown above the line as you strum. If you find yourself struggling to change chords cleanly or in time, try playing just one strum per bar: let the chord ring for as long as possible while counting through the bar. The most important thing is that whatever you do choose to play, however busy or sparse, it should be played in time.

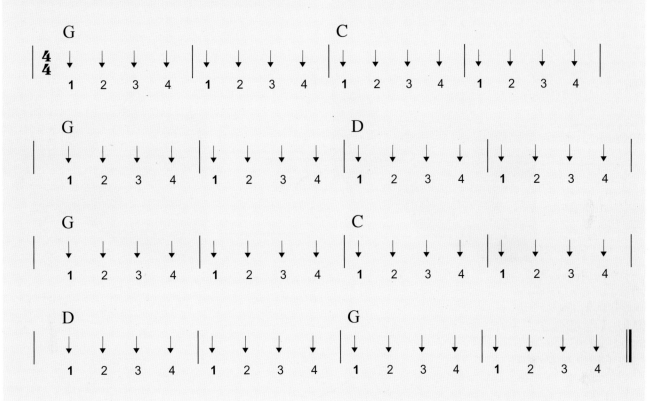

Bob Dylan

A much better guitarist and all-round musician than he is usually given credit for, Bob Dylan is a master of the craft of simple songwriting, often using only three or four chords to underpin some of the most memorable songs of the 20th century. Dylan's guitar playing and early songwriting were both heavily influenced by his hero Woody Guthrie, whose spirit can be felt in the lyrical themes, vocal mannerisms and guitar style of early albums such as *The Freewheelin' Bob Dylan* and *The Times They Are A-Changin'*. Seen as the leading figure of the American folk music revival of the early '60s, Bob Dylan triggered a surge in the popularity of the acoustic guitar across the world. The Beatles, Rolling Stones and other major acts of the time were all drawn to incorporate 'folky' elements into their records as a direct result of Dylan's success.

ABOVE: *Bob Dylan with a Dreadnought acoustic guitar in the early 1960s.*

More chords and strumming

You will greatly expand the number of songs you can play in G by adding two chords to your repertoire: E minor and A minor, usually abbreviated as Em and Am. Notice that these chords have a different character from the first three, which were all major chords. Minor chords are often said to sound 'sad', but they are actually much more expressive than is suggested by that simple description.

E minor and A minor

These chord diagrams and photographs show how to make E minor and A minor. They are both fairly easy shapes to make. What is more, it is not difficult to move between the two.

When changing from Em to Am, fingers 2 and 3 move across one string together. As they arrive at strings 3 and 4, the first finger will naturally be poised to come into play on the second string, first fret.

Am

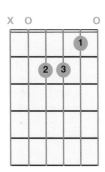

ABOVE: *The Am chord has two fretted notes in common with the C chord; when changing between the two, only the third finger need move.*

Em

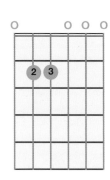

ABOVE: *The Em chord is a relatively simple shape as it requires only two fingers – usually the second and third as shown here.*

Four-chord sequence

The exercises on these pages will help you get used to playing these new chords in combination with the ones you have already learnt, but first try this progression, which involves C, G, D and Em.

| G | Em | C | D |

Like the three-chord trick, this four-chord sequence (here in the key of G) has been used in hundreds of songs. It is known as the '50s sequence' or "Stand by Me", after one of the many songs which use it. Others include "Every Breath You Take", "Earth Angel", "Up on the Roof" and "I've Just Seen a Face". Once you have looked at the strumming exercises, come back and try singing along to some of those songs while you play.

EXERCISE 1

In this exercise you will be applying the simplest downstroke-upstroke strumming pattern to the E minor chord you learnt earlier.

Make sure that you are strumming downwards on the beat (1, 2, 3, 4) and upwards on the offbeat (each 'and'), not the other way round.

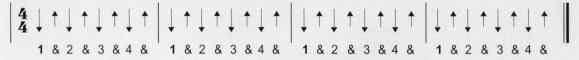

Strumming upwards

One way to use these new chords in more musically interesting ways is to expand the strumming technique at your disposal. So far we have used down strums only. Deliberately missing the strings on the way up again actually requires extra effort, so adding up strums in between should come fairly naturally. In most strumming styles, down strums are used on the beat, while up strums are used in between beats, otherwise known as the offbeat. In other words, staying with our metronome click of 60 beats per minute, we would play down strums in time with the click, and up strums exactly halfway between clicks. By convention, this is counted as follows: '1 and 2 and 3 and 4 and 1 and 2 and 3 and 4 and…'. Practise the exercise shown here until you feel intuitively comfortable with it.

1 Strum downwards across all of the strings that need to be used in the chord shape.

2 Now strum upwards. Up strums between down strums are usually a little lighter/softer than the down strums. Repeat steps 1 and 2.

EXERCISE 2

Offbeats with missed up strums are shown in brackets below the arrows. Don't play the upstrokes shown in grey type: they are there just to show you which direction your hand should be going at that point. The important thing is that the right hand should always move downwards on the beat, and upwards on the offbeat, whether strumming or not. It may help to tap your foot on the beat and imagine that your right hand and foot are connected by an invisible string.

EXERCISE 3

The following piece makes use of all five chords encountered so far, and incorporates various combinations of the above strumming patterns.

We have dispensed with the grey arrows: you should now know instinctively which way your strumming hand should be moving.

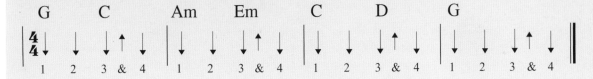

Syncopated strumming

All your strumming so far has involved playing downstrokes on the beat, plus upstrokes on one or more offbeats. But it is also possible to create different patterns where the downstrokes are missed out, and the offbeat is accented. This effect is known as syncopation; it is common in many styles of music from classical to dance music, and it is subtly present in most pop rhythm playing.

Using syncopation

To understand syncopation, start by counting quavers (half beats) in $\frac{4}{4}$ time: '1 and 2 and 3 and 4 and…'. Now modify this so that the offbeats ('and') are louder, while the beats are barely muttered: '(1) AND (2) AND (3) AND (4) AND…'. This accent on the offbeat is so prevalent in most jazz melodies and solos, for example, that removing it would make them sound strangely wooden.

Other styles characterized by heavy syncopation include jive and ska, which simply would not work without it. Many familiar pop songs are driven by less obvious syncopation: the 'recommended listening' examples listed in the box opposite are all memorable mainly because of syncopated strumming patterns which manage to bring to life otherwise very ordinary-sounding chord sequences. In some styles, the presence of bass and drums means that the guitar can play offbeats only, but this does not really work when the guitar is played on its own.

Recommended listening:
- George Harrison: "My Sweet Lord"
- Oasis: "Wonderwall"
- Paul Simon: "Me and Julio Down by the Schoolyard", "Kodachrome"

Two new chords

Before you practise some simple syncopated strumming, take this opportunity to enlarge your chord vocabulary with two new chords: E major and A major.

These, together with the chords learnt already, make several new keys available on the guitar. Any three-chord song can be played in the key of A using the chords A, D and E.

E

A

You will notice that the E major chord is the same shape as the A minor chord, but played on different strings. This is convenient, since a change from E to Am and then back again is a very common progression.

When changing between them, try not to break up the shape of your hand as it moves across the strings; instead, aim to lift the whole shape smoothly off the strings and then place in the new position. This chord may also be viewed as the same shape as Em, but with the index finger added to turn it into a major chord. Try alternating between the two to highlight the difference between major and minor qualities.

The A major chord is slightly unusual in that three fingers are placed at the same fret. If you have large hands, it can be difficult to squeeze the fingers together for this shape. Although the chord box represents all three fingers in a straight line, this is physically impossible; in reality, the three fingers form a diagonal back from the second fret, with the index finger furthest away.

If you do have large hands, you may continue to find this shape difficult. Later, you may wish to try another way to fret these three notes, using just one finger (see 'Barre chords'). For now, some perseverance may be necessary.

Syncopated strumming patterns

As with all the downstroke–upstroke patterns that you have already encountered thus far, it is crucial that the right hand should move down on the beat and up on the offbeat, whether striking the strings or not. If you find yourself playing upstrokes on the beat, or downstrokes on the offbeat, it may help to tap your foot on the beat and imagine that your right hand and foot are connected by an invisible string.

Repeat symbols

The symbols |: and :| found in these exercises are repeat marks. They are often encountered in standard music notation and tablature (see 'Guitar notation'), and unless accompanied by further instructions or symbols, they simply mean 'play everything between these symbols twice'. Musical pieces often repeat, so this is a way of saving space on the page.

EXERCISE 1

This exercise explores some possible syncopated patterns. Ghosted (missed) strokes are greyed out, and shown in brackets on the counting line.

Remember, it essential to maintain consistent down/up motion, whether striking or missing the strings – anything else will prevent the development of fluid strumming.

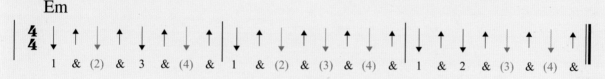

EXERCISE 2

This sequence uses a one-bar syncopated pattern created by missing the downstrokes on beats two and four. This works well when playing with a drummer, as the snare drum is usually played on these beats.

For an even more syncopated effect, the down strum on beat 3 may also be ghosted; in this case, the down strum on beat 1 should be made louder so that the ear can still identify a clear downbeat in the rhythm.

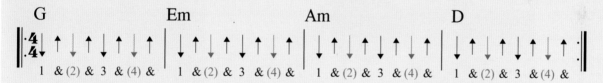

EXERCISE 3

The first beat of the second bar is the only missing downstroke in this two-bar pattern. Set your metronome to a comfortable speed and concentrate on maintaining the rhythm of each piece in time with the click; gradually increase this speed.

Try working up from 60 to 90 beats per minute with these exercises. For added colour, try changing the Em chord to E major the second time through. Coming after Am, this would lend the sequence a slightly Spanish flavour.

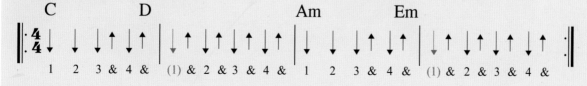

Seventh chords

Major and minor chords are the main building blocks of most Western music, but there is another essential type of chord, the dominant seventh (usually known simply as the seventh, written as E7, for example). It is formed by adding a fourth note to the basic three. This additional note is most easily found by playing the note a whole tone below the root note of the chord.

The importance of seventh chords

Dominant seventh chords have a darker, richer sound than ordinary major or minor chords; this is because they contain four unique notes rather than three. In classical music, the dominant seventh is only carefully used in certain contexts, but in all these styles it is almost ubiquitous, and our ears have become very used to it.

To form the seventh of G, you add an F to the G, B and D – because F is one tone below G. To play F7, you add an E♭ (meaning 'E flat') to F, A and C, because E♭ is one tone below F. The simple addition of one note can totally alter the character of the harmony. Play any dominant seventh, and

you will hear that the ear (and the heart) yearns for it to go somewhere else: there is a tension built into the sound that needs to be resolved by its going 'home' to another chord.

For this reason, the dominant seventh chord is crucial to all Western harmony, particularly to the sound of the blues and all styles derived from it, including jazz and rock 'n' roll. Its unresolved nature means that it often functions as a pivot chord when changing keys. And it is no secret where sevenths want to go. They resolve as shown below.

E7   ⟶   A (or Am)

A7   ⟶   D (or Dm)

D7   ⟶   G (or Gm)

G7   ⟶   C (or Cm)

BELOW: *First-position seventh chords are all easy to learn, because their shapes are closely related to the major chord shapes. Here are four of the most common sevenths. Learn the shapes, and try them out in various combinations with the chords that you already know.*

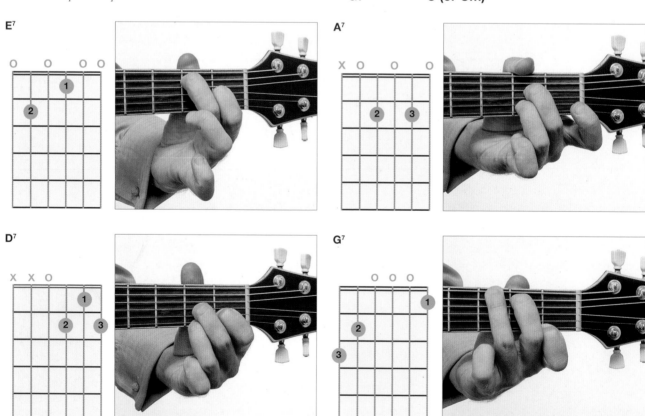

The least movement principle

Sevenths are a good illustration of the 'least movement principle'. In order to move from one chord to the next as cleanly and efficiently as possible, it is important not to make the fingers of the left hand do more work than necessary. For example, the second and third fingers need not move at all when changing from G to G7. And when changing from E to E7, the third finger is simply lifted while the first and second fingers stay in place. For many other chord changes, one or more fingers may slide between frets on the same string while the other fingers move around. For an example not involving sevenths, try moving from A to D. The first finger stays on the B string but slides from the second fret to the third fret: no need to lift it. But finger pressure should be relaxed when doing this so that the slide is not audible (and so as to avoid hurting your fingertips).

James Taylor

This artist would figure near the top of any list of influential singer/songwriters; he was at the height of his success in the early '70s. His successful *Greatest Hits* album sold more than 11 million copies and burned deeply personal yet instantly memorable songs such as "Fire and Rain" and "Carolina in My Mind" into the hearts of a generation, along with definitive versions of other writers' songs, including Carole King's "You've Got a Friend". Many of Taylor's best-known songs are written around his own highly accomplished fingerstyle guitar playing, which combines elements of jazz harmony with country/folk roots.

RIGHT: *Most critics agree that James Taylor is one of the finest acoustic guitarists in the world.*

EXERCISE

This exercise uses syncopated strumming patterns, and also mixes seventh chords with some of the major and minor shapes learnt previously. All of the seventh chords here either resolve to a major/minor chord or form part of a sequence that eventually resolves. They are a good way to become acquainted with the eloquent effect that can be achieved with just a few standard chords. The exercise also use a new key signature: $\frac{3}{4}$ i.e. 3 beats in the bar.

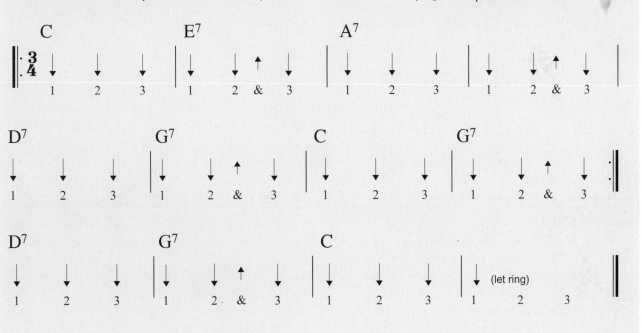

Guitar notation

Guitar music can be written down in a number of different ways. One is the strumming system that we have already looked at – but those arrowed diagrams can only express whole chords. They are not suited for putting melodies down on paper, or even for complex rhythms. For these tasks, there is standard music notation and also a specifically guitar-based notational system called tablature.

Standard music notation

The best way of understanding standard notation is to think of it as a kind of musical alphabet. It is a way of writing down any note of any length, any combination of notes (chords), as well as the gaps between them. It also includes ways of indicating the manner in which the notes should be played – loudly, softly, slurred together or crisply distinct.

Standard notation uses a system of five horizontal lines, called the stave (or staff), to represent musical pitch (how high or low each note is). In most cases, the lines – and the spaces between them – represent steps of one tone up or down. The adjacent pairs B-C and E-F span only a semitone (half a tone).

Most guitar music, in common with most melodic music, is written in the so-called treble clef – also known as the G clef. This is simply a way of indicating which note corresponds to which line. In the G clef, the second line from the bottom represents the note G, and is indicated by an elaborate stylized G anchored on that line, thus: 𝄞. All the other notes can then be worked out from that one: the bottom line must be E, the space above F, and so on.

The other component of standard notation is rhythm. The appearance of each note tells us its rhythmic value – how long it is in terms of beats or parts of a beat. A crotchet is usually used to denote one beat; a minim is two beats long; a quaver half a beat long. (Different terms are used in American English – see the chart below.) A corresponding set of symbols is used to indicate rests – gaps or silences – of specified lengths. All of the note values in any bar must add up to the total defined by the time signature. The chart below gives all the basic symbols with their values in $\frac{4}{4}$ time (four beats in a bar).

BELOW: *Note values in British and American English. The majority of Western music can be notated using very little else.*

Music notation: the basics

Single note	Group	Note name (UK)	Note name (US)	Duration in $\frac{4}{4}$	Rest
o	-	semibreve	whole note	4 beats	▬
♩ (minim)	-	minim	half note	2 beats	▬
♩	-	crotchet	quarter note	1 beat	𝄽
♪	♫	quaver	eighth note	½ beat	𝄾
♬	♬♬	semiquaver	sixteenth note	¼ beat	𝄿

Finding the notes

The beauty of standard notation is that it is universal; the music written for one instrument can usually be played on any other. A violinist or pianist who can read music can play a piece written for the guitar, and vice versa.

One thing this system doesn't tell you on its own is where to find these notes on the guitar. Many instruments, such as keyboards and wind instruments, have just one place to find each note. On the guitar, any given note can often be found in two, three or four places on the fretboard. As a result, playing from standard musical notation is harder for guitarists than for some other instrumentalists, because they have to work out for themselves where to put their fingers.

This is often used as a lazy excuse for not learning to read music at all, but getting to understand musical notation is something that all guitarists will benefit from doing.

David Gray

Few musicians have successfully crossed over from the British folk scene to international chart success, and none have done this as spectacularly as David Gray. More important than this transition, however, is Gray's success in combining many of the hallmarks of the acoustic folk sound with elements of contemporary pop production: layers of guitars, often using open tunings and making prominent use of the capo (raising the guitar's pitch for sonic effect), combined with drum loops and synth washes in a musical blend. Gray succeeded in achieving prominence in the late '90s music scene, which was dominated by electric Britpop and bleeping electronica.

ABOVE: *David Gray has played a leading role in returning acoustic sounds to the pop mainstream.*

ABOVE: *Most beginners start playing the guitar simply by strumming – but guitar music, like any form of music, can be read and played from the page.*

Tablature

There is a notational system designed specifically for the guitar, which is known as tablature, often abbreviated to TAB. It does the very thing that standard notation cannot: it tells you exactly where to place your fingers in order to play each note. Tablature looks superficially like standard notation in that it is written on a stave-like set of horizontal lines. However, the six lines of the tablature stave represent not pitch, but the strings of the guitar. A number placed on a given line indicates that the string in question should be played at the specified fret.

As with standard notation, you scan left to right – playing the notes in the order in which they occur. In the example below, three notes are played on the bottom E string: on the third fret, the second fret and finally the open string indicated by a zero (0). Chords are shown vertically, as notes on several strings are played simultaneously.

The weakness of tablature is that it gives little indication of rhythm. This omission may be solved in several ways. Some publications add tails and stems to the notes on the TAB stave in order to convey rhythms corresponding to those found in standard notation. In recent years, however, most publishers and guitar magazines have opted to combine standard notation and tablature. The TAB stave is placed underneath the music stave, in effect acting as a companion to the otherwise complete top stave. Chord symbols or boxes are usually placed above the top stave.

This combined system has many advantages for the guitarist: confident sight-readers can follow the top stave and ignore the TAB; learners can follow the TAB but glean crucial rhythm information from the top stave. Each system of notation compensates for the disadvantages of the other, creating a solution that is greater than the sum of its parts.

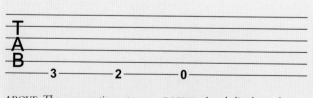

ABOVE: *Three consecutive notes on the bottom E string (third fret, second fret, open string).*

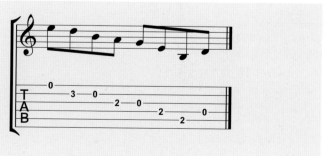

RIGHT: *A melodic phrase shown in notation and tablature – the complete picture.*

Using the fingers

The guitar is an incredibly versatile instrument, capable of strummed chords, fast melodic playing and anything in between. Fingerstyle technique, while still mainly based on chord shapes and primarily focused on accompaniment, may be seen as a first step away from pure strumming towards melodic playing. The simplest fingerstyle technique involves picking bass notes with the thumb and strumming with the fingers.

Bass/strum style

The technique of bass/strum playing is particularly popular in country and folk music. As its name suggests, the bass/strum style involves alternating between bass notes (played with the thumb) and strums (which are usually played with the first, second and third fingers together).

Bass/strum style also requires you to strum without the use of the plectrum, although we will be coming back to it later. The plectrum can in fact be used to play many 'fingerpicking' ideas, but it is useful to be able to use the fingers of the right hand independently. If you can play with your fingers a wider range of techniques are open to you; the musical effect can sound rather different from notes played with a plectrum.

Fingerpicking involves using the nails of the right hand to pluck the strings. Serious fingerstyle players devote considerable attention to shaping their fingernails to this end. Don't worry if your right-hand nails are too short for fingerpicking, since you can initially get by using the fleshy part of the fingertips. The fingernails don't have to be long or well shaped for strumming, anyway; it matters more when you come to play single picked notes (see 'Simple fingerpicking patterns').

You may also wish to investigate an alternative to using your own fingernails: a set of fingerpicks. These are attached to the individual fingers and thumb of the right hand and act as nail extensions. For maximum control, it is important to find a set that fits your fingers snugly, without protruding too far.

LEFT: *Fingerpicks are often favoured by country players, and provide an alternative which cuts out the need for nail care. Some players also prefer the resulting angle of the thumb.*

Recommended listening:
- The Beatles: "Rocky Raccoon"
- Bob Dylan: "North Country Blues"
- Johnny Cash: "Ring of Fire"
- Paul McCartney & Wings: "Mull of Kintyre"

Johnny Cash

One of the towering figures of country music, Johnny Cash became known for the distinctive 'boom-chick-a-boom' style of his rhythm section. Cash forged a path that combined a deep respect for the traditions of country music with a range of other influences, from blues to gospel. The common thread in much of his output is simplicity: simple chord sequences and a simple guitar-accompaniment style geared to serving his songs, which often deal with the themes beloved of country music without falling prey to its most obvious clichés. As one of the major artists in the Sun Records stable (along with Elvis Presley, Carl Perkins and Jerry Lee Lewis), he was almost automatically propelled to legendary status; this association, as well as doing his own standing no harm at all, helped keep simple guitar-driven country music central to American culture when it might otherwise have been completely dominated by rock'n'roll.

RIGHT: *Johnny Cash epitomized one of country music's favourite sayings: "All you need to write country music is three chords and the truth."*

Practising the bass/strum

There is more than one way to do the bass/strum – or at least the strumming part of it. Many players bring the fingers into the palm of the hand and then 'flick' them outwards to strum; others maintain a looser hand position and strum from the wrist.

As with many issues of guitar technique, the general rule is: if it feels relaxed, it's probably alright. If it feels awkward, it's probably not going to result in fluid playing. Either way, it is going to feel odd at first if you are used to playing with a plectrum. Try the exercises below and persevere: the technique will start to feel natural with practice. Remember, if a chord box has an 'X' on any string, this string should not be used as a bass note.

RIGHT: *This breakdown of a basic bass/strum pattern uses the D chord. Practise this for a while, then attempt the exercise below, which also begins with D.*

1 The left hand forms the D major chord. The right hand plays the open D (fourth) string (beat 1).

2 The first, second and third fingers of the right hand strum the top three strings (beat 2).

3 Pick the D string again (beat 3). For variety, try the A string instead.

4 Strum again (beat 4). You will need to practise this until it feels natural.

EXERCISE

This bass/strum exercise involves chord changes, and also asks you to pluck the bass on different strings. Follow the tablature: notes stacked on top of each other should be played simultaneously – as a strum, in other words.

Tip

For musical variety, you may want to vary this pattern by repeating the bass note on beat 3 (instead of strumming), as shown in the step-by-step sequence above.

Simple fingerpicking patterns

The next step in fingerpicking is learning to use the right-hand fingers and thumb independently. You will still be making chord shapes with your left hand, but you will be playing them in a succession of rising and falling notes. The effect can be beautiful, almost magical, as if you were weaving melodic tapestries on the air. This style works well if a less dense texture is required.

Arpeggios and fingerpicking styles

Many fingerpicking styles are built on arpeggio patterns. The term 'arpeggio' is from the Italian word *arpeggiare*, which translates as 'to play on a harp'. It means that the individual notes of a chord are played in sequence. In guitar circles, arpeggios are sometimes known by the less technical term 'spread chords'. Stringed instruments, by their nature, lend themselves to arpeggios, because a number of notes are always simultaneously available to the player: four to the violinist, six to the guitarist, dozens to the harpist.

Arpeggios played on a guitar can be very simple – say, the top three strings played one after the other in a repeating cycle – or they can take the form of complex patterns. Guitar arpeggios are usually produced by the thumb and first three fingers of the strumming hand (the little finger is rarely used). As a general rule, the thumb moves between the bass strings as necessary, while each finger covers just one of the top strings. The labelling system is shown below.

Each note of an arpeggio pattern should be allowed to ring for as long as possible – generally until the same string is played again. This effect is not always directly reflected in written note durations, as it would be visually messy. But it is taken for granted wherever fingerpicked arpeggios are shown, and sometimes reinforced by the indication 'let ring'.

Now try the fingerpicking exercises opposite. Notice that both of these exercises are in the 3/4 time signature. This seems to lend itself particularly well to arpeggio-style guitar accompaniments, since there are six quavers (notes of half a beat), which is exactly enough for the ascending/descending motion described above.

You may also wish to try these patterns using a plectrum. At slow tempos, this can be achieved using downstrokes only, but for greater fluency (and usually a more musical result), alternating down/upstrokes are recommended, following the general rule established for strumming 'downstrokes on the beat, upstrokes on the offbeat'.

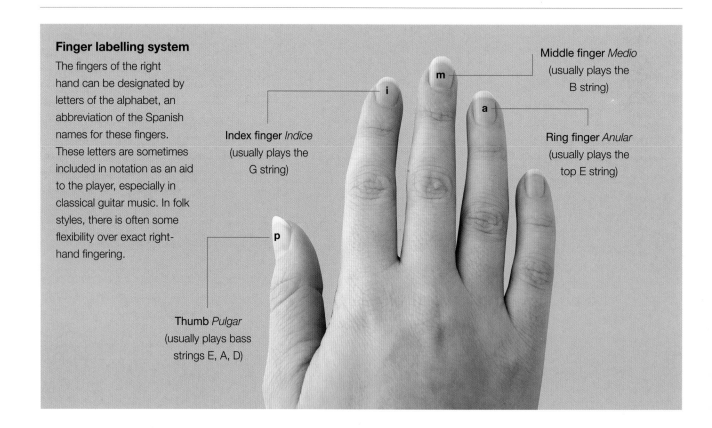

Finger labelling system

The fingers of the right hand can be designated by letters of the alphabet, an abbreviation of the Spanish names for these fingers. These letters are sometimes included in notation as an aid to the player, especially in classical guitar music. In folk styles, there is often some flexibility over exact right-hand fingering.

Middle finger *Medio* (usually plays the B string)

m

i

Index finger *Indice* (usually plays the G string)

a

Ring finger *Anular* (usually plays the top E string)

p

Thumb *Pulgar* (usually plays bass strings E, A, D)

EXERCISE 1

While the left hand frets the C major chord, the right hand arpeggiates the notes of the chord: first ascending, then descending. This exact right-hand pattern will also work for any other chord that has the root on the A string, including C major and A major. Other chords may have the bass note on the D string or low E string, as seen in Exercise 2 (below). For these chords, the right-hand fingers may also move down by one string (to the D, G and B strings).

Recommended listening:
● Garth Brooks: "If Tomorrow Never Comes"
● Eva Cassidy: "Songbird"
● Simon and Garfunkel: "Scarborough Fair"
● James Taylor: "Sweet Baby James"

EXERCISE 2

The arpeggio picking piece here uses the same right-hand picking pattern throughout – the fingers do exactly the same thing in each bar; the only elements that change are the chords and strings picked by the thumb. Remember to let each note ring for as long as possible; this is particularly important in the case of the bass notes: their sound underpins each chord and so helps to create an effective bass line.

Using the thumb in fingerpicking

The right thumb fulfils the same role in fingerpicking as the bassist does in a band: it plays the low notes that add depth to the sound. But this job need not be pedestrian or dull. The guitarist's thumb (like a creative bass player) can put notes together in a variety of ways to produce a satisfying melodic bass line. At its best, this can sound like a second melodic strand accompanying the voice or melody instrument.

Additional notes

Simply introducing an additional note to the bass line is enough to create a much more interesting effect when playing arpeggios. This might mean no more than using the thumb to pluck two of the lower strings in turn, while keeping the same chord shape. Some pairs of bass notes sound better than others, but one combination that nearly always sounds good is the root (the note on which the chord or scale begins) together with the fifth note of the scale.

Root and fifth

For details of how to construct chords, see 'Chord construction'. For present purposes, you need only know where to find the root note and fifth of each chord of the chords you have learnt so far. Almost all of them naturally contain the fifth on one of the bass strings, so the left hand does not need to move for the thumb to alternate between them.

Look at the chord diagrams below. Available root notes are shown in red, and fifth bass notes in blue. Sometimes they are on open strings, in which case the **O** at the top of the diagram is coloured. Notice that playing a C chord with the fifth in the bass requires you to move the third finger to the bottom E string. None of the other chords here require movement of the left hand to achieve this. Only the major chords learnt so far are shown. As for the minor and seventh chords learnt so far, they are all variations on these major shapes, and both the root and fifth are to be found in the same places. Practise finding the root and fifth with your thumb, then try Exercise 1, opposite.

Passing notes

Another way to create interesting bass lines is to introduce passing notes – bass notes that bridge the gap between chords. These are notes that do not belong to the chord, but are (usually) part of the scale or key of the piece. When combined with chord notes, passing notes make it possible to construct bass lines that add melodic interest.

One easy approach is to find notes that lie between the root notes of consecutive chords and see if they sound good. For example, many songs use the sequence C–Am. The root notes of these chords are found on the A string, third fret and open A string respectively. Therefore, either one or both of the notes in between (A string, first and second fret) could in theory be used as passing notes; which one sounds best will depend on the key of the piece.

As a rule, passing notes between chords should be fretted using whichever left-hand finger is most easily available. The aim is to cause the least disruption to the chord shape, and to allow other sounding notes to continue.

RIGHT: *The use of a thumb pick can add a brighter, crisper quality to bass notes, but can take some time to get used to.*

root and fifth of D	root and fifth of C	root and fifth of A	root and fifth of G	root and fifth of E
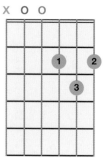				

EXERCISE 1

This exercise applies the concept of moving between root and fifth to a simple arpeggiated pattern using first-position chords. To get even more value out of this exercise, try re-ordering the notes on the G, B and top E strings in each chord pattern (for example, try P a m i or P m i a).

EXERCISE 2

This exercise uses root notes, fifths and passing notes to create a simple 'joined up' bass line. The time signature of this piece is $\frac{6}{8}$. This means that there are six quavers (eighth notes) in each bar. Although the number of quavers is the same as in $\frac{3}{4}$, they are accented as two groups of three: ONE two three, FOUR five six. This time signature also lends itself particularly well to arpeggiated accompaniment, and is often encountered in ballads.

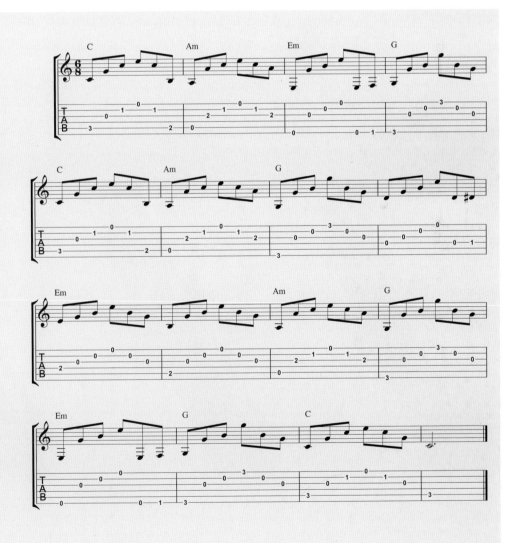

Using a capo

The capo is a device that raises the pitch of the guitar by placing a 'clamp' over all the strings at a given fret. This makes it possible to change the key of a song to suit a singer's vocal range and style, while retaining the sound and shape of chords being played. In folk styles, in particular, many players use a capo almost all the time so the song falls comfortably within their vocal range.

How to change key

Transposing a song into a different key is a tricky business on some instruments – a piano or a clarinet, for example – because all the fingering has to change. But it is easy on a guitar if you use a capo: you play all the same chords, but higher up the neck. All that has changed, in effect, is the position of the nut. If you are transposing with a capo to suit your own voice, you may not need to know the names of the sounding chords. Just find a capo position that works for you.

If you are playing with other musicians or singers, however, you may need to agree on a key. The basic unit of pitch on Western instruments is the semitone. On the guitar, two notes that are one fret apart on the same string are also one semitone apart. Most other musicians will understand if you tell them how many semitones you have transposed. For details of transposition, see the chart opposite.

The capo can also be used on the higher reaches of the fretboard to make the guitar sound more like a mandolin (which has a shorter neck).

In the Beatles' "Here Comes the Sun", for example, the bright, zingy tone of the guitar part is achieved by playing with a capo way up at the seventh fret.

Types of capo

It is essential that your capo is the right shape for your guitar. Some are designed to be used on guitars that have a completely flat fretboard (as almost all classical guitars do); while others are shaped for a curved fretboard (as is the case with most steel–string acoustics). There are many different types of capo are available, and each has its own advantages. The mechanism is usually designed either to enable fast application or removal, or to prioritize tuning accuracy and clean-sounding notes. Only the best types of capos manage to achieve both. The most common varieties of capo are shown below.

ABOVE: *The clamp capo offers the most precise adjustment. However, the disadvantage of it is that it cannot be moved quickly between frets. The reason for this is because the clamp tension has to be adjusted for each position.*

ABOVE: *The quick-release capo cannot be adjusted as accurately as a clamp capo, but is very easy to move between frets. This is the best type for most guitars, and is the one to use if you are performing on stage.*

ABOVE: *The advantages of the wrap-around capo are that it is inexpensive, and can be moved quickly around the neck. However, the downside is that the tension of the elastic cannot usually be adjusted precisely.*

FAR RIGHT: *Though his main instrumental role in the Beatles was to play the bass, Paul McCartney has played both the acoustic and electric guitar throughout his long career..*

BELOW: *This chart shows the actual sounding notes achieved by six familiar major chords at capo positions up to the seventh fret.*

Paul McCartney

Every pop band needs a bass player, and when the Beatles' original bassist left the band, the role naturally fell to Paul McCartney, who inhabited the position superbly, bringing a fresh approach to the instrument. McCartney has never stopped playing the guitar, and many of his best-known songs feature his acoustic guitar playing and often incorporate highly original techniques and ideas, ranging from hybrid fingerpicking/strumming for his lyrical "Blackbird", to tuning the guitar down a tone (the reverse of using a capo) for "Yesterday". By doing this, he managed to transpose the song into a comfortable key, while keeping the rich sound of first-position chords.

Transposition guide

No capo	E	A	D	G	B	E
1st fret	F	Bb (A#)	E♭ (D#)	A♭ (G#)	C	F
2nd fret	F#	B	E	A	C# (D♭)	F#
3rd fret	G	C	F	B♭ (A#)	D	G
4th fret	G# (A♭)	C# (D♭)	F# (G♭)	B	D# (E♭)	G# (A♭)
5th fret	A	D	G	C	E	A
6th fret	B♭ (A#)	E♭ (D#)	A♭ (G#)	D♭ (C#)	F	B♭ (A#)
7th fret	B	E	A	D	F# (G♭)	B

Tuning with a capo

In theory, one should be able to apply the capo at any given fret and, so long as the guitar is already in tune, it will remain in tune with the capo in place. In fact, the capo exerts a lot of pressure on the strings, and this is enough to affect their tuning. So it may be necessary to adjust the tuning once you have put the capo on. A small amount of relative tuning should be sufficient.

If you use an electronic tuner that needs to be set manually, you will need to know the pitch of all six strings at the fret where you are fitting the capo. The chart above shows the pitches of the 'open' strings (with capo) up to the seventh fret. Notes in parentheses are alternative names for the same note. Your tuner may describe these as sharps (#), flats (♭) or both.

ABOVE: *As with fretting fingers, the capo should generally be placed as close as possible to the active fret to avoid buzz. However, make sure the strings aren't pushed out of alignment (see above).*

Playing tunes

So far we have been dealing mainly with ways of playing chords. However, the guitar is not just for rhythmic accompaniment; it is also an instrument on which you can play tunes. If you can get to grips with the guitar's melodic potential, a whole new world of musical possibilities will open up to you – from improvised blues to gypsy jazz. In fact, just about any conceivable melody can be played on the guitar.

The musical vocabulary

When strumming on the guitar, you can get by without really knowing much about the components and musical construction of the chords. But to play a tune, you really need to have some familiarity with the notes. You probably already know that there are 12 notes in the musical vocabulary: on a piano, these correspond to the seven white keys plus the five black ones that occur before the pattern of keys repeats itself. On a guitar, they are the 12 frets that you have to climb before you get to the note where you started – but an octave higher.

Few tunes use all these notes – and many fine melodies can be played using five notes or fewer. The first five notes that you are going to learn are C, D, E, F and G. They are shown below in ascending order in standard musical notation and in 'TAB'. The fretted notes here should be played with the

finger number corresponding to the fret number: so the second fret is played with the second finger and the third fret with the third finger. This approach, known as *position playing*, is the most efficient way of achieving this since it involves the least finger movement.

When playing an ascending figure on one string, such as the three notes played here on the D string, fingers may stay in place on lower frets as higher notes are played: after playing the note E (second finger, second fret), there is no need to remove this finger before playing the next note (F: third finger, third fret). However, when moving from one string to another, care should be taken that notes sounding on the first string played should not ring on over notes on the next string. For example, in playing the ascending figure here, the third finger should be lifted after playing the first note (C) and again after playing the note F.

LEFT: *The first five notes of the C major scale, in first position. Remember to play the fretted notes using one finger per fret, as described above.*

Pat Metheny

Although his records are usually filed under 'jazz', Pat Metheny's output spans a far broader range of styles: folk, rock, Latin and classical influences are often prominent, to name a few. Equally at home on both electric and acoustic guitars of various types, Metheny has been stretching boundaries ever since he came to prominence in the mid-'70s, while remaining one of the few players with such a distinctive 'voice'.

The right hand

Strumming with the plectrum often involves the whole right forearm, but melodic playing requires greater precision, and so demands a lighter touch from the right hand – a delicate rocking of the wrist at most. The right hand may rest lightly on the bridge when playing single notes, but it should also be poised so that it can be lifted at any time in order to go into strumming mode.

RIGHT: *The right hand in picking position.*

LEFT: *Pat Metheny is widely recognized as one of the most fluent melodic guitarists of his generation. He has accomplished this through both his own work as well as collaborations with Steve Reich, Joni Mitchell and many other musicians.*

FIVE-NOTE MELODIES "WHEN THE SAINTS GO MARCHING IN"

Many well-known tunes can be played using just the five notes that you now know – from simple pieces, such as "When the Saints Go Marching in", to magnificent uplifting melodies, such as Beethoven's "Ode to Joy".

Be sure to take account of the rests when playing this piece – including the one that is the first beat of the first bar.

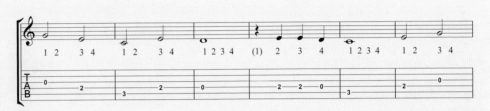

FIVE-NOTE MELODIES "ODE TO JOY"

Beethoven's famous piece is not ideally suited to the guitar, but it is still excellent practice. The beat is very regular throughout, but watch out for those two pairs of quavers in the third line.

Now see if you can work out some tunes for yourself. This is one of the best possible ear-training exercises. Try your hand at the following melodies to start with:

"Jingle Bells"
(hint: the first note is E)

"Hot Cross Buns"

"Au Clair de la Lune"
(first part)

The C major scale and first position

You already know the first five notes in the scale of C major; now you will learn the rest of it. The whole scale can be played in 'first position', meaning that the four fingers of the left hand never leave their base on the first four frets. Once you know the whole scale, you can play tunes in the key of C major. All other major scales can be found in first position, although some are easier to play than others.

Positions

In first position, notes at the first fret are played by the first finger, notes at the second fret by the second finger – and so on. In second position, the first finger is at the second fret, and the other fingers take up their posts at the third, fourth and fifth frets. This is the most economical way of getting to the note you want to play, and it is a principle that you should aim to absorb: one finger to a fret, wherever musically possible.

RIGHT: *The left hand in first position – each finger covers one fret. In first position, open strings also form part of many scales, whereas higher positions usually use fretted notes only.*

Playing the scale of C major

Below is the scale of C major, beginning on the lowest C note that a guitar can play. The musical notation shows you the scale rising and falling one step at a time; the TAB shows you how far you can go while keeping the fingers in the first position (as far as G on the third fret of the top string – an octave plus a fifth).

The scale is written out in quavers. As we have seen, these occupy half a beat each. As with quaver-strumming patterns in $\frac{4}{4}$ time, this means that every other note here is on the beat, while those in between are on the offbeat.

While it is possible to play every note here using only downstrokes, greater speed and fluency can be achieved by alternating downstrokes on the beat with upstrokes on the offbeat. Here, the direction of the picking action is marked on the score:

ABOVE: *The right hand playing a downstroke. This is usually used on the beat.*

ABOVE: *An upstroke, usually used on offbeats (between beats).*

The symbol ⊓ indicates a downstroke, and V indicates an upstroke.

The tunes opposite both use the major scale in first position and only the note/rest values we have used so far. Try recording yourself strumming the chords, and then play the melody along with this, or get a friend to play the chords while you play the melody. Or various software programs will allow you to generate a complete backing track by simply typing in the chords.

BELOW: *The C major scale in first position, using upstrokes and downstrokes. The picking pattern in the first bar is repeated throughout.*

Dots, ties and upbeats

The exercises below introduce a few new symbols and conventions. Neither of the two pieces of music begins on beat 1. Sometimes a piece can begin with an incomplete bar, also known as a pickup bar or *anacrusis*. This usually means that the final bar of the piece is also incomplete (especially if there is a repeat marked), so that the two add up to a full bar, enabling the piece to be repeated seamlessly.

EXERCISE "CAMPTOWN RACES"

A dot placed immediately after a note indicates that its duration is half as much again as its undotted value.

So, a dotted minim 𝅗𝅥. is read as three beats (2+1), and a dotted crotchet ♩. is one and a half beats.

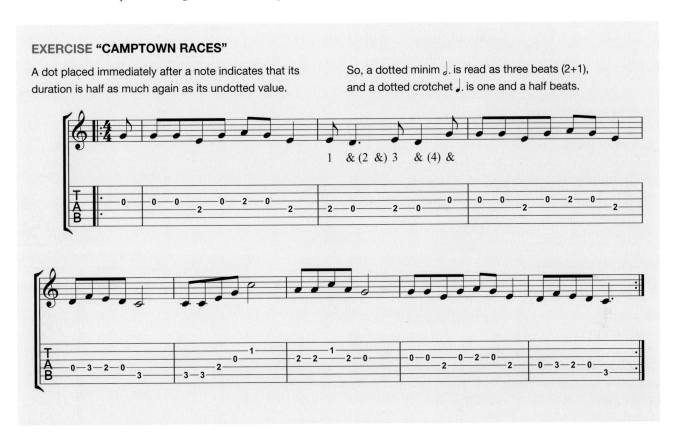

EXERCISE "ON TOP OF OLD SMOKEY"

The curved horizontal line seen between notes is called a tie. This symbol is used to join the durations of notes together, even across bar lines, so they become one long note. In this piece there are two points where two dotted minims are joined across a bar line, meaning that the note lasts for two whole bars of $\frac{3}{4}$, or six beats.

The major scales

Learning scales is a useful discipline in many ways. Committing scales to memory expands your musical vocabulary, and strengthens your command of the instrument. If you practise your scales regularly (as all serious players do), you will become better acquainted with your guitar, undertake a good practical workout and at the same time expand your theoretical knowledge of music.

What is a scale?

A scale consists of all the notes in a particular key. When we play a tune in C, we expect that most or all of the notes will be drawn from the scale of C. The scale is an inventory of structural elements of a tune, a map of the melodic landscape. When you know your scales, you are less likely to be caught out by the direction that a tune takes.

Daily practice

Starting to play the guitar can be physically wearing, particularly for the fingertips of the left hand. Calluses (pads of hardened skin) will develop but, in the meantime, don't overdo things, and stop practising if your fingertips become painful.

Understanding scales

An excursion into music theory may be helpful at this point. A Western musical scale can be seen as an arrangement of tones and semitones. Notes that are one fret apart on the same string of a guitar are one semitone apart; a tone is equal to two semitones, and is two frets apart.

The piano keyboard provides a useful way of visualizing how scales work. On the piano, adjacent keys are one semitone apart, whether they are black or white. The scale/key of C major is defined as having no sharps or flats. On the piano, this means that if you start on C and play the white notes in succession, you will hear a perfect major scale.

Most adjacent white notes are one tone apart, but the adjacent pairs B–C and E–F have no black note between them, and so are only one semitone apart. It follows that the third and fourth notes of the major scale are a semitone apart, as are the seventh and eighth.

It further follows that a scale starting from any note other than C will not have the same internal configuration of tones and semitones if only the white notes are used. One note or more will have to be adjusted (raised or lowered) in order to preserve the intervals of the major scale/key. This is where sharps and flats are introduced. If you start a scale on G, to get the semitone gaps to fall in the right place you will have to play one black note, F#; that is the note a semitone above F. It can be said that the scale of G is defined by the fact that it contains one sharp. In fact, every key is defined by the number of sharps (or flats) that it contains.

BELOW: *Two octaves from G–G on the piano. Notice that there are no black notes (sharps/flats) between E–F or B–C.*

Middle C

Some new scales

Try playing the three major scales that are shown here. They are all in first position and use open strings where possible. Each scale starts on the lowest available root note, ascends to the highest note available in first position, descends to the lowest note in first position, and finally returns to the root – so this version of the C major is a little more extensive and challenging than the one you have already tried. Remember to stay in first position: one finger per fret.

EXERCISE C MAJOR SCALE

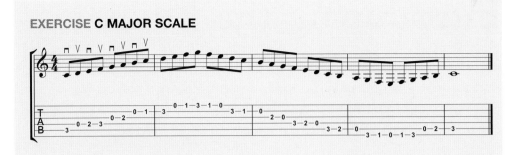

EXERCISE G MAJOR SCALE

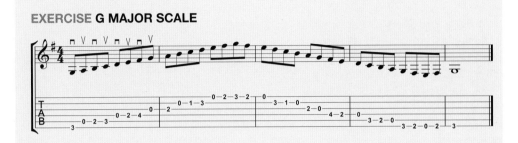

Tip

Short daily practice sessions are far more beneficial than longer, infrequent ones, even if the total time spent is the same overall.

EXERCISE D MAJOR SCALE

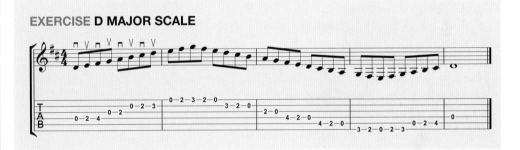

EXERCISE CHROMATIC SCALE

This exercise is not a major scale but the chromatic scale – which simply means that it involves playing every available note. This makes it an excellent practice tool, since every fret in the first position is covered. You will notice in the musical notation that the scale contains sharps on the way up, and flats on the way down. These are the piano's black notes. A sharp or flat symbol remains in force for the rest of the bar in which it is written, unless cancelled by a 'natural' sign (symbol).

Since a sharp is a semitone above a given note, and a flat a semitone below, there are some notes that can be described either in terms of the note above or the note below: the note between A and B could be called A♯ or B♭. It is a convention of chromatic scales that notes are given as sharps in the ascending form, and as flats in the descending form.

Introducing the blues

It is hard to overestimate the importance of the blues to modern popular music. Without the blues, there would be no Elvis, no Beatles, no Rolling Stones, no jazz... Blues guitar can be a lifetime's study in itself, but there are two important starting points when studying the blues: the blues scale (for melodic playing and solo construction) and the twelve-bar blues chord sequence.

The blues scale

Most blues-based music gets its distinctive sound from certain notes being flattened (that is, lowered by one semitone) in relation to the major key. If you take the most important notes in the major key and add to them the flattened notes, the result is a set of notes usually known as the blues scale. Like any scale, the blues scale can generate an infinite variety of melodic effects, but the basic formula is straightforward, and it is easy to get to grips with on the guitar.

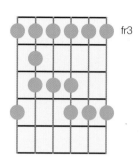

fr3

LEFT: *The notes of the blues scale form this pattern on the fretboard of the guitar. The pattern is the same whatever the key you play in (that is, wherever you start on the neck). Stick to these notes when you jam, and the result is bound to sound right.*

The 12-bar blues sequence

Many blues and rock songs are based on a simple progression of three chords – the first, fourth and fifth in the scale – played in a sequence of 12 bars. For the purposes of learning the basics, we are sticking to the key of G in all the examples and exercises on this and the opposite page.

G7	G7	G7	G7
C7	C7	G7	G7
D7	C7	G7	D7

Play this chord sequence with a simple pattern of four strums per bar at first, to get used to the sound. Singing any 12-bar blues song will further help to internalize the structure of the sequence. Try "Sweet Home Chicago", "Johnny B. Goode" or "Shake, Rattle and Roll". Better still, use the blues scale to improvise a solo of your own on top of these chords. To play the blues in G, place your fingers in the third position (that is, with the first finger based on the third fret).

Recommended listening
- B. B. King: *Live at the Regal*
- John Mayall: *Bluesbreakers with Eric Clapton*
- Stevie Ray Vaughan and Double Trouble: *Texas Flood*
- Taj Mahal: *Taj Mahal*

Charlie Patton

Often called 'The Father of the Delta Blues' as so many styles have evolved from the blues, Charlie Patton must rank as one of the most important figures in the history of popular music. Patton grew up in Mississippi around the turn of the 20th century, and developed a diverse and adaptable guitar style. Many of the best-known Delta blues musicians hailed from Patton's corner of Mississippi, and he is thought to have influenced most of them, from Robert Johnson to Howlin' Wolf and John Lee Hooker.

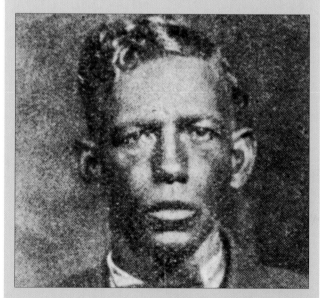

ABOVE: *Charlie Patton's voice and guitar, through the medium of scratchy and faint recordings such as "Pony Blues", provide a compelling insight into the birth of the blues.*

EXERCISE G BLUES SCALE

Play this blues scale in third position by placing your first finger at the third fret, your second at the fourth, and the third and fourth fingers at fifth and sixth frets. Notice the flattened fifth notes in each octave.

EXERCISE SIX BLUES LICKS

One of the great things about blues styles is that more or less any melodic idea constructed using the blues scale will work over any part of the chord sequence. Here are six classic blues 'licks' to get you started with this process.

EXERCISE "BEGINNER'S BLUES"

This piece combines a simple melody using the G blues scale with the 12-bar chord sequence. The best way to hear this to full effect is to record yourself playing the chord sequence (or programme the sequence using accompaniment software such as Band In A Box) and play the melody over the top.

The sixth shuffle

The sixth shuffle is a simple guitar trick, widely used in acoustic blues and electric rock 'n' roll. It is a variant of the 12-bar sequence that combines the root note with a pattern that alternates between the fifth and sixth note of the prevailing chord. That is the technical explanation; the reason the sixth shuffle is so popular is that it sounds great and really adds momentum to a song.

Using the sixth shuffle

The sixth shuffle creates a kind of driving bass rhythm that works well in any kind of bluesy jam session. Only three notes are involved, but the motion between the fifth and sixth is such a strong musical figure that the chord sequence is implied – even though the full chords do not sound in the most basic version of the idea.

Recommended listening:
- Chuck Berry: "Johnny B. Goode"
- Gary Moore: "Movin' on Down the Road"
- Tommy Tucker: "Hi-Heel Sneakers"

The basic moves

The key of A is the simplest key in which to learn the blues shuffle pattern as the root note of each chord can be found on an open string. The left hand stays in second position throughout: fretted notes are played by the first finger at the second fret and the third finger at the fourth fret. The key of A is unique in that all three chord roots of the 12-bar blues (I, IV and V) can be found on open strings. In order to transpose the sixth shuffle into other keys, the right hand forms a movable shape, with the root and fifth on the bottom two strings; the little finger stretches to play the sixth. This is simply shifted up the neck for chords IV and V. For example, C is found at the eighth fret while D is found at the tenth.

sixth shuffle

LEFT: *The left hand in position for the sixth shuffle. The first finger stays at the second fret, while the third finger 'rocks' on and off the string at the fourth fret.*

Adding the seventh

The basic sixth shuffle pattern can be elaborated in a number of ways. In the key of A, the left hand may stay in second position but proceed up to the seventh of each chord; this extra note is played by the little finger at the fifth fret. Adding the seventh in other keys requires that the movable shape explored above (G) be turned into a G7 barre chord (see 'Barre chords').

sixth shuffle G chord

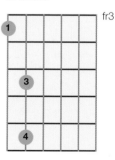

ABOVE: *The sixth shuffle G chord. The first and third fingers play the root and fifth; the little finger stretches to play the sixth.*

Swing/shuffle feel

The shuffle pattern here is written in quavers (eighth notes), or half-beat notes in $\frac{4}{4}$, but the indication 'swing' or 'shuffle' tells us something important about how these quavers should be played. In the absence of such an indication, offbeats should be played exactly halfway between beats: '1 and 2 and 3 and 4 and...' This is also known as a straight feel. Swing feel changes this by making the offbeat arrive late: '1 and2 and3 and4 and...'

The exact timing of swing offbeat depends on the tempo of the music and also varies between players and styles. It is important to be familiar enough with the swing/shuffle feel to be able to play it naturally, since it forms the rhythmic basis of most blues and jazz. To this end, all of the listening recommendations given below demonstrate the shuffle feel. However, very many classic rock'n'roll songs use a straight feel, so you need to be able to do both.

EXERCISE **BASIC SHUFFLE**

This exercise uses the basic shuffle pattern to play the twelve-bar blues sequence. The pattern remains the same except that it is transferred up to the D and G strings (for the D chord) and down to the low E and A strings (E).

Tip

Some blues songs simplify the structure by staying on the tonic chord in the last bar. In this example, this would mean staying on the A pattern for the last bar rather than changing to E.

EXERCISE **ADDING THE SEVENTH**

This exercise adds sevenths to the blues shuffle sequence – the fourth finger is added to play the seventh at the fifth fret for each chord.

Tip

A different effect can be achieved by alternating between the two strings used for each chord rather than playing them simultaneously, somewhat in the manner of the classic "James Bond Theme" guitar line.

Building a blues solo

The blues scale is the blues guitarist's road map, but to improvise well on the guitar, you need to know your way around the fretboard instinctively. Learn licks and make up your own, but beware of trotting out the same figures every time. Instead, explore the blues scale: one route to finding new and even better solos is shown on the page opposite, but this is by no means the only way.

Tension and release

The blues scale works by creating and releasing tension in relation to the chord sequence. Some notes are consonant (they belong together) against certain chords, while others are dissonant (they clash) against others.

Arguably, the defining note of the blues scale is the flattened third (the note Bb in the key of G). When played over chord I (G7), this creates the dissonance that is characteristic of all blues-related music. However, when played later in the sequence over chord IV (C7), this note actually belongs to the chord and therefore does not sound dissonant. It is therefore possible to play a phrase over chord I in the first line, which creates tension; this is released when the same phrase is played over chord IV in the second line. In any case, repetition usually works well in a blues context.

This 'tension and release' approach is found in many blues themes and improvised solos. Although it is possible to extend this effect into the third line of the blues, another popular soloing ploy involves modifying the melodic material used in the first two lines to create an 'answer'.

This call-and-response style has been central to the development of the blues, and is reflected in the lyrics of many blues songs. The first line of the verse is an opening statement or question, the second line repeats this (usually exactly), and the third line 'rounds off' the verse in the form of an answer or explanation.

Blues classics such as "Dust My Broom" (Robert Johnson), "Stormy Monday" (T-Bone Walker) and "Before You Accuse Me" (Bo Diddley) all contain this idea. Exercise 1 (opposite) is a blues solo using this pattern.

Outside the blues

The blues scale is such a powerful vehicle for improvisation that it often works well even when the chords are not strictly a blues sequence. When used in the minor key, the flattened third is no longer dissonant, because it belongs to the key. The scale still has a bluesy flavour, however, especially if you lean heavily on the flattened fifth. This possibility is explored in Exercise 2 on the opposite page.

When using the blues scale over any chord sequence, the important thing is to identify the key correctly. Using a blues scale in the wrong key will generally result in some strange dissonances that do not contribute to a blues feel. The key may be identified from a music theory perspective, but it is also important to be able to hear where the key centre lies: listen for the chord that sounds like 'home', the point in the music where the harmony feels as though it has come to rest. For this reason, the tonic chord (chord I) is often found as both the first and last chord of many chord sequences.

Recommended listening:

- Buddy Guy & Junior Wells: *Alone & Acoustic*
- Eric Bibb: *Natural Light*
- Eric Clapton: *Unplugged*

RIGHT: *Brownie McGhee's name is often omitted from the 'front rank' of 20th-century blues guitarists, perhaps because he focused so well on accompanying Sonny Terry's harmonica.*

Brownie McGhee

Best known as one half of a duo with the harmonica player and singer Sonny Terry, Brownie McGhee bestrode the worlds of blues and folk, creating subtle but powerful accompaniments to Terry's wailing, honking, pleading harmonica lines. One of the 'classic' Southern bluesmen born in the second generation of the 20th century, McGhee's career included fruitful collaborations with some of the biggest names in blues, from Champion Jack Dupree to Big Bill Broonzy. Brownie McGhee's style is often sensitively minimal, but he was not afraid to embark on gutsy solo ideas, even with no supporting musicians.

EXERCISE 1

A new rhythm value is introduced in this solo: the quaver triplet. A group of three quavers with a '3' above indicates that the beat here is divided into three (rather than two, as with an ordinary pair of quavers).

Tip

The triplet is arguably the basis of the swing feel, at least at slow/medium tempos: the swing offbeat is in time with what would be the third note of a quaver triplet.

EXERCISE 2

This exercise overlays the G blues scale on a G minor chord sequence. For maximum benefit, either record yourself playing the chords or get a friend to play them while you play the solo.

Tip

Automatic accompaniment software can also be very useful for the purpose of this exercise, and may even inject some blues 'feel' for added inspiration.

Advanced blues

The blues scale, powerful as it is, is not the sum total of the melodic possibilities that are available to blues players. For increased melodic potential when improvising in a blues style – or in any other style – you can also make full use of all the notes that make up the chords in the progression, paying attention to which of these chords you are playing over at any one time.

Using notes with chords

Almost every note in the octave can be used in a blues context. Fluid improvisation is about knowing which notes can be used over which chords. The table below represents an analysis of each note in relation to the three chords of the 12-bar sequence. For this exercise, we are using the key of G: I7 (G7), IV7 (C7) and V7 (D7). Bear in mind that the relationships of the notes to the chords will be the same in any other key. So, for example, the note that is a semitone above the tonic (A♭ in this instance) is always to be avoided.

BELOW: *All the notes shown here in the notation and in the tablature relate to the blues scale in third position.*

Note	Part of chords	Comments	Note	Part of chords	Comments
G	G7 C7	The tonic (key) note	C#/D♭	-	Dissonant/bluesy against all chords in the sequence; resolves down to C or up to D
A♭	-	AVOID	D	G7 D7	Usable anywhere
A	D7	Not used much, but part of the dominant (D7) and used as a passing note	E♭	-	AVOID
B♭	C7	The flattened third – THE blue note in relation to the key, also part of the C7 chord	E	C7	The third of C7; also used as a passing note
B	G7	The third of G7; the flattened third resolves to this note; to be avoided over C7	F	G7	The seventh of G7 and a blue note in relation to both the key and the D7 chord
C	C7 D7	Usable anywhere	F#	D7	The third of D7; avoid this note over G7

The blues sequence

This is much the same as saying that the blues scale itself can be used over any part of the blues sequence. Notes that are not present in the blues scale may be used either as chord tones or as passing notes against other chords.

Recommended listening:

- Big Bill Broonzy: *Big Bill Broonzy Sings Country Blues*
- Lightnin' Hopkins, Sonny Terry & Brownie McGhee: *Blues Hoot*
- Jimmy Reed: *Jimmy Reed at Carnegie Hall*

ABOVE: *Brownie McGhee and blues singer/harmonica player Sonny Terry. Their on-and-off blues partnership lasted for several decades (1958–80).*

RIGHT: *Hopkins usually played alone, owing much to Blind Lemon Jefferson's fingerpicking style, maintaining a full accompaniment of bass and chords under his vocal line.*

Lightnin' Hopkins

Sam 'Lightnin' Hopkins was one of the handful of bluesmen with a direct link to the blues tradition through the early musicians who were active into the late 20th century (he died in 1982). Hopkins grew up in the heart of Texas and learnt both from family members who were steeped in the blues, and also from the legendary Blind Lemon Jefferson, one of the first singers to record the blues. Jefferson's influence is one of many that can be heard in Hopkins' guitar work, as well as in his singing style. Although his contemporaries John Lee Hooker and Muddy Waters achieved greater fame, Hopkins continued the 'lone bluesman' tradition of Jefferson; his influence can be heard in the next generation's acoustic and electric players alike.

EXERCISE **ADVANCED BLUES**

This blues solo here uses both chord notes and passing notes. Note the hammer-ons (slurring to produce a smooth sequence) between B♭ and B natural (and later between F and F♯): the first note is written as a cue note (small) with a line through it, often called a grace note, indicating that it should be played as quickly as possible just before the main note. Every note here can be found in third position; any notes outside the blues scale do not require moving the left hand out of position.

The 12-bar sequence is also modified slightly here, by introducing chord IV7 (C7) in bar 2.

Barre chords

In all the chords that you have learnt so far, the fingers of the left hand have fretted one note each. But in order to make some chords, especially the more unusual ones, it may sometimes be necessary for one finger to act like a movable capo that frets some or all six strings at once. The chords that are formed in this manner are called barre chords, and form an essential part of most players' chord repertoire.

Making barre chords

Barre chords (sometimes called 'movable chords') make it possible to move the standard chord shapes up and down the neck, and so to access the full range of chords. Making the barre involves flattening a finger – usually the first finger – across all the strings (or most of them). This will feel difficult and unnatural at first – but you will get used to it. It is worth the effort, because you will be limited in what you play if you can only manage the first-position chords.

Since your first finger is occupied in making the barre, you have only three fingers available to make the rest of the shape – and not the three fingers that you are used to using. For example, the F major chord here uses fingers 2, 3 and 4 to form the fretted notes of the E shape.

Fretting the F chord

1 Form the barre with the first finger at the first fret. For the F chord, the barre should span all six strings.

2 Consulting the chord box, form the E shape with the second, third and fourth fingers relative to the barre (one fret higher than the standard E shape).

3 Check that the chord sounds clearly, paying particular attention to fret buzz, which may occur if the barre is too far away from the fret.

Moving the barre

An alternative way of forming a G major chord can be achieved by moving the barred shape up to the third fret. Sometimes this is the most economical way to move from F to G or vice versa.

The barre is shown in chord-box format as a curved line linking notes at the same fret. For visual simplicity, only the sounding notes are shown, even though the barre is in place behind the other fretted notes.

F

G

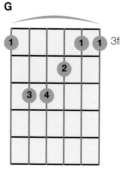 

ABOVE: *F and G major barre chords based on the E shape. Exactly the same shape is used for both chords.*

ABOVE: *The symbol '3fr' indicates that the G chord box starts at the third fret.*

Other shapes

In principle, almost any three-finger chord can be moved up the neck using a barre. In practice, some shapes are much more convenient than others. The E major shape is essential; E minor and A minor are also extremely useful shapes from which to make barre chords, and quite easy to do. The C shape also works well, but is harder to hold down, because it stretches over four frets, making it more susceptible to accidental buzzing and muffled sounds.

B♭m

Fm

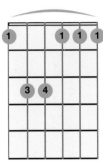

D♭

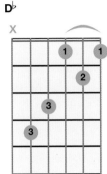

Chord slash notation

The chord sequences below are shown in a form of notation generally known as chord slashes. Each bar contains four diagonal slashes, corresponding to four beats in the time signature, but these are not necessarily intended to dictate four strict strums per bar. Rather, the exact strumming (or even picking) pattern is left to the player's own taste. Where there are exact rhythms that are required in the piece, these are integrated by adding stems and tails (as in the final bar of Exercise 2 here); the note-heads remain in the 'slash' style to indicate that only rhythm (rather than pitch) is being conveyed. Even here, there is some freedom in the exact technique that is used to deliver the rhythm.

EXERCISE 1

If you form barres from E, Am and C at the first fret, these three shapes result in Fm, B♭m and D♭ chords respectively. These are all useful chords. This exercise combines Fm and B♭m with open chords to produce an interesting sequence.

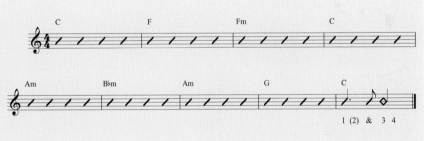

EXERCISE 2

Barre chords can be hard work, even a little painful at first. The easiest way to bring them into use is to employ them in combination with open chords to allow the fingers some rest. This exercise uses the E-shaped F chord within a chord sequence in the key of C major.

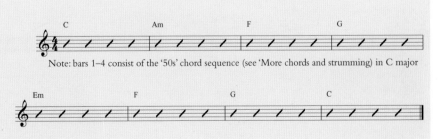

Note: bars 1–4 consist of the '50s' chord sequence (see 'More chords and strumming') in C major

More on barre chords

The beauty of barre chords is that they make hundreds more chords available to you as a guitarist and are therefore widely used in many styles of music. You don't have to learn every chord separately: instead, you deploy a few shapes – most of which you already know – combined with some barre technique and a little theoretical knowledge. The E shape and the A shape alone will take you a long way.

The two magic shapes

If you knew just one barre chord shape for each chord type, you would theoretically be able to use this shape anywhere on the neck, and so open up the full range of musical keys. But this would still require a lot of movement, and would sometimes take you into the difficult upper areas of the neck.

RIGHT: *The A-shaped barre. On the first fret, this makes B♭, which is an important chord when you are playing in the key of E.*

But if you knew two shapes in different parts of the scale, you would always have an option. You could barre any chord in a sensible, economical way. This route is in fact open to you. Once you know all the important chord types associated with the E shape and the A shape (that is: major, minor, seventh and minor seventh), then you will have a way of playing the vast bulk of rock, pop, blues and folk songs – and a fair amount of jazz, too.

Some players find the A shape hard to use in barre chord form, as it involves all four fingers in a rather awkward stretch: the first finger barres all six strings; the other three must crowd into one fret that is quite a stretch away.

Chords for the shapes

Here are all the chord types for both the E shape and the A shape. None of them are as difficult to master as the A major shape that you have just learnt, and there is in any case an alternative way of playing that shape – that is, by using the first finger on the fifth string and a short barre across the second third and fourth (the top E string is usually not played).

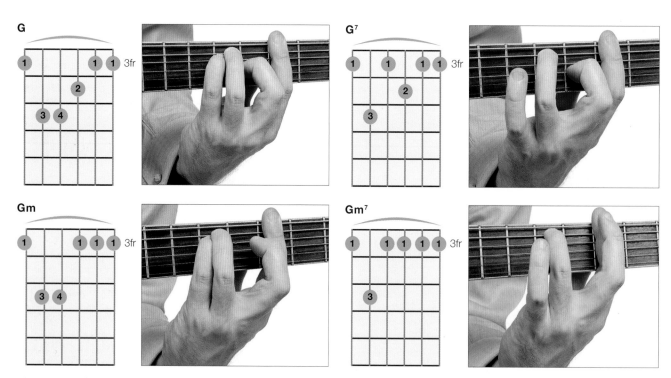

ABOVE: *Barre chords – root E string. All of these chords are based on first position chords (E, E7, Em, Em7).*

Third-fret barre chords

For comparison, barre chords are shown here at the third fret. As this corresponds to the note G on the E string and the note C on the A string, this produces 'G' chords and 'C' chords respectively. This fact demonstrates the benefit of knowing two shapes for each type: you can go from, say, Gm7 to Cm7 while staying at the third fret (a very common chord change). With only one shape in your repertoire, a shift up the neck of five or seven frets would be required.

C

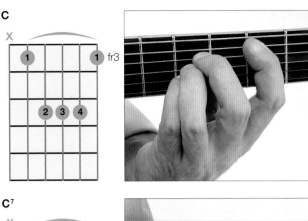

C Alternative shape

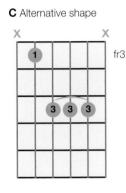 

C⁷

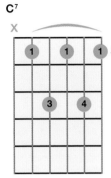 

Cm

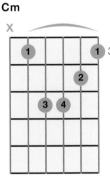 

Cm⁷

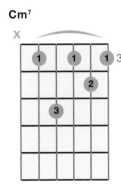 

Finding the root

To get the maximum potential out of these shapes, you need to know where to find the root of any given chord. With practice this becomes second nature; until then, the fretboard chart to the right shows every note on the bottom two strings.

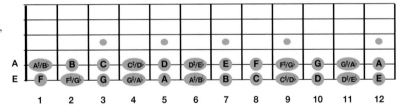

EXERCISE

The best way to memorize the note locations on the fretboard chart is to have to find them yourself. To this end, any chord sequence can be used as two separate exercises; choosing an 'E'-based shape for the first chord will result in one set of shapes, while an 'A' shape will result in another. In this exercise the first two

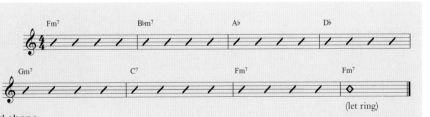

(let ring)

chords may be played in two ways: Fm7 (1st fret) followed by B♭m7 (1st fret) or Fm7 (8th fret) followed by B♭m7 (6th fret).

Understanding keys

Getting to grips with how key signatures work makes it possible to play melodies and construct chord sequences in any key. It also opens up the entire fretboard for practice and for musical exploration. The relationships between the major keys are built on a few simple principles, which are explained here. Each major key is also closely related to a minor key – equally important in many styles.

THE CIRCLE OF FIFTHS

As we have seen, the key of C major is unique in that it has no sharps or flats (which are the 'black' notes on the piano). It is constructed entirely using 'white' notes, also known as naturals. All other keys contain sharps and flats. These occur in a logical arrangement that can be described with a device called the circle of fifths.

In the circle of fifths, each key has one more sharp (going clockwise) or flat (going anti-clockwise) than the preceding one. And each key is one fifth above the one that comes before it. For example, D major is a fifth above G major, and has two sharps in the key signature where G major has only 1.

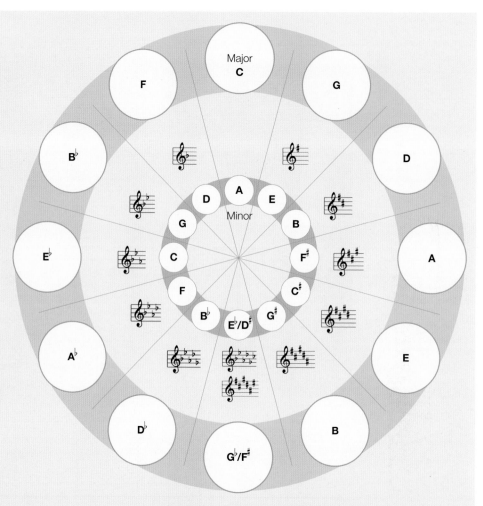

Davey Graham

Among the most influential of British folk guitarists, Davey Graham was one of the first musicians to expand the bounds of 'folk' music to flavours from beyond the UK or even Europe. His compositions incorporated elements of Indian and Arab music, and borrowed blues ideas for use in a Celtic folk context. His most famous composition, "Anji", has become one of the classic guitar instrumentals, with recorded versions by Simon and Garfunkel, Gordon Giltrap and John Renbourn, among others. The early date of this composition (1962) makes a strong case for him as the inventor of the modern folk instrumental.

LEFT: *As well as pioneering DADGAD tuning (see 'DADGAD tuning'), which was later widely adopted among folk players, Davey Graham is sometimes credited as the father of World Music for using elements of folk music from other cultures.*

The major keys: sharps

The scale of G major is a perfect fifth above C. It contains one sharp (F♯), and so is the first key in the cycle of 'sharp' keys. Each new key in the circle is a perfect fifth above the last, and introduces a new sharp that is also a perfect fifth above the last and the leading note of the new key.

Ascending in fifths gives us the keys C – G – D – A – E – B – F♯. The 'new' sharpened notes in each key are F♯ – C♯ – G♯ – D♯ – A♯. New sharps appear in the key signature at the start of each line in this order.

Although we have defined sharps and flats as 'black notes' on the piano keyboard, there are actually only five black keys in each octave, and we have still only defined eight keys in this way. In fact, the last sharp in this sequence, E♯, is not even a black note, but the same physical note as F. Likewise, the note Cb (physically B natural) is found in the key of Gb major.

The relative minor

Each major key shares its key signature with another key: its relative minor. For each key signature, the relative minor is found a minor third below the major (or the sixth step of the scale). For example, the key signature with no sharps or flats is shared by C major and A minor; one flat indicates F major or D minor. Because the key centre is different, the internal arrangement of notes in the scale is different, resulting in a different mood from the major key (just as minor chords sound different from major chords). The natural minor scale uses the same set of notes as its relative major; other types of minor scale are constructed by modifying it in various ways, for example by raising the seventh note by one semi-tone, resulting in the harmonic minor scale (see 'Gypsy jazz').

The flat keys

It is important to understand that just as the notes of the C major scale can be sharpened (or raised), they can also be lowered, or in other words, flattened. In the same way as F becomes F♯ to give us the first sharp key, the note B is lowered to B♭ (B flat) to give us the key of F major, the first 'flat' key. F is a perfect fifth *below* C. The flat key side of the circle is constructed by proceeding downwards in fifths, which gives guitar players each new key, as well as giving them each new flat note.

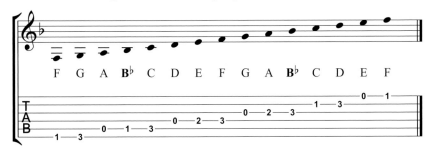

F G A **B♭** C D E F G A **B♭** C D E F

LEFT: *The F major scale in first position. Every note is a natural except for B♭, which defines the key signature.*

EXERCISE FINDING NEW KEYS ON THE FRETBOARD

All of these new keys can be located easily in first position on the guitar. The fretboard chart here shows the name of every note on the first four frets. To play any major scale, proceed as follows:

1 Find the lowest available root note (for example, for an F major scale, find the lowest F: bottom E string, first fret).

2 Using the circle diagram, check which notes of the scale will be sharps or flats (in F, the note B is lowered to B♭).

3 Play all the available note names in first position, from the lowest root note to the highest available root note, remembering that all notes will be natural except those specifically modified by the key signature (e.g. F major: F, G, A, B♭, C, D, E).

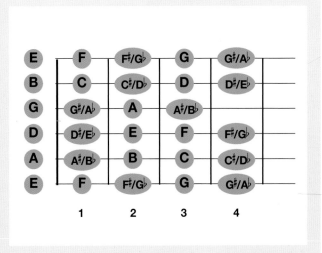

Chord construction

Some combinations of notes sound pleasing, while others sound dissonant – but why should this be? Fundamentally, the effect of a combination of notes derives from the intervals between them. The space between any two notes represents a harmonic relationship to which we instinctively have an emotional reaction. A minor third is inexplicably melancholy; a major third, universally upbeat.

Understanding intervals

The interval between two notes simply describes how far apart they are. The interval is defined by the number of steps up the scale from the lower note to the higher one. For example, the interval C–E is a third, because we can count three steps (C, D, E), whereas A–E is a fifth because it represents five steps (A, B, C, D, E).

These simple terms do not give the whole picture, however. Consider the two intervals C–E and D–F. Both are thirds, yet they sound different. Closer inspection reveals that the interval C–E spans two tones, whereas D–F is only one tone and a semitone. The former, being the larger interval, is called a major third, and the latter a minor third. All other intervals are also broadly defined by the number of scale steps, and precisely defined by the number of semitones.

A few intervals are particularly important if you want to understand basic chord construction. The best way to view them is in relation to a fixed lower note. Using the note C on the A string (third fret), we can find all the important intervals in first position and listen to them for comparison (see below).

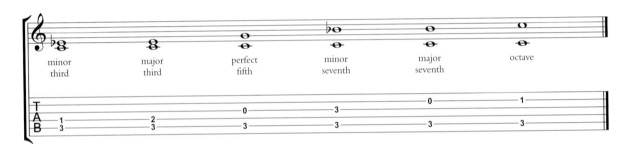

What makes a chord?

Any simultaneous sounding of two or more notes may be considered a chord. Western classical harmony uses mainly three-note chords (also known as triads), but jazz, pop and rock often use more complex chords with four notes or more (for example, dominant seventh and minor seventh chords contain four notes). It is important not to confuse the number of different notes in a chord with the number of strings played in a guitar chord shape. Open guitar chords such as E and G use all six strings but many notes are doubled in different octaves (for example, the familiar E shape contains three E notes), so there are still only three unique notes.

C triad (C major triad)

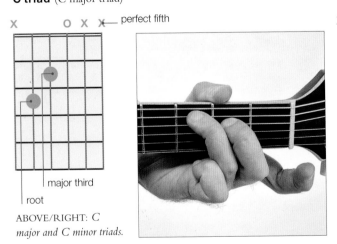

ABOVE/RIGHT: C major and C minor triads.

Cm triad (C minor triad)

Thirds

Chords are usually constructed as a stack of thirds. Starting with the root note of the chord, we add a note a third above, and then another note a third above that.

To minimize confusion, both of these are usually defined in terms of their relationship to the root note, and therefore known as the third and fifth of the chord. The third and fifth are defined independently in relation to the root. For example, a major chord is said to contain a major third and a perfect fifth; a minor chord contains a minor third and perfect fifth. From the intervals chart shown on the opposite page, we can simultaneously play the root (C), perfect fifth (G), and either the major or minor third (E or E$\flat$). These combinations will result in the major and minor triads respectively.

More complex chords

Chord construction may be continued in this way, becoming progressively more complex as we add more thirds: after the third and fifth various sevenths, ninths, elevenths and thirteenths may be added (although these notes are not often used all together to avoid internal clashes, and for the simple reason that the guitar has only six strings).

Seventh chords are commonplace in most popular music styles; more complex chords, originating in jazz, have also found their way into many pop styles, perhaps the most notable of these is soul music. We have encountered two types of third interval and two types of seventh. When combined with the root and perfect fifth, this results in four types of seventh chord. These are shown below as extensions of the C major and minor triads that are illustrated on the opposite page.

Normally in C the fifth would be played on the open G string. In some of the chords below, we use the G string to play the minor seventh – a B$\flat$ on the third fret. This means that there is no fifth in the chord as it is played, but this does not matter as seventh chords sound strong even when the fifth is omitted, and in fact this is often the case in jazz, where seventh chords are very often outlined using just the root, third and seventh.

Cmaj⁷ (C major seven)

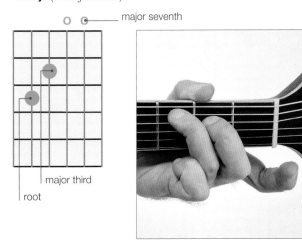

major seventh

major third

root

Cm⁽ᵐᵃʲ⁷⁾ (C minor, major 7)

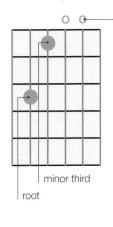

major seventh

minor third

root

C⁷ (C seven)

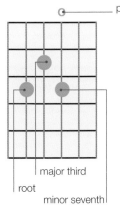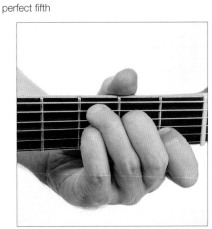

perfect fifth

major third

root

minor seventh

Cm⁷ (C minor seven)

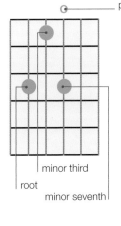

perfect fifth

minor third

root

minor seventh

How to find any note

Acquiring total knowledge of the guitar fretboard is a gradual process. Being able to name any note on the fretboard instantly (or, in reverse, to be able to find any named note on a given string) is the first step towards this. If you have the right theory knowledge, you can then start to construct chords yourself from first principles, rather than looking them up each time.

Knowing the notes

There are several ways to become familiar with all the available notes on the fretboard. You could simply learn the names of all the notes on all the strings by memorizing them individually, but this is time-consuming and dull, and it is hard to make use of the knowledge in a practical playing situation. There are other, more helpful ways to get to know your way around the neck, and to learn the names of all the places your fingers might want to stop. One approach involves thinking about the relationships between known and unknown notes.

Octave relationships

It makes sense to prioritize memorizing the notes on the two bottom strings (E and A). This is because the root notes of movable chord shapes are usually found on one of these strings. Playing as much material as possible using movable shapes (while also excellent practice in itself) will help these names to sink in. The chart of barre chords (see 'Barre chords') is a useful reference.

Once you know the names of the notes on the bottom strings, you can quickly find other notes by 'referring back' to those strings, using the octave interval and its shape on the fretboard. Two notes an octave apart (with the same letter name) will have a fixed physical relationship on the guitar fretboard: they are separated by a certain distance of strings and frets. Thus, a note on the upper strings may be named by quickly finding the note one or two octaves below. The shapes represented by these octave relationships are also important in themselves to many playing styles.

BELOW: *Octave intervals span two strings in all cases and two frets if the lower note is on the bottom E or A string, or three frets if the lower note is on the D or G string.*

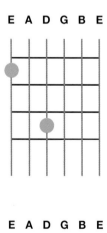

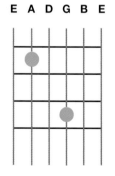

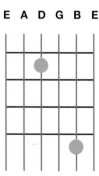

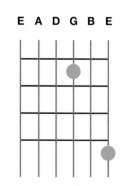

Identifying notes

The process for this is as follows:

• To identify an unknown note on the D or G string, find the note an octave below by jumping two strings down and two frets back.

• To identify an unknown note on the B string, find the note an octave below by jumping two strings down and three frets back. If this note is also unknown, repeat the process for finding an unknown note on the D string.

• The low and high E strings are two octaves apart and thus share the same note names at any given fret, making it unnecessary to learn the notes on the top E string separately.

ABOVE: *To find the note name of the D string, on the sixth fret, relate back to the E string on the fourth fret (G♯/A♭).*

ABOVE: *To find the note name of the G string, on the seventh fret, relate back to the A string on the fifth fret (D).*

Horizontal relationships

The octave relationship is complemented by a horizontal relationship: the fixed interval of one semitone between frets. Therefore, an unknown note can be related to a known note on the same string by counting the frets between and proceeding up or down the chromatic scale, remembering that there is no sharp/flat between the notes B and C, or between E and F.

Any notes at or above the 12th fret can also be related back to the lower frets: the 12th fret is an octave above the open string. Therefore, the 13th fret is an octave above the first fret; the 14th fret corresponds to the second, and so on.

ABOVE: *Because there are 12 frets to a complete octave, note names start again above the 12th fret. Therefore, the top E string at the 13th fret produces an F (an octave above the first fret).*

EXERCISE 1

Place one left-hand finger anywhere on the fretboard, without looking. Then, using the methods outlined above, work out the name of the note.

EXERCISE 2

In reverse: choose a string and a note name at random. Then find it, either working up the string one fret at a time or by relating to a known note.

How to transpose without a capo

As we have seen, the capo is extremely useful in that it enables quick transposition without any knowledge of music theory. Sometimes we need to transpose a song without using the capo. The chords in the new key will have different shapes, and in some cases will only be playable as barre chords. Finding the chords in the new key can require a little more knowledge.

Interval analysis

There are several ways to transpose a chord sequence into a new key, but they all require a good working knowledge of both intervals and keys.

The most direct approach simply involves analyzing the relationship between the two keys and applying that relationship to each chord in the sequence. For instance, if we wish to move a song from the key of C major to D major, as C and D are a major second (one tone) apart, each chord in the sequence will have to be transposed upwards by this interval. It is important to note that the chord type is always unaffected by transposition: only the chord root changes. In this example, C major becomes D major, Dm becomes Em, G7 becomes A7, and so on.

The safest way to analyze any interval relationship is in terms of semitones: on the guitar this is equivalent to a number of frets on the same string: count the number of semitones between the original key and the desired new key, and apply this to each chord in the sequence. It is also important to realize that the absolute direction of transposition is unimportant: there are ten semitones between G to F when counted upwards, but only two (or a whole tone) when counted downwards, and this is a far easier interval to deal with. In this way, you will never have to deal with any interval greater than a fifth.

Picking the key

If you have any freedom to choose (for example, when playing with a singer who simply needs a song a little higher rather than being restricted to a certain key), it is usually a good idea to bear in mind the relative difficulty of the chord shapes you will encounter in the new key. For example, a chord sequence in G major may be entirely composed of easy first-position shapes, but will require barre chords (or other movable shapes) throughout if transposed up one semitone to A♭ major. The key of A major (another semitone up) would usually be a better choice, as the main chords in this key can also be played in first position.

When deciding on a new key for a song, you may wish to consult the table below. This shows the main chords in the six most guitar-friendly keys; the really important chords (the major chords or three-chord trick) are shown in bold. Each row shows the main chords in one key; simply locate the original chord in that key, and then find the new chord in the appropriate row of the same column. For example, when transposing from the key of A to D (one row down), the D chord becomes a G chord.

The majority of songs can be transposed in this way, and of course any chord types not found here can still be transposed in the same way – only the root note or 'letter' name of the chord is important in determining the transposed chord.

Transposition table

	I	II	III	IV	V	VI
E major	**E**	F#m	G#m	**A**	**B**	C#m
A major	**A**	Bm	C#m	**D**	**E**	F#m
D major	**D**	Em	F#m	**G**	**A**	Bm
G major	**G**	Am	Bm	**C**	**D**	Em
C major	**C**	Dm	Em	**F**	**G**	Am

1950s chord sequence

This chord sequence (see 'Syncopated strumming') can be transposed easily. Let's go from the key of G to the key of E.

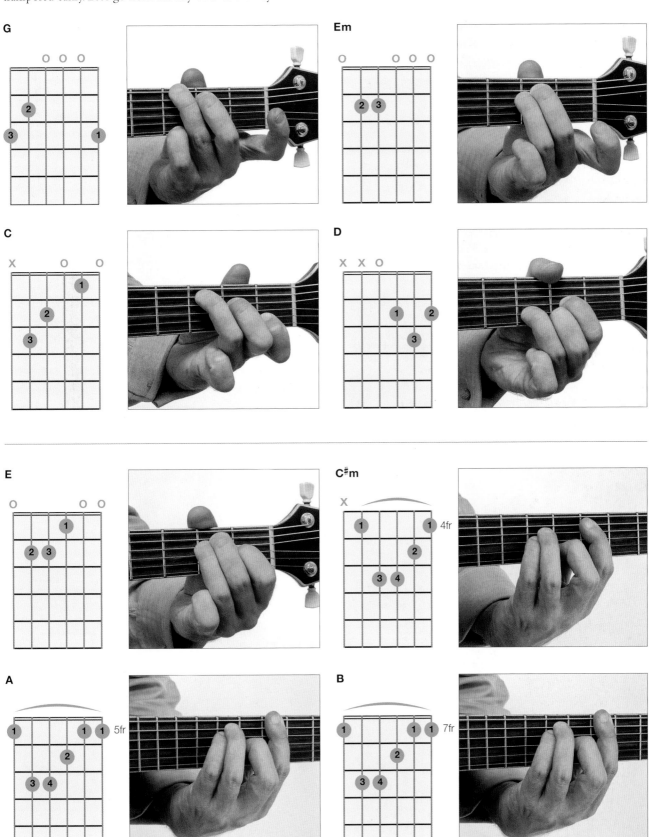

G

Em

C

D

E

C#m

A

B

Left-hand embellishments

The left hand can do more than fret the strings while the right hand plays the notes. It can fret the strings when they are already sounding, so as to elicit two notes from each right-hand stroke. You can add a finger at a higher fret to raise the pitch of a ringing string (a hammer-on), or remove a finger to lower it (a pull-off). Some styles incorporate both techniques liberally.

Slurring
Hammer-ons and pull-offs are fundamental techniques that can add a great deal of texture to your playing. They are both forms of 'slurring', which is a musical term that means deliberately altering the pitch without separately enunciating the change. Hammer-ons and pull-offs are often used sequentially in order to produce a smooth sequence of three or more notes – a kind of extended slur.

Hammer-on
In its simplest form, this technique involves a sequence of two sounding notes, but only the first is played by the right hand. As the name suggests, the second note is produced by 'hammering' a left-hand finger on to a string which is already ringing. The first note may be either an open string or a lower fretted note. This technique can be integrated into fingerpicking, on either bass or treble strings and in either bass/strum or arpeggio styles. Hammer-ons are also often used in melodic playing; a two-note phrase played in this way can sound more fluid than two individually picked notes. The hammer-on is usually shown in both standard notation and tablature using a slur (curved line) joining two ascending notes on the same string, sometimes with the letters 'H' or 'HO'.

1 Hammer-on from open string: play the open D string, then hammer on to the second fret (E).

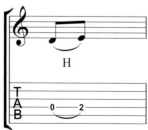

2 Hammer-on between fretted notes: play the second fret (E), then hammer on to the third fret (F).

Slur symbol
Pull-offs are also shown using a slur symbol, and may be accompanied by the indication 'PO'. The 'H' and 'PO' symbols are not always used, though, because the context differentiates them: if the slur is ascending, it is accomplished by hammering-on; if it is descending, then it must be a pull-off. Slurs should not be confused with ties (see 'The C major scale and first position').

Pull-off

The pull-off creates a descending figure that is, in effect, the opposite of a hammer-on. After playing the first note conventionally, the fretting finger is pulled away from the string to allow a second note to sound. Again, this can either be an open string or a lower fretted note.

Most pull-offs involve some downward motion of the finger. This has the effect of setting the second note ringing; in effect the left-hand finger is lightly plucking the string.

This is done because pulling-off, in its basic form, can have the effect of deadening the string, so the volume would be reduced if it were not given a little extra boost.

This type of pull-off is particularly effective on the top E string, since there is no adjacent string in the way, and is often used in folk guitar styles as an embellishment when finger-picking the chord of D major. Although not his unique invention, this is one of James Taylor's stock-in-trade ideas (see 'Using the fingers').

1 Pull-off to open string: play the second fret (E), then pull off to the open string (D).

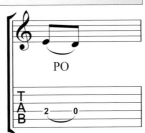

2 Pull-off between fretted notes: play the third fret (F), then pull off to the second fret (E).

EXERCISES 1 and 2

The major scale can be adapted into an excellent exercise, which manages to incorporate these techniques. The two examples here use hammer-ons in the ascending G major scale and pull-offs on the way down. Exercise 1 uses hammer-ons and pull-offs involving open strings, while Exercise 2 places the two of them between fretted notes.

Exercise 1

Exercise 2

Country picking

The acoustic guitar is central to the sound of country music. But country-style guitar is defined more by the technique than the instrument itself. The terms *banjo style*, *clawhammer* and *chicken pickin'* are often used to describe country guitar-playing. These involve busy thumb movement in the right hand, combined with fluid chordal figures and percussive rhythmic stabs played on the treble strings.

Elements of the style

In country-picking style, the thumb maintains a constant 'rocking' motion, alternating between bass notes on every beat of the bar. The root and fifth (see 'Chord construction') work well for this purpose with most chord shapes, although the driving rhythm is actually more important than the exact choice of bass notes. Merle Travis, regarded as the founder of this style, often struck several bass strings together for added power. The bass notes should be combined with the fingers in such a way as to give the impression of independent parts, rather as a pianist may maintain a bass line with the left hand while playing chords or a melody with the right hand. While arpeggio-based fingerstyle work uses the index, middle and ring fingers separately, country picking often uses two or three of them together to pluck chords on the treble strings.

The B7 chord

The B7 chord, another dominant seventh in first position, works well in the key of E major – a popular key in country, blues and rock'n'roll. Particular care should be taken not to let the open bottom E string sound when playing this chord.

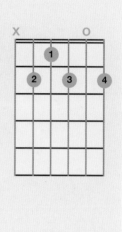

Pick 'n' fingers

As we have seen, conventional fingerstyle players use the nails of the right hand, which may be supported by a thumbpick and one or more fingerpicks. Many players also use a plectrum for strumming or melodic playing, but it can be awkward to have to pick up and put down the plectrum when shifting from one manner of playing to the other.

A solution to this technical problem, one favoured mainly by country players, involves playing the bass line with a plectrum held between the thumb and index finger, while the other three fingers do the picking on the top three strings. Since the rarely used index finger is occupied holding the plectrum, the rarely used little finger is then brought into play to cover the top string.

Some players find it hard to get the fourth finger to work independently of the third, so it is worth focusing on this aspect by practising arpeggio figures with this combined plectrum/fingerpicking technique.

Recommended listening
- Chet Atkins: "Travelin'"
- Elizabeth Cotton: "Freight Train"
- Dolly Parton: "Jolene"
- Elvis Presley (Scotty Moore): "Mystery Train"
- James Taylor: "Oh Susannah"

LEFT: The right hand here is using a hybrid pick/fingers technique. Some work may be necessary to achieve independence between the third and fourth fingers.

Merle Travis

Born in 1917, Merle Travis belonged to the generation that laid the foundations of modern country music before World War II. Although he contributed a clutch of songs that have earned a place in the American songbook (Tennessee Ernie Ford, a recording artist and TV presenter, had a huge radio hit with Travis's classic "Sixteen Tons"), Travis will probably be remembered even more for his style of guitar playing. As one of the first players to adopt and popularize the thumbpick, Travis developed the combination of constant bass motion and syncopated chords or melodic ideas that is today so instantly identifiable as 'country picking', but is in fact a rich mix of stylistic influences, including jazz, blues and ragtime (which was strongly represented in Travis's instrumental recordings). His influence can be heard on many country records, not least via Chet Atkins, who adopted and refined Travis's picking technique.

ABOVE: Merle Travis is one of the few who can justifiably be said to have invented a whole style of guitar playing.

EXERCISE 1

This exercise shows a bass line in the Merle Travis style. It should be played with the thumb only, and needs to be fluent before you can add the treble strings. Don't worry if the moving thumb sometimes cuts notes off: this staccato effect is often a key part of the style.

EXERCISE 2

Here, chord notes are added separately and together. Unlike the bass movement, these chord notes should be allowed to ring on for as long as possible, even when shown as quavers (half beats). You can use the staccato effect here, too, for a contrasting result. The notes on the top string, if accented and allowed to ring on, will function as a melodic strand.

Advanced country guitar

Country guitar often combines left- and right-hand techniques such as arpeggiated chords and the fluid use of hammer-ons and pull-offs. First-position chord shapes are favoured since they require little movement in the left hand. These chords also make for an effective sound: all the notes can ring freely, and melodic ideas can be integrated into the accompaniment.

Adding melody

The next step in developing banjo-style fingerpicking is to embellish a chordal accompaniment by adding fragments of melody. The easiest approach, particularly for fast playing, is to start with a familiar chord sequence so that the bass (thumb) motion will remain secure. Hammer-ons and pull-offs form an important part of this style, as they allow rapid melodic motion between beats. These slurs help to create a melodic line, and at the same time they sound much more fluid than the same notes picked individually.

Country ballads are often supported by sparse instrumental accompaniment dominated by the acoustic guitar. As the vocal line is often delivered using long, slow notes, the guitar maintains a sense of motion using continuous arpeggio patterns. This is sometimes known as 'ballad style', and is explored in Exercise 2, opposite.

Two new chords

You will encounter the E7 chord in Exercise 1, below. Here, the seventh is added on the B string (third fret) instead of the open D string. This is useful here, as it allows the top notes of the chords in bars 5 and 6 to form a descending melody.

Exercise 2 features the B minor barre chord. This is formed by barring the A minor shape at the second fret. The B string hammer-on used in the exercise (from the barre to the third fret) is a stock-in-trade folk/country guitar figure. Another popular move, as used in Dolly Parton's classic "Jolene", involves a simultaneous hammer-on by the second, third and fourth fingers: strum or pick the notes formed by the barre alone, then hammer the rest of the fingers into place.

E⁷

Bm

ABOVE: This is an alternative E7 shape with the seventh on the B string.

ABOVE: The chord of B minor (the Am shape barred at the second fret).

EXERCISE 1

This exercise builds on the country-picking exercise (see 'Country picking'): the chords and bass/thumb motion are the same. The E chord is often embellished here by using a hammer-on from the open G string to the first fret (G♯). This gives a bluesy effect, as the note G is the flattened third of the chord (see 'Introducing the Blues').

Chet Atkins

One of the towering figures of commercial country music, Chet Atkins was influential as both a guitarist and a record producer, and played both roles on scores of hit records by the biggest names in country music (as well as being a key figure in the development of Elvis Presley's career). Chet's famous 'Atkins style' right-hand technique, itself a development of Merle Travis's style, has been widely imitated, although his use of two fingers per string to pick melodies while maintaining bass motion is actually very difficult to master. In a career spanning five decades, Atkins collaborated with other guitarists of a similar stature, including Les Paul, Mark Knopfler and Tommy Emmanuel. Jazz influences abound in Atkins's own work; these, together with his apparent debt to classical right-hand technique, may have played a part in his migration from the Gretsch electric guitar to the Gibson nylon-strung acoustic model that bore his name.

RIGHT: Chet Atkins may have won countless Grammy awards as a record producer, and is remembered as the father of 'The Nashville Sound', but his contributions to guitar playing are arguably even greater.

A new chord sequence

The eight-bar chord sequence used for Exercise 1 is one of the standard chord sequences found in many styles of popular music, from ragtime and jazz to rock 'n' roll, and the second half of the progression turns up as an ending in many other songs. As with other stock chord sequences such as the '50s sequence and the 12-bar blues, it is well worth learning this progression in as many keys as possible.

I	IV	I	V7
I I7	IV IVm	I V7	I

ABOVE: The eight-bar chord sequence in Exercise 1 is easy if you apply the harmonic analysis method (see 'Chord construction'). This sequence can be analyzed as above.

EXERCISE 2

This exercise shows a typical example of a country/folk ballad accompaniment. The hammer-ons and pull-offs are illustrated using slurs. Each note here should be allowed to ring on for as long as possible. It is important to take particular care not to cut off ringing notes when performing hammer-ons and pull-offs.

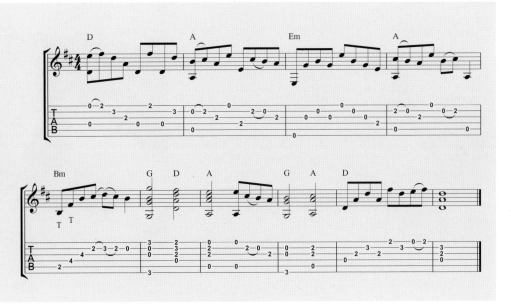

Integrating a melody

We have seen how to make musical patterns by fingerpicking, and we have also learnt how to embellish those figures by using passing notes and other techniques. From here, it is a short step to playing melody and chords simultaneously on the guitar. This may take many different forms, but as a rule, you pick out a tune on the top strings, while plucking the lower strings to provide a bass accompaniment.

Rhythm and melody

Generally speaking, melodies are made up either of chord notes or the passing notes found between them. That is to say, when you make a chord in first position, some of the notes you need to pick out a tune are already there, at your fingertips. The other notes are unlikely to be far away – you might only have to move one finger to find them. The difficult part is keeping the accompaniment going in a rhythmic way – maintaining the arpeggios on the lower strings – while you play the tune.

Ringing strings

The left-hand fingers have to do a little extra work to play the melody, and it is the job of the thumb to compensate and provide the arpeggio motion. The right-hand fingers may also have to shift around the strings to some extent. That is to say, you may have to depart from the beginner's principle whereby the first three fingers are anchored to the top three strings. For example, it is often better to deploy two fingers when playing consecutive notes on the same string (one finger naturally has to move off its 'home' string to do this). The result is likely to be more fluent than when one finger-plucks the same string twice in a row.

First-position chords using two or three left-hand fingers lend themselves to melodic embellishment, because the fourth finger can be used to fret the passing notes without disrupting the shape of the chord. Other notes not in the chord can be found on open strings by lifting fingers.

Occasionally, however, the chord shape will have to be disrupted in order to fret a passing note. For example, the notes B–G are available on the top two strings when playing the C chord: C and E are part of the chord; the open B string is revealed by lifting the first finger; D and G can be added using the fourth finger.

Sometimes you will have to be inventive to find the note you want. Say your melody contains an F over the C chord. It can be found on the top string's first fret, which means that your first finger is close by – on the right fret, one string away. You might move that finger to make the F if you can do without it for a moment, or you might flatten it into a partial barre covering both strings. As long as there are notes sounding from the lower part of the shape (and the open B string does not sound), this need not disrupt the sense of harmony. This is exactly what happens in the first bar of Exercise 2 (opposite).

Tommy Emmanuel

Few players have caused as much excitement in the acoustic guitar world in recent years as the Australian Tommy Emmanuel. Emmanuel's style owes much to the lineage of Merle Travis and Chet Atkins, the latter of whom was one of Tommy's childhood heroes (and later a musical collaborator: their duo album was Atkins's last recording). Although often overtly country-based, Tommy Emmanuel's dazzling solo acoustic work draws on a far wider spectrum of styles and musical resources, including folk, jazz and classical guitar. An Emmanuel performance epitomizes the solo guitarist's dream of juggling multiple strands so skilfully that they meld into one.

RIGHT: In a Tommy Emmanuel performance, the bass line, chords and melody seem to pour forth simultaneously, belying the fact that there really is just one man playing.

EXERCISE 1

This exercise explores the melodic possibilities that can be found on the top E and B strings, while maintaining an arpeggio accompaniment using the chords of C, Am and G.

EXERCISE 2

This exercise is a melodic study using the main chords in G major. The melody consists of both chord notes and passing notes. All right-hand fingerings are shown on the stave to help you. In the first bar, you will have to use the partial barre, as described above.

EXERCISE 3

This is the traditional melody "Greensleeves", with a harmony constructed from first-position chords.

Tip

Sometimes you will have to interrupt the flow of bass and chords to fit in a melodic idea. Try to do this with confidence and without interrupting the basic pulse.

Altered tunings

The guitar's standard tuning, E A D G B E, is just one of many possibilities. There are other ways to tune a guitar, and these alternatives can make the instrument sound and feel very different. This can be a refreshing experience, but also a confusing one. However, different tunings are an experiment worth trying, because they might open up new avenues for you as a guitarist.

Non-standard tunings

There are many approaches to changing the guitar's tuning. Broadly speaking, the non-standard tunings can be divided into two groups: altered tunings, where the starting point is standard tuning but one or more strings are tuned differently; and open tunings, where the open strings are tuned to the notes of a chord. We will be looking at open tunings later. For now, let's take a look at a couple of altered tunings.

Described on the right are two tunings that require you to alter the pitch of just one string. This means that standard chord shapes will now sound different. Depending on the shape and context, the result may be either musically interesting or alternatively very dissonant.

E A D G B D# – the top E string is lowered by one semitone. To achieve this quickly with relative tuning, tune the guitar as normal and then tune the top E string to the B string, fourth fret. This has an interesting effect on many familiar shapes: E and G become maj7 chords and the simple A shape turns into a very complex-sounding 'add#11' chord. (This is a major chord and added note which is an augmented fourth above the root note.)

E A D G A E – the B string is lowered by one tone. (After tuning to standard tuning, the B string should be tuned to the G string, second fret.) This has an equally complex effect on basic shapes such as E, A and G.

Retune with care

Acoustic guitar strings are designed to produce optimal sound at fairly high tension. The string gauges in a standard set are designed with standard tuning in mind, so that string tension will be even across all the strings. So, tuning a string higher than its standard intended pitch can result in breakage. A semitone, or even a tone, is usually safe, but going beyond this is generally unwise. It is no coincidence that altered tunings tend to involve lowering strings more often than raising them.

LEFT: Be prepared for string breakages if you turn the strings too far above their normal range. Tuning down is safer.

Joni Mitchell

Without exaggeration, Joni Mitchell can be described as one of the most influential musicians of the late 20th century. Although she emerged from a folk background, playing clubs and coffee bars in late 1960s New York, within her first few albums Mitchell had staked out a musical territory encompassing folk, rock, modern jazz and avant-garde sonic experimentation. As a guitarist, Mitchell has probably explored the world of altered tunings more deeply than any other major singer/songwriter: many of her musical ideas stem from the harmonic possibilities of a unique tuning; she has claimed that she originally did not know there was such a thing as standard tuning.

RIGHT: Joni Mitchell often works with some of the world's finest jazz musicians, but her folk roots and her own highly innovative guitar style are ingredients that are vital to most of her well-known songs.

USING DIFFERENT STRINGS

String breakage, at least at home, is only a big problem when you run out of strings, so you should keep spares if you intend to experiment with tunings. Having spare strings around the house also allows you even more room for experimentation. If, for example, you would like to try raising the D string by a fourth to G, replace it with a standard G string, since this is the pitch it is designed for.

Recommended listening:

- Coldplay: "Yellow"
- Crosby, Stills, Nash & Young: "Guinevere"
- David Gray: "My Oh My"
- Joni Mitchell: "A Case of You"

EXERCISE TUNING: E A D G B D♯

This exercise uses the first of the two non-standard tunings described opposite. For comparison, many shapes are the same in both pieces, although they sound different and have different names. Where a shape corresponds to a familiar chord's standard tuning, this is given in brackets. All the chord shapes are shown; some of them, you will notice, are new and unfamiliar, but in fact they are all essentially just simple shapes.

Tuning: E A D G B D♯

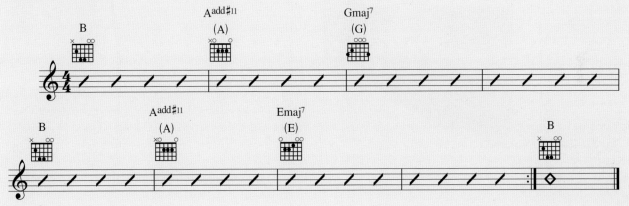

EXERCISE TUNING: E A D G A E

Dropping the B string down to A creates some interesting tensions, particularly against shapes with the third on the G string, such as E and Em.

Tuning: E A D G A E

Tip

In some instances, familiar shapes from standard tuning can result in really dissonant chords in other tunings, but usually only a slight modification will produce something usable and often interesting.

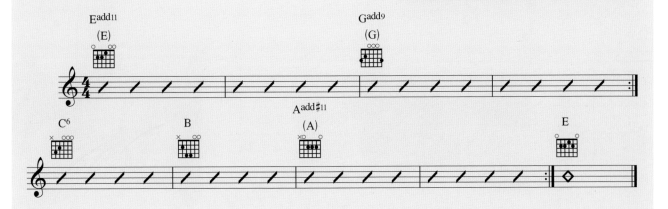

Drop D tuning

Perhaps the most useful of the altered tunings, drop D is very popular with guitarists. As with the tunings we have already looked at, drop D involves adjusting just one string: the bottom E, which is tuned down a tone to D. This extends the range of the guitar and adds a resonant bass thrum to the sound – this is especially effective when you are playing in the key of D or D minor.

The bass D note

In standard tuning, a bass D note is not really available. The lowest D you can have is to be found on the open fourth string. So, tuning the bottom string down to D slightly extends the range of the guitar and has a surprisingly profound effect on the character of the chords you play. Songs to listen to include "Fat Bottomed Girls" (Queen), "Stuck in the Middle" (Stealer's Wheel) and "Polly" (Nirvana Unplugged).

Detuning the bottom string

To retune to drop D, pick the bottom E string together with the D string while dropping the pitch of the E string. It should be very obvious when the two notes are exactly an octave apart, as the slight rhythmic 'beating' effect, caused by two notes that are almost but not quite in tune, will disappear.

One advantage of drop D tuning is that open D chords (major and minor) can now be supported with a truly deep bass note. The disadvantage is that familiar chords with the root on the E string need to be modified to work in drop D. The principle is easy to learn: since it has been detuned by one tone, the bottom string must be fretted two frets higher than in standard tuning to play the same note. This is easier to achieve with some shapes than others.

As with most non-standard tunings, most players tend to utilize the strengths of drop D and avoid using shapes that do not lend themselves to smooth execution.

LEFT TOP, CENTRE AND BOTTOM: Some important chords modified for use in drop D. Notice the muted A string in the G chord for strumming; this should be muted with the side of the third finger.

BELOW: The D minor chord is especially sonorous with the deep low D bass available in drop D tuning. (As with the D major chord, the bottom E string would not be played in standard tuning.)

E

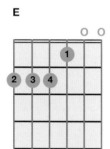

Em

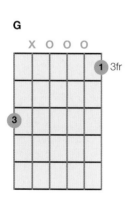

G

Dm

Barre chords in drop D

Although the open E chord is easy to modify to drop D, barre chords based on the E shape cannot be used in this tuning (at least, not with the bottom string sounding). However, the rich sound of the three lowest open strings can easily be moved around using a partial barre: the first section of the index finger (usually) plays the three lowest strings simultaneously at the same fret. This produces a movable chord consisting of the root, perfect fifth and octave. As there is no third, this chord is neither major nor minor, and is usually known as a '5' chord (A5, C5 etc) or a 'power chord'. '5' chords are playable in standard tuning too (simply play the bottom three strings of an E-derived barre chord), but there is something especially gutsy about the sound of a '5' chord in drop D tuning.

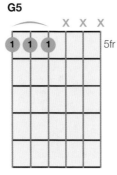

G5

RIGHT: The G5 chord in drop D, played with a partial barre.

EXERCISE 1

This exercise is an introduction to the sound of drop D: a simple arpeggio accompaniment in D major, using the D major chord (the standard shape, but including a low open D), as well as modified G and Em shapes (see opposite). The Am shape is unchanged, as the bottom string is not used.

EXERCISE 2

This exercise uses the full ringing open Dm chord along with the movable one-finger power chord (F5 and G5). This type of riff works well in many settings, from folk-rock to grunge.

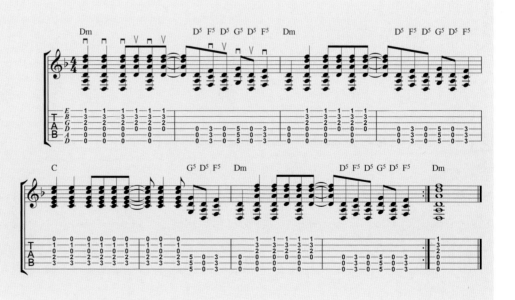

Open tunings

In open tunings, all six strings are tuned to the notes of a particular chord, meaning that the open strings ring pleasingly together. This euphony serves as a kind of platform on which complex harmonies can be built, often using simple movable shapes. So open tunings can lead to unexpected musical results, and for that reason they are popular among singer/songwriters.

Tuning for songwriting

Many great songs have been written around open tunings. Some very fine players – Nick Drake, John Martyn, Richard Thompson, for example – have used open tuning in preference to standard tuning most of the time.

In theory, any chord of any type can be used as the basis of open tuning. If you wanted to, you could tune your guitar to a minor chord, a seventh, or something more complex. In practice, however, straightforward major chords work best – and only a few of the major chords at that. The most widely used open tunings are D, C and G. We will deal with open D and C overleaf. Here, by way of introduction to the possibilities of open tuning, we will look at open G, sometimes known as 'Spanish' tuning.

Open G

To tune to open G, start in standard tuning and drop both the E strings and the A string down by one tone. The open strings are now tuned to D G D G B D (the notes of a G major triad are G, B and D). Just as for drop D tuning, this can be easily achieved by comparing octaves: the new string pitches should be tuned to the existing D and G strings.

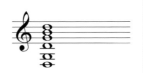

ABOVE: The pitches of the open strings in open G.

EXERCISE OPEN G TUNING: D G D G B D

This exercise introduces some partly familiar shapes on the G, B and D strings, ringing against open strings.

Strum the shapes shown in the given rhythm below, changing the chords where indicated, playing all the strings shown as open or fretted. Be careful not to play the bottom string where marked with an 'X'.

After this, feel free to try a sparser approach, picking individual strings or strumming only some of them. Don't worry too much about the names above the chord boxes: when playing an open tuning, simple shapes can result in complex harmony, but most players using open tunings tend to think in terms of shapes rather than theory.

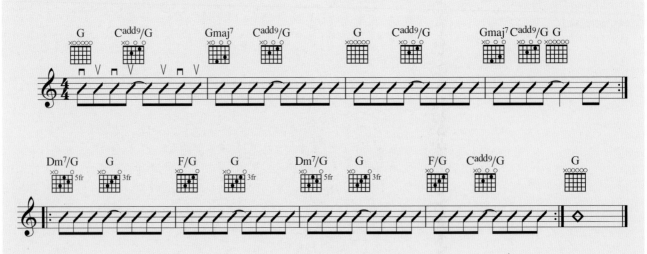

G, B and D

You will notice that three adjacent strings – G, B and D – are tuned the same way as in standard tuning. In other words, half the notes you might potentially want to play are in the places you are used to finding them. This is one of the things that makes G a popular open tuning, as well as the best introduction to the device. The familiar harmonic relationships here can be exploited, either on their own or against one or more open strings.

Of course, entirely new chord shapes are also possible and sometimes necessary, as you will see when you come to do the exercises. Open tunings lend themselves well to barre chords, because the simplest way to play any major chord is simply to make a full barre on the appropriate fret.

ABOVE: A very simple chord shape – in open tunings, major chords can be found by barring across all six strings. In open G tuning, this full barre at the fifth fret produces a C major chord.

EXERCISE OPEN G TUNING: D G D G B D

Many ideas in open tunings are constructed from very simple melodic movement using fretted notes against open strings. This piece is played entirely in quavers (half-beat notes) and will sound great if you allow all the notes, whether open or fretted, to ring until another note is played on the same string. This instruction is not reflected in the note values shown here, since it would look extremely messy. Note also that changing the tuning changes the normal correspondence between the top stave (with the musical notation) and the tab stave. If in doubt, follow the tab. This dreamy piece may be played using either fingerstyle or picking technique. Note the use of double hammer-ons (see 'Left-hand embellishments') to play an ascending melody. This is a popular folk guitar move.

More open tunings

In all open tunings, the open strings contain the notes of the tonic chord, while full barres at frets 5 and 7 are a way of making chords IV and V very easy to play. However, open tunings are much more than merely convenient. Their value also lies in the interesting effects that can be achieved when single fretted notes, or very simple shapes, sound against the open strings.

Open D

Sometimes called 'Sebastopol' tuning after a famous tune of the same name, open D is probably the most widely used open tuning after open G. It was popular with many of the early acoustic blues guitarists, and it has also been favoured by more contemporary players, such as Ry Cooder and Joni Mitchell. Open tunings tend to have a set of shapes or 'moves' that bring out the essence of the tuning. In the case of open D, particularly in a folky context, double-stopped sixths on the bottom A and the F♯ (G) strings have this effect. Each shape outlines a chord in the harmonized D major scale. The remaining open strings (all either D or A, the tonic and fifth of the key), either 'agree' with the fretted notes or create interestingly tense chords.

LEFT: The strings in open D: D A D F♯ A D.

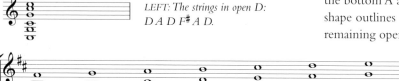

LEFT: Double-stopped sixths in open D tuning.

Open C

Any tuning with a low C on the bottom string is bound to have a rich, dark sound. This pitch is about as low as you can go with a standard string, and you get some 'rattle' from the string because it is so much slacker than usual. Some players consider this effect part of the charm of such tunings; if you don't agree, then change the bottom string for a heavier one. The beauty of open C tuning is that the upper strings are in their usual range, so there is plenty of 'zing' that contrasts intriguingly with the murkiness of the bottom string.

LEFT: The strings in open C: C G C G C E.

There are open tunings for other keys, too. Many of them are actually the same tunings as some of the ones already described, but at different pitches. The most popular open A tuning, for example, is open G transposed up a tone. Likewise, the most popular open E tuning is the open D given above, but raised by a tone across all the strings.

If you want to play in open E, bear in mind that it will necessitate raising the pitch of three of the strings above the pitches that they have in standard tuning, so both the neck and strings are placed under greater strain. A safer way to achieve open E is to tune to open D and place a capo at the second fret. Apart from effectively reducing access to the very top of the fretboard, there is no musical difference.

Phil Keaggy

During the course of a career spanning more than 50 albums, Phil Keaggy's eclectic style has crossed musical barriers with breathtaking ease, all the way from folk-rock to contemporary jazz; his technical virtuosity is always in evidence and yet it never gets in the way of his musical vision. Keaggy often explores a far wider range of sonic possibilities than most players: unusual tunings, two-handed tapping, drumming on the body and strings, and even managing to simultaneously play the shaker with his picking hand. His live solo performances frequently make use of electronic delays to create loops, enabling him to build up complex harmonies, textures and rhythms.

RIGHT: Phil Keaggy lost most of his right-hand middle finger in an accident at the age of four, yet he has often been voted one of the greatest fingerstyle guitar players in the world.

EXERCISE **OPEN D**

All of the chords here contain just two fretted notes, which sound against open strings. To avoid congestion on the stave, each chord is spelt out in full initially; rhythms using slash notation mean 'keep playing this chord in the rhythm shown.'

Tip

Although the shapes here use all six strings, it can also be appropriate to vary the number of strings used to create musical accents.

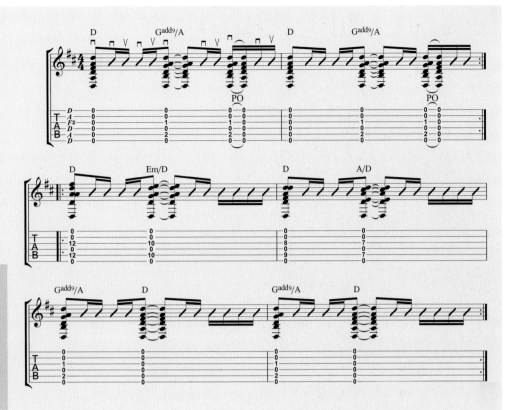

EXERCISE **OPEN C**

This piece looks much harder than it really is. The F and G bars are played using a full barre at the fifth and seventh frets respectively – no other left-hand finger movement is required here. C bars require a little more attention: take care not to cut off ringing open strings as you play the fretted notes. The final chord at the 12th fret may also be played as harmonics (see 'Advanced left-hand techniques').

DADGAD tuning

DADGAD occupies a special niche because it is neither an open tuning nor an altered tuning. It is so called because those are the notes the strings are tuned to. It is especially dear to acoustic folk guitarists, and it has an instantly identifiable, unmistakably Celtic flavour, but is also found in rock music. There are dedicated DADGAD players who have made a lifetime's study of the tuning.

How to achieve DADGAD tuning

DADGAD tuning can be reached by using standard tuning as a reference. First, drop the low and high E strings to D (using the octave interval to get them in tune with the D string), then drop the B string to A (an octave above the open A string). DADGAD can be seen as a close relative of the open D tuning that you have already encountered. The difference is that in DADGAD, the third string is tuned to G rather than F#.

ABOVE: This shows the pitches of the open strings when using DADGAD tuning.

Recommended listening:
- Dick Gaughan: "Song for Ireland"
- Led Zeppelin: "Black Mountain Side"
- Lee Westwood Ensemble: *Nymph Suite*

The nature of DADGAD

DADGAD is an unusual type of guitar tuning. Most guitar tunings are built on combinations of thirds, fourths and fifths between adjacent strings. In DADGAD, two of the strings (G and A) are tuned just a major second (one whole tone) apart. This 'crunch' interval plays a large part in the unworldly sound of DADGAD. If the open strings can be said to make a chord at all, it is not a major or minor chord, but a 'suspended' chord (Dsus4 or Gsus2, depending on which note is considered the root), and most simple fretted shapes in this tuning can be given similarly complex names. The suspended open chord can be turned into a D5 power chord using just one finger: the G string, second fret. Try executing a rapid hammer-on from the open string to this note while you are strumming all six strings. This high-impact sound can be achieved only in DADGAD tuning.

Muting strings

Some of the chords in Exercise 2 opposite contain unplayed muted strings. As we have seen, these can often be muted 'as if by accident' with the side of a fretting finger. However, it is not possible to mute the bottom string in this way, and the energetic strumming style required here makes it difficult to control which strings are struck with the right hand. The solution is to wrap the left-hand thumb around the neck to mute the bottom string, a technique that would incur disapproval from most classical guitar teachers.

RIGHT: The left-hand thumb muting the bottom string. The thumb should touch the string with enough pressure to mute it but not enough to produce a note.

An ear for open tunings

If you have a good ear, you may be tempted to approach retuning by making approximate adjustments and then fine-tuning until strumming all six strings simply sounds 'right'. This approach has pitfalls in open tunings especially, as the guitar's frets are spaced according to equal temperament, a compromise system in which all the intervals sound equally good, although none is quite perfect. Tuning the open strings by ear (even in standard tuning, but especially in open tunings and DADGAD) will give an uneven result, where some chords are built on the intervals that sound really good, while others will sound really bad. In open tunings, use the strings that are an octave apart as the basis of your tuning by ear, because the octave interval is constant regardless of temperament. This rule may be relaxed when using open tunings for slide playing (see 'Advanced left-hand techniques').

EXERCISE 1

This is a classic DADGAD folk accompaniment. As with open tunings, some of the chord names here get rather complex, but the basic ideas are simple. This piece is strummed in semiquavers; this means doubling the usual rate of down/upstroke motion, as shown in the first bar. To reduce visual congestion, each chord change is reflected in the TAB stave, but after this slashes in the top stave only are used until the next chord change.

Tip

Fast strumming does not always have to be extremely loud: playing slightly softer most of the time leaves some room to create accents when you need them.

Tuning: D A D G A D

EXERCISE 2

This exercise is written in a similar strumming style. The indication 'cont. sim.' means 'carry on like this'. While continuing to play in a similar way, there is also some freedom to vary the strumming pattern while staying true to the style established in the previous measure. Feel free to use hammer-ons and pull-offs with both the D5 chord (as in Exercise 1) and the A7sus4 chord. Placing the pull-off on beat 4 (so that the last three semiquavers are played on open strings) allows plenty of time for changing chord. Don't worry too much about this, however: occasional muffled notes just before a chord change let the ear know that the player is human rather than a machine!

Tip

Try playing this exercise with a metronome, slowly at first, making sure that strums on the beat (the first of each group of four) occur exactly on the beat.

Tuning: D A D G A D

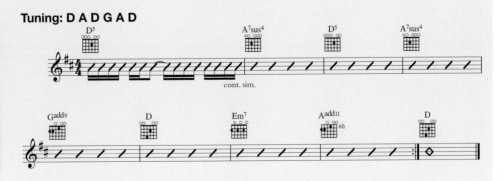

Introducing jazz chords

To play jazz chord sequences, you have to take a slightly different approach to chord construction. Instead of using first-position open chords or movable barre shapes, you will have to adopt a minimalist approach where only the essential notes are played. This pared-back method is the essence of jazz guitar and, when done right, it makes for a highly sophisticated sound.

Voice leading

There are two main reasons why jazz harmony requires a different approach. The first is the principle known as voice leading. Ideally, each note except the root should move to the nearest available note within the next chord, rather than leaping randomly around the neck, as can often happen with barre chords.

So, voice leading means thinking 'horizontally' about the melodic sequence that each note in the chord is making. This is far removed from the bar-by-bar block of sound that

ordinary strumming produces. And if some notes are doubled on several strings, as is the case with ordinary chord-making, then voice leading becomes practically impossible.

The other reason for the fact that jazz chords take a sparse form is that jazz, by its nature, uses many notes beyond the root, third, fifth and seventh.

If these extensions are added to the full chord, the result is likely to sound messy or to contain internal clashes. In any case, the guitar has only six strings, so an economical approach to basic chords is very useful.

Three essential notes

The simplest jazz chord shapes contain just three notes, but these are rarely the standard root, third and fifth of the scale. Seventh chords form the basis of jazz harmony, but normally, a seventh chord contains four notes: root, third, fifth and seventh. To achieve a jazzy three-note voicing, the fifth is omitted. The third is what tells you whether a chord is major or minor, and is therefore essential. The seventh note has to be there to make the chord a seventh. The fifth does not define the chord, and so is dispensable.

We now come to the key question of where to find the three required notes. Placing the root on either the low E string or the A string results in two sets of chord shapes with the third and seventh on the D and G strings in both cases. The conventions of jazz harmony mean that most chord sequences can be played by alternating between these two types, thus enabling the thirds and sevenths to move in steps rather than by leaps. It is only the bass note that needs to move in larger leaps.

There are three basic types of seventh chord: dominant seventh (7), major seventh (maj7) and minor seventh (m7). These are shown below, based on root notes at the third fret. This gives us a set of G chords (root: E string) and a set of C chords (root: A string).

These shapes (often used without the bass note when playing with a band) form a useful basis for more advanced harmony using extensions such as ninths and 13ths (see 'More jazz chords').

Recommended listening:
- Count Basie Quartet (Freddy Green): "I Don't Know"
- James Taylor: "Gorilla"
- Joe Venuti & Eddie Lang: "Wild Cat"
- Jim Hall: "Bossa Antigua"

BELOW: The three basic seventh chords in G and C, with the root on the E string and A string at the third fret. These six shapes form the basis for a lifetime's worth of exploration.

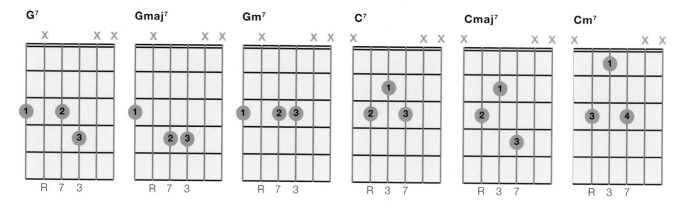

G7   Gmaj7   Gm7   C7   Cmaj7   Cm7

Muting

A chord shape with three sounding notes inevitably has three unplayed strings. It is of course possible to pick only the three fretted notes with the thumb and first two fingers. However, many jazz accompaniment styles are based on rhythmic strums. In order to be able to strum with some rhythmic drive, it is not feasible to use only the right hand to control which strings will sound. Instead, the left hand should mute the unplayed strings.

The fretting fingers therefore do two jobs: the fingertips fret the notes of the chords while the sides of the fingers mute the unwanted strings. Experimentation is the best way to arrive at your own version of this technique. By way of an example, here is a G7 shape. Note that the fretting fingers fall across the unplayed strings to mute them.

ABOVE: The G7 chord at the third fret.

EXERCISE 1

This exercise strings together dominant seventh chords. Alternating between shapes with the roots on the E and A strings allows for elegant voice leading: the thirds and sevenths move largely in semitones.

EXERCISE 2

This exercise uses a series of moves called the II-V-I progression. It consists of the harmonized seventh chords on steps II, V and I of any key, and is such a strong progression in its own right that it effectively establishes a temporary key centre each time it is transposed. This effect is exactly what happens in this exercise.

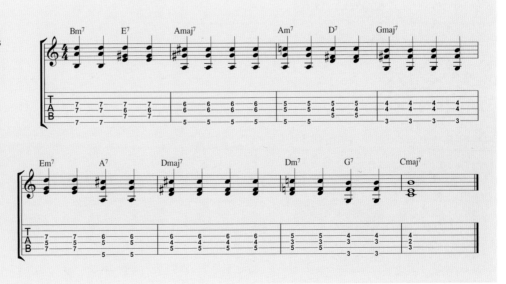

More jazz chords

Jazz harmony is based on seventh chords, but has gradually evolved in complexity. Dominant seventh-type chords, in particular, are often spiced up further by the addition of various other notes. The theory behind these additional notes can get a little complicated, but fortunately it is possible to take a guitar-based approach that avoids most of the theoretical complexity.

Building a jazz chord vocabulary

Our two basic three-note dominant seventh shapes (see 'Introducing jazz chords') provide an excellent basis for adding extensions without tying our fingers in knots. The simplest approach is to look at all the notes that can be added on the B string. With the root either on the E string or the A string, all notes at nearby frets on the B string can be added to produce usable extended jazz chords.

Our basic three-note shapes all use the first three fingers of the left hand. Most available notes on the B string can be added easily with the fourth finger, but this does not work for all permutations: for some shapes, the fingers need to be swapped around. These chords are again shown with the root at the third fret (G7 and C7 chords).

The ninth chord shown here can also be played using a partial barre with the third finger for the G and B strings.

Natural and altered tension

Extended dominant seventh chords are used almost constantly in modern jazz. If you play through the six chords shown below, you will notice that the '9' and '13' shapes (C9 and G13) have a simpler, less dissonant sound than the rest. The ninth and 13th chords are known as natural tension chords, whereas the rest are altered tension chords. These are usually easy to spot, because the chord symbols are longer and more complicated.

The two natural tension shapes can be used in any part of a chord sequence in place of a dominant seventh (7) chord. Altered tension chords should be used with a little more care, generally only in place of a dominant seventh chord that is resolving up a fourth (or down a fifth – see 'Seventh chords'). For example, if a G7 chord is followed by a C chord (whether major or minor), an altered tension chord may be used. If it is followed by anything else, it is usually safer to stick to a natural tension chord (9 or 13).

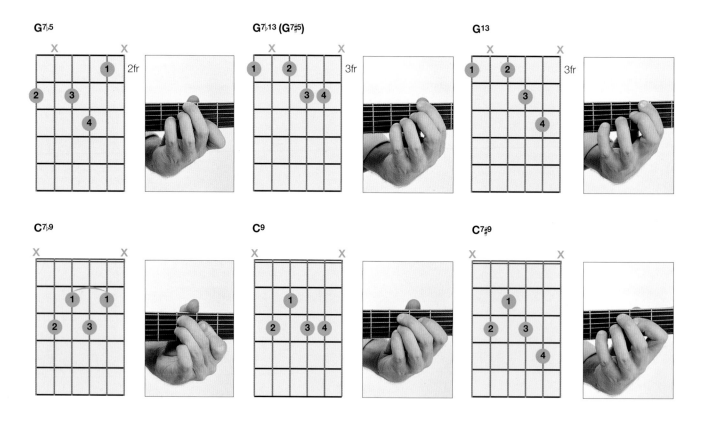

EXERCISE 1

This exercise is based on the cycle of fifths (see 'Understanding keys') – a sequence in which each chord resolves up a fourth. The sequence could therefore use altered tension chords throughout, but in fact it alternates between natural and altered tension for ease of fingering; each 'voice' (string) moves musically nonetheless.

EXERCISE 2

This exercise is based on the same sequence as the exercise above, but it reverses the tensions. Doing this results in a slightly richer sound. This is because the 7$^{\sharp}$9 chord has a particularly 'spiky' dissonant quality, which makes it a popular choice not only when playing jazz but in blues and rock, too.

EXERCISE 3

As before, the chords here may be strummed with the plectrum, but you may also wish to try picking the notes of each chord simultaneously, either using the thumb and first three fingers, or the plectrum and fingers in hybrid right-hand technique (see 'Country picking'). This immediately lends the piece a Latin jazz flavour; feel free to experiment.

The 12-bar blues in jazz

The basic three-chord blues can be modified in a great many ways. It is almost infinitely adaptable, and it crops up in musical genres that, on the face of it, appear to have little to do with the blues. The 12-bar sequence runs like a thread through jazz (which is related to the blues), but the chords and their uses are altered in some quite intriguing ways; the possibilities explored here are just the beginning.

Blues with a jazzy accent

In a jazz context, almost every chord in the 12-bar sequence can be substituted by a different chord. Such is the strength of the underlying blues structure that the result is always recognizable as a 12-bar blues.

As we have seen, the II–V progression is central to modern jazz. There are many places in the blues sequence where a II–V progression can be added. One way is to change the last line so that the chords V–IV (D7–C7 in the key of G) become II–V (Am7–D7).

This simple move is the most important in turning the sequence into a jazz blues. The same II–V progression can also be added in the final bar. Exercise 1 (opposite, top) puts these two changes into effect, along with the use of chord IV (C7) in the second bar.

The dominant seventh chord always 'wants' to resolve to a major or minor chord a perfect fourth above. So it can be said that almost any chord has its own related V chord. For example, the dominant seventh chord in G major is D7. The chromatic chord of A7 can be used in the key of G major, even though it does not strictly belong to the key. The A7 chord resolves to D7, which makes it 'chord V of chord V', or the secondary dominant. Secondary dominants can be used freely in the jazz blues.

In the same way, any dominant seventh-type chord can be preceded by a m7 (minor seventh) chord a fourth below to give a II–V progression. In our example, the blues in G, the II–V (Am7–D7) can be preceded by its own secondary II–V (Bm7–E7). Exercise 2 (opposite, below) adds some secondary II–V progressions to the sequence.

The last two bars of the structure now take the form of a jazz turnaround: as the name suggests, this is a short chord sequence which rounds off a chord structure and leads us back to the first chord. These four chords can be analyzed in terms of the key as follows: I7 – VI7 – IIm7 – V7. This is a very useful sequence to learn in as many keys as possible.

Pulling off the turnaround

The turnaround can also be modified by means of tritone substitution to G7 – B♭7 – A7 – A♭7 – another stock-in-trade jazz progression. The tritone is an interval of a diminished fifth or augmented fourth, so called because it spans three tones. This interval sounds rather dissonant on its own, especially in the context of simple harmony. Banned in church and known by the term *diabolo in musica* ('the devil in music'), it was rarely found in classical music until the 19th century.

However, the tritone is crucial to the sound of modern jazz, because it is at the heart of the dominant seventh chord. The fact that every tritone interval is actually present in two seemingly unrelated chords makes it possible to substitute one for the other.

In the jazz turnaround described above, the chord B♭7 can be substituted for E7, because they have a tritone in common. (D7 becomes A♭7 in the same way, C7 becomes G♭7 and so on.)

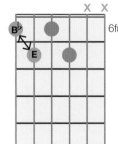

B♭7 & E7

6fr

LEFT: E7 and B♭7 chords – note the common tritone (shown in red).

FAR LEFT: The tritone interval – two notes that exemplify the sound of jazz. Many 'spiky'-sounding jazz compositions have been written around this sound.

EXERCISE BASIC JAZZ BLUES

This sequence uses three-note jazz voicings (see 'Introducing jazz chords') rather than full/open chords.

Tip

This sequence may be transposed into any key by simply moving it up the fretboard. Beyond approximately the eighth fret, however, the bass notes will sound rather high, so it would usually be better to start with a shape that has the root on the fifth string.

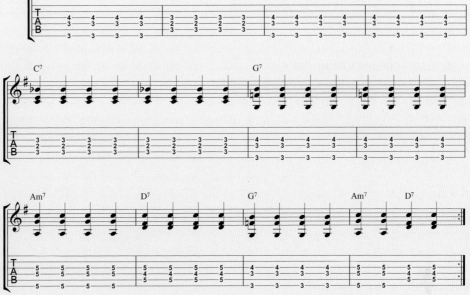

EXERCISE JAZZ BLUES NO. 2

This exercise expands the blues sequence further by adding relative II–V progressions and a jazz turnaround at the end.

Tip

The turnaround here can be modified using tritone substitutions in any number of ways; all of them will resolve to G7 for the next repeat of the sequence.

A dozen classic blues licks

Every musical style has an associated vocabulary of melodic and harmonic devices. In the blues, certain guitar 'licks' (short phrases) are so widespread that they have become the common currency of every player. It is worth learning these licks off by heart, so that you can deploy them at will while jamming, or use them as a starting point for your own improvisations.

Building your blues vocabulary

Some of the riffs on the opposite page go right back to the roots of the blues. Nobody can claim to have written them – any more than a composer or songwriter can claim to have invented the basic chord sequences.

As with chord sequences, what matters with these riffs is how you play them, and how you imbue them with your own individual style. If you do nothing but wheel out these tried and trusted set phrases, your playing will sound clichéd. But if you use them in combination with your own musical ideas, they will add instant authenticity to your playing.

Many of these licks can also be treated as starting points for explorations of your own. The trick here is to identify the core concept, and then do something else with it: transpose it to a different part of the scale, move it up or down an octave, change the rhythm…

Some sort of accompaniment is highly recommended, to help you try these in context once you have got them under your fingers – either a recording of yourself or an automatically generated accompaniment using a keyboard or computer software, or both together (automatic accompaniment plus rhythm guitar for a full sound with some natural 'feel').

Seasick Steve

In an age dominated by youth and the cult of celebrity, Seasick Steve's story is refreshingly different. Steve Wold first achieved widespread public recognition and commercial success in his 60s. He is one of the few current blues musicians who can claim real experience of lifestyles such as sleeping rough, jumping freight trains and working as a farmhand, having spent nearly 20 years of his life living like this in the American South. Steve also worked as a session musician and sound engineer for many years, but was as surprised as anyone when his performing career took off, initially in the UK. His guitar style is deeply rooted in the blues tradition, but has also been shaped by necessity and his own resourcefulness. As well as his more conventional guitars, many of Steve's instruments are highly individual creations, including a one-stringed slide guitar and one made largely from the hubcaps of a Morris Minor.

ABOVE: There is not a shred of revivalism in this version of the blues. Seasick Steve's blues represent a rare commodity sometimes called 'the real deal'.

LEFT: Seasick Steve is well known for his range of customized electric and acoustic guitars.

EXERCISE 12 RIFFS

The licks given here are classified harmonically: some work best over chord I, some over chord IV and some over chord V. In addition to these, you will find a couple of stock blues endings, which act as a kind of flourish when used in the last two bars of the structure. All the licks are shown in the key of G, and work best using a shuffle rhythm (see 'The sixth shuffle'). The chord symbols show which part of the sequence each lick works best with, but many can be used elsewhere.

Chord I

★ Slide: see 'Advanced left-hand techniques'

Chord IV

Chord V

Endings

Double stopping

So far we have looked at chord-based playing and single-note melodic work. However, there is an extremely effective technique, double stopping, that falls somewhere between the two. Double stopping simply means playing two notes at once. It makes for a very expressive sound which can be seen as a sequence of incomplete chords, but could also be described as two melodies running in tandem.

Movable two-note shapes

Double stopping, in its usual form, involves two notes moving melodically in parallel. The interval between the two notes can be anything, but the most widely used intervals for double stopping are thirds and sixths. This is no accident: thirds always harmonize in a pleasing way (to take an example from the world of pop music, think of the two voices in Abba's "Fernando": they are moving side by side in strictly parallel major and minor thirds). As for sixths, they are no more or less than inverted thirds: that is, the lower note of the third has been transposed up an octave.

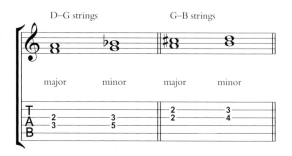

ABOVE/BELOW: Major and minor third shapes.

Fingering double-stopped shapes

To double stop effectively on the guitar you need a working knowledge of the guitar fretboard and the key signatures. For example, if you want to play double stops in the key of G major, you really have to know where the notes of G major (including the F♯) are to be found on the fretboard.

You also have to know what your chosen interval looks like on the fretboard. Thirds are usually played on two adjacent strings. On most adjacent pairs, the higher note is found one fret back from the lower note on all the strings.

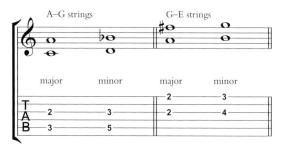

ABOVE/BELOW: Major and minor sixth shapes.

G and B

The exception is the G and B pair. Here, the interval between the open strings is already a major third (on all the others it is a perfect fourth), so to form a major third anywhere on the neck, you play the same fret on these two strings.

The minor third interval is one semitone narrower than the major third, so to make a minor interval you fret two frets back on the higher string on all pairs except G and B, where you fret one fret back. Sixths can be played in several shapes. The easiest shapes are found using two strings separated by one unplayed string. If you know where the notes of a given scale are to be found, all you need to do to be able to play it in thirds is to find pairs of notes a third apart which belong to the scale. This is complicated by the fact that open strings cannot usually be used to play the lower note, as there is no room for the upper note on the string above (see Exercise 2 for an example of this).

ABOVE: Van Morrison devised possibly the most famous double-stopped guitar theme ever for the introduction to his song "Brown-Eyed Girl".

EXERCISE 1

This is a simple melody in G major harmonized in thirds. All the shapes used can be found on the harmonized major scale.

EXERCISE 2

This exercise is derived from the G major scale in first position. Instead of being harmonized in thirds, it is harmonized in sixths (the upper line is transposed down an octave).

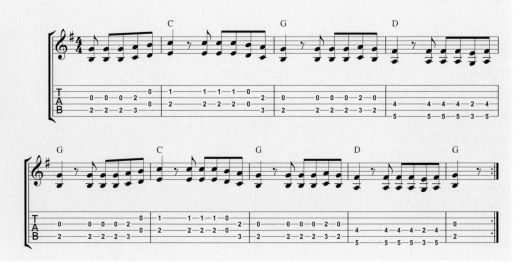

Half-open chords

These types of chords are shapes that can be moved around like barre chords, but include some open strings. Using this technique allows you to make complex-sounding chords with simple shapes, moved up and down the neck. The ringing open strings, top or bottom, provide a sense of harmonic continuity. This very fruitful manoeuvre is popular in many genres, especially pop and folk.

Lazy barres

The most common form of half-open chord is sometimes known as a 'lazy barre', because it is like a barre-chord shape but features some open strings (which makes it easier to play than a full barre).

The E shape works well as a half-open chord or lazy barre. Instead of making a full barre behind the E shape, you use the index finger to fret the low E string only, leaving the B and top E strings open. When the shape is moved up the neck, the E and B notes sound against the rest of the chord.

In some positions, the half-open E-shape delivers some complex-sounding (but usable) chords as well as some rather dissonant (and generally unusable) ones. The most usable positions for this shape are: first fret (this gives Fmaj7#11 – a rather dark sound with a flamenco flavour); second fret (F#7add11); third fret (G6), fifth fret (Aadd9); seventh fret (Badd11), eighth fret (Cmaj7); and tenth fret (D6/9). In fact, only three positions are too dissonant to be of much use.

If your guitar allows access, try the shape at the 12th fret, which results in a richly sonorous E major).

Aadd9

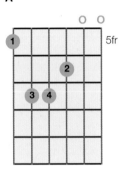 

ABOVE: The 'lazy barre' E shape at the fifth fret. The chord produced is Aadd9.

Dmadd9

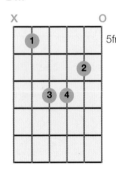 

ABOVE/BELOW RIGHT: Two easy movable shapes at the fifth fret: Dmadd9 and Am9.

Am-based shape

The Am-based barre shape sounds great in many positions with the top E string left open, as does the Em7 shape with the root on the E string with open top E and B strings. The best way to familiarize yourself with the possibilities here is to experiment to see what sounds good. Don't worry about the exact names of the complex resulting chords: it is more important to know what works here. At the ninth fret, the open strings duplicate the fretted notes on the G and B strings, producing a rich 'chiming' C#m7.

Am9

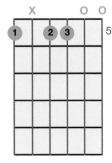 

Bass notes in open chords

Good effects can be achieved by making fretted shapes on the higher strings and moving them in relation to an open bass string. Try playing a standard first-position D chord, then moving the fretted notes up first by two frets (E/D) and then one more (F/D). This slightly mysterious effect has always been popular in folk-rock and related styles. Note the use of the slash in these chord symbols: E/D ('E over D') signifies an E chord with a D in the bass. Chord symbols like this are also very common in contemporary jazz.

EXERCISE 1

This exercise uses the E shape in a typical indie-pop sequence. To achieve the maximum effect, you should aim to keep both the B and top E strings ringing throughout the whole sequence.

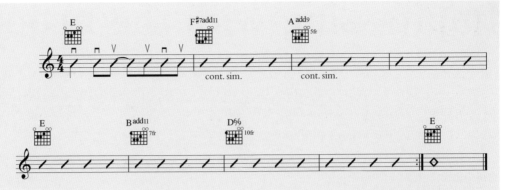

EXERCISE 2

This exercise uses just two half-open shapes to achieve some rather complex sounds, which become increasingly dissonant towards the end of the sequence. The tension is ultimately released with the simple Em chord ending.

EXERCISE 3

This exercise introduces a folk/rock cliché – moving the C chord shape up two frets (D$^{add9/11}$). Unlike the other shapes that are shown here, the C shape doesn't work very well anywhere else.

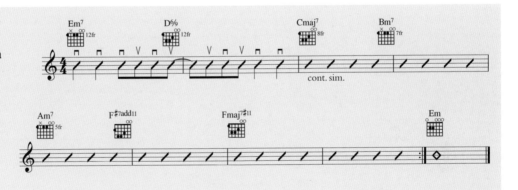

Paul Simon

Although it took a back seat for most of his later solo career, Paul Simon's deft acoustic-guitar work powered a string of hits for Simon & Garfunkel in the 1960s, on both steel-string and classical guitars. His relaxed, rolling fingerpicking style, influenced by British folk players such as Bert Jansch and John Renbourn, often incorporates melodic elements that weave a third strand in counterpoint with the duo's vocal harmonies; songs such as "Homeward Bound", "I Am a Rock" and "The Boxer" are memorable as much for their distinctive guitar figures as for their lyrics or melodies. Paul Simon's influence can in turn be heard in both the songwriting and guitar styles of many singer/songwriters from later decades, including Suzanne Vega and Edie Brickell.

ABOVE: Paul Simon's early work with Art Garfunkel epitomizes the tradition of a folk duo with a single accompanying instrument.

Improvising with the major scale

For the past 500 years, almost all Western music has been based on the major–minor key system. The ability to improvise using the major scale is an important part of learning to play *ad lib* solos in any style, including jazz. The major scale, familiar to millions as 'do, re, mi, fa, so, la, te, do', is the musical foundation on which most other melodic building blocks stand.

The importance of listening

Improvisation is at least as much about listening as it is about playing. At any given moment, the note you are playing produces a certain sound, or flavour, in relation to the underlying chord sequence.

This can only be properly appreciated if that chord is actually sounding, so it is far more useful to practise improvising with a friend playing chords (or you could try a recording of yourself playing chords) than if the chords are only present in your head.

Constructing an *ad lib* melody

Having played your first note over the underlying chord, the next step is to listen and react musically. Knowing which notes of the scale are present in each chord is essential: these notes, which agree with the harmony, will sound 'sweet' or stable. But if no other notes are used, the result may be rather bland. When we were exploring the blues scale, we looked at the mechanism of 'tension and release'. The same mechanism applies in relation to improvisation in the major scale: a note that does not belong to the underlying chord results in dissonance, or tension, but this tension can be released by resolving to a note belonging to the chord. Try playing up and down the parent scale of the chord sequence (for example, the scale of G major over the chord sequence used for the exercises opposite), and try to hear whether each note is or is not present in the chord.

All melodies essentially consist of a combination of chord notes and other notes (known as neighbour notes or passing notes). For example, if you start a solo using the note A over a G major chord, moving to either G or B will resolve the tension generated, as these notes are both found in the chord.

The next step to improvising an effective melodic line is simply to mix things up a little. Try combining arpeggio notes with step-wise motion, vary the rhythm (this immediately produces a more 'natural' result than a constant stream of crotchets or quavers), add interest with hammer-ons, pull-offs or other embellishments – and dare to leave a few rests.

Another ingredient of successful melodic improvisation is structure. Having played a musical idea (even just two or three notes) that seemed to work, try repeating them. Using the same melodic idea in different parts of the chord sequence will automatically create an element of structure.

Eddie Lang

This talented guitarist can justifiably be called the father of jazz guitar. Born at the dawn of the 20th century, Lang was working professionally by the end of the World War I, and was one of the first players to make the transition from the banjo (ubiquitous in 'Dixieland' – the very earliest recorded jazz and its various revivals) to the guitar. Such changes in instrumentation were an important part of the evolution of swing jazz in the 1920s and '30s. Eddie Lang worked in ensembles both large and small, appearing with many of the big names of the day including Paul Whiteman, Bing Crosby and Bix Beiderbecke. It is chiefly for his collaboration with violinist Joe Venuti that he is remembered today, however. The duo context liberated Lang's guitar from the 'padding' role usually required in big bands, allowing his unamplified acoustic guitar to be heard loud and clear.

ABOVE: Eddie Lang playing an archtop acoustic guitar typical of the era.

EXERCISE 1

This exercise is a chord sequence using four chords in the key of G major: G, Am7, C and D7. The melody line consists entirely of notes belonging to these chords, or arpeggios, all drawn from the major scale in second position (see 'Practice patterns').

EXERCISE 2

This exercise uses the same chord sequence as Exercise 1, but here each arpeggio note is preceded by a neighbour note, which creates a temporary dissonance before it is resolved.

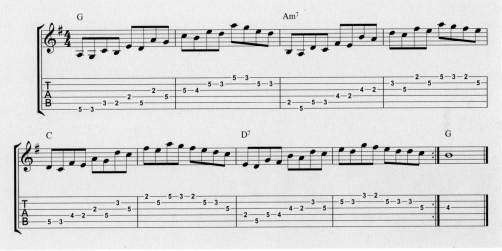

EXERCISE 3

Still using the same chord sequence, this exercise combines arpeggio notes with step-wise motion, using varied technique and rhythm.

Advanced left-hand techniques

The standard interplay of the left and right hands, where the right hand picks each note and the left hand changes the pitch of the notes in question by fretting the strings, is only a small part of the range of available guitar techniques. There are two other techniques involving the interplay of both hands which are useful to get to know: harmonics and slides.

Harmonics

These are notes with a pure, bell-like sound produced by touching the string lightly rather than pushing it down on to the fretboard. Unlike ordinary notes, harmonics can only be produced at certain points along the string. These points are mathematically defined, and correspond to exact fractions of the string's length. The easiest harmonics to produce are found at the 12th, seventh and fifth frets (a half, one third and one quarter of the string's length, respectively).

To produce a harmonic, touch the string lightly with any left-hand finger and pluck the string with the right hand. The left-hand finger should make contact with the string

without moving it. It may help to concentrate on using only the very tip of the finger; if you have very large hands, you may find that the little finger works best at first. The exact position is critical: for 12th, seventh and fifth fret harmonics, the note is found exactly above the fret, rather than in the area between frets, as for ordinary notes.

If you stray from this position even very slightly, the result will be a 'dead' or muted percussive sound rather than a pitched note. Higher harmonics can be found between the fifth fret and the nut, but these are both harder to find (the position of each will not be exactly above a fret) and harder to produce clearly.

ABOVE: The twelfth fret harmonic on the top E string.

LEFT: Multiple harmonics can be produced at the same fret, using the side of the finger.

ABOVE: This shows harmonics across all six strings at the 12th, seventh and fifth frets.

EXERCISE HARMONIC CHORDS

This exercise uses harmonics as chords (sometimes supported by fretted bass notes). In each case, as several ringing harmonics are to be played at the same fret, use the side of the left-hand finger, as shown. Harmonics are shown as diamond-shaped note heads.

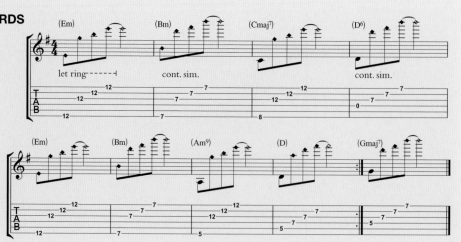

Slides

The slide technique (also known as *glissando* or *gliss*) is both simple and effective: the left hand slides between notes on the same string. To play a slide between two notes, pick the first note, then slide the fretting finger along the string while maintaining finger pressure until you reach the second note. It is important to maintain enough pressure so that the sound does not die off before the second note is reached; however, be careful not to apply too much pressure either, as it is quite possible to cut your finger tip on the guitar string, especially if you have not yet developed calluses.

Slides are shown using straight diagonal lines between notes. Each of these is usually accompanied by a slur (curved line). To produce a grace note slide (shown using a small note preceding the main note), use the same technique, but make the first note as short as possible, emphasizing the second note.

Sliding from C to E on the G string

Slide and re-pick   Slide (do not re-pick)   Grace note slide

LEFT: Three major scales in second position. Remember to maintain alternate picking throughout, as shown in the first bar.

1 Begin by playing the note C (G string, fifth fret).

2 Maintain finger pressure and slide the finger to the ninth fret (E).

3 Allow the note E to sound once your finger is in position.

EXERCISE SLIDES AND HARMONICS

This exercise is a simple melody constructed using both slides and harmonics. The piece moves around the neck considerably; therefore recommended left-hand fingerings are shown using small numbers above the notes where necessary.

Practice patterns

The major scale contains enormous potential for generating practice material that will expand your knowledge of the fretboard. While there is nothing wrong with the traditional approach of simply playing up and down each scale, this represents only one possibility. The number of ways in which a scale can be arranged is limited only by the imagination, and borders on the realm of musical composition.

Scales and positions

The first-position scales we have encountered so far have all included open strings. Like first-position open chords, these cannot be transposed. The first requirement for a movable scale shape is that it should contain no open strings. Learning just one movable major-scale shape enables us, to some extent, to play any major scale, by moving this shape up the neck.

However, the ultimate aim for much more elegant results is to know all scales in all positions. There are a number of scale shapes to learn, as a first step towards this goal. Here, we will concentrate on three shapes. In second position, these shapes give us the scales of C, G and D major. We have seen these scales before, but in second position they have no open strings

and are therefore movable. The G and D major scales shown below are both in strict second position: that is to say, the first finger always plays the second fret, the second finger plays the third fret and so on. Because of the guitar's tuning, this strict approach sometimes has to be relaxed in order to make some notes accessible. The C major scale in second position can only be played by incorporating two stretches – the index finger stretches out of position by one fret, in this case to play the note F on both the high and low E string.

BELOW: Three major scales in second position. Remember to maintain alternate picking throughout, as shown in the first bar.

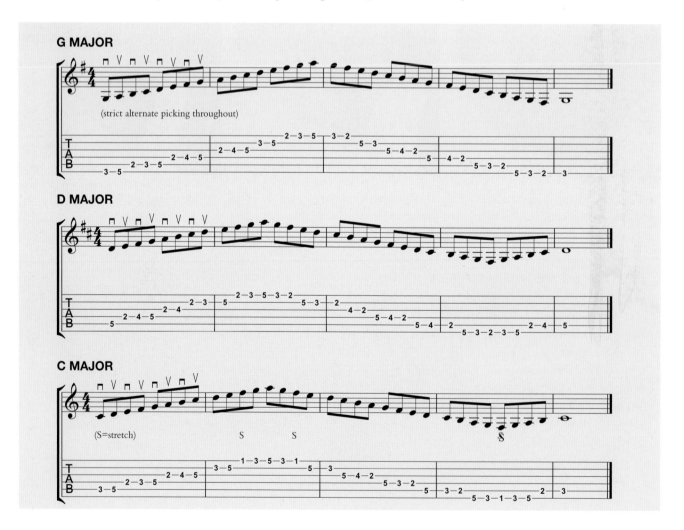

Generating patterns

The G major scale 'workout' below introduces some of the possibilities for practice material generated from the major scale. These ideas are all consistently realized: a simple interval or melodic idea is generated from the tonic note (G).

This idea is then transposed to begin on the second note (A), and so on all the way up and then down the scale, taking in every available note in the given position. The first idea in the workout is a simple ascending third interval (G–B), which is transposed to begin on every note in the ascending scale. This becomes a descending third on the way down the scale (although maintaining the ascending third would be equally valid; try both versions for variety).

The patterns contained in this workout may also be applied to the D and C major scale, or to any other scale in any other position – the combinations are almost infinite.

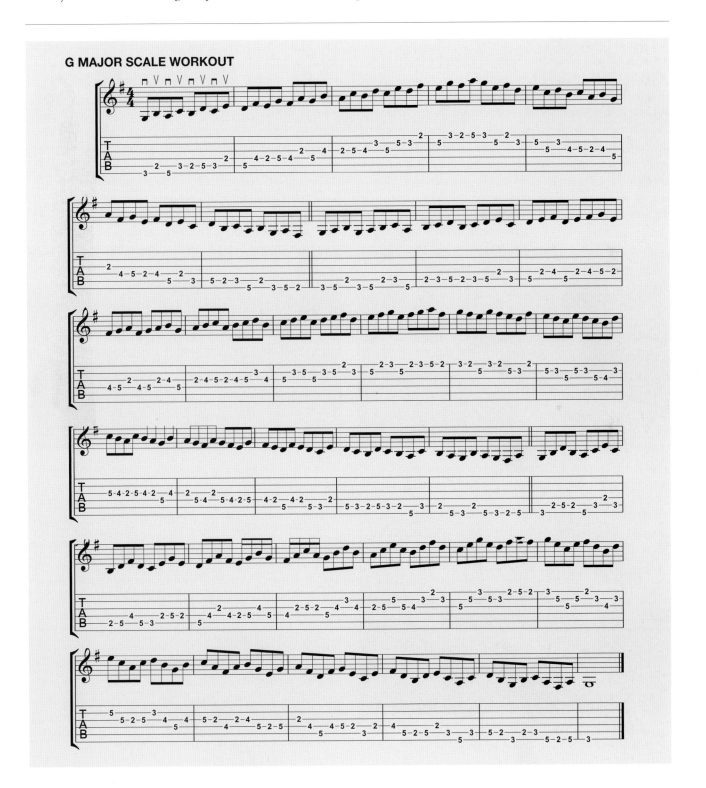

G MAJOR SCALE WORKOUT

Party tricks

We are now going to look at some novel ways of getting sounds out of your guitar. Artificial harmonics allow you to produce any harmonic you like, and thumb chords make new chord shapes possible high up the neck. Or you can try right-hand tapping, which is an unusual way to fret notes and produce a note in places other than where the left hand happens to be.

Artificial harmonics

As we have seen, to produce a natural harmonic on an open string, you lightly touch the string at a certain point with the left hand, and pick with the right. But the open strings can produce only a limited range of natural harmonics. To access a wider range of harmonic notes, it is first necessary to change the basic pitch of the string by fretting a note in the normal way. For example, if the left hand frets the first fret, the octave harmonic is now located at the thirteenth fret rather than the twelfth, and the next harmonic is at the eighth fret rather than the seventh. To sound the note, the fingers of the right hand

must be deployed both to touch the string at the correct point, and to pick the note. Harmonics produced in this way are generally known as artificial harmonics, and they are trickier to pull off than they sound. There is more than one way to produce them – see below. All these methods take practice, because it is hard to keep the finger that is touching the string quite still while also moving other fingers to sound the string.

In practice, most players only ever use harmonics an octave (12 frets) above the fretted note. This is usually shown in notation using diamond-shaped note heads, as for natural harmonics, but with the additional indication 'AH'.

ABOVE: Fingerstyle technique: the thumb picks the string while the index finger produces the harmonic.

ABOVE: Plectrum technique: the plectrum is used between the thumb and middle finger, and the index finger reaches over to produce the harmonic.

ABOVE: Pinch harmonic: the string is played holding the plectrum conventionally, but the thumb simultaneously 'digs' into the string at exactly the right point to produce a harmonic.

Tapped harmonics

An alternative technique may be used to produce a harmonic one octave above the fretted note. This involves a sharp but light tap with a left-hand fingertip. The string is tapped directly above the active fret; as for artificial harmonics, this is 12 frets above the note fretted by the left hand. The idea is to push the string down so that it makes momentary contact with the fret; the tap should have enough energy to set the string in motion, but should not remain in contact for long enough to have a muting effect. Like the other techniques here, some practice is required to master tapped harmonics, but the effort is worthwhile as no other technique produces quite this sound.

Thumb chords

In normal play, the left-hand thumb stays behind the neck most of the time. However, as we have seen, it may also be used to mute the bass strings. Many players take this technique one step further, and use the thumb to fret the low E string. Some guitarists use this technique as an alternative to barre chords: the index finger covers only the top E and B strings, while the thumb covers the bottom E string. This technique enables otherwise impossible shapes, such as the descending suspension/release sequence used by Pete Townshend in the verse pattern of The Who's "Pinball Wizard": as an alternative to barre chords based on the E shape, Townshend uses his thumb to fret the root of each chord on the bottom E string and mute the A string at the same time. This frees the fourth finger to add the suspended fourth on the G string without moving the rest of the fingers.

ABOVE: This thumb chord is a popular alternative to the F major barre chord.

Right-hand tapping

There are many ways to produce a note without using both hands simultaneously. Hammer-ons and pull-offs fall into this category. The right-hand fingers can also be used directly on the fretboard – a technique known as 'tapping'. Practitioners of the most advanced version of this technique use the two hands to tap on the fretboard independently, enabling an almost piano-like independence of lines and chords.

Most players limit themselves to occasionally using a single right-hand finger to tap an otherwise impossible note. This is often encountered as a 'party piece' ending: the left hand plays a high chord on the upper strings; while the chord is ringing, the right hand 'crosses over' the left hand to tap a low bass note and finish the piece. This crowd-pleasing manoeuvre is actually much easier than it looks, and is definitely worth trying to master.

ABOVE: The right hand crossing behind the left hand to tap a bass note.

EXERCISE

This exercise uses artificial harmonics and adds a right hand-tapped ending. Note that the fret numbers given for artificial harmonics apply to the left-hand fingering; the harmonic is produced by the right hand 12 frets higher, unless otherwise noted.

Slide guitar

The sounding lengths of the strings can be changed by using a technique known as slide guitar, whereby a metal or glass tube is used as the primary means of sliding. This produces a very different sound from regular left-hand work. It makes for a kind of plangent twang that works well in a blues or folk context, but it is also a distinctive ingredient of country music.

Basic bottleneck

The slide is often called a 'bottleneck', because the neck of a bottle can serve as a rough-and-ready slide. It is far preferable, however, to invest in a slide designed specifically for the task. These hollow cylinders – usually made of brass, steel or glass – come in various sizes to suit different players. The slide is usually worn on the little finger; the other fingers are used to damp the strings behind the slide to control the sound.

Some slide players employ conventional fretting technique using the other fingers. It is also common practice among players to use the right hand to pick one note at a time to play melodically, or several strings simultaneously to produce chords. The most effective slide ideas tend to use a combination of both of these approaches.

ABOVE: Glass and metal slides come in a range of sizes.

Using the slide

Slide guitar (like the steel-string acoustic guitar itself) is a quintessentially American invention, and it lends itself to American styles of music. As its name suggests, slide playing often involves sliding between notes or chords. Although this is a crucial part of the slide style, it can also be over-done – hence the need for damping by the other fingers. It should also be noted that for most purposes the slide needs to be positioned exactly above the corresponding fret, otherwise the notes will sound out of tune. When playing blues, however, the in-between positions of notes and chords have considerable expressive possibilities.

When you are sounding notes with the right hand, you must keep the slide parallel with the frets (perpendicular to the neck) in order for the result to be in tune. Since all the notes that you can play at any given moment are on the same fret, it makes a great deal of sense to use open tunings when using the slide. That way, you will always have a major chord at your disposal. Melodic slide playing is perfectly possible, however, and not unusual in standard tuning.

One of the first things you will notice if you try using a slide with an ordinary acoustic guitar is that it can be rather difficult to produce a clean sound without also making unwanted noises as the slide strikes the fretboard and frets. There is a fine line between exerting enough pressure to produce a clean note, and pressing so hard that the string makes contact with the fret.

ABOVE: The slide in use – it should be exactly parallel to the frets.

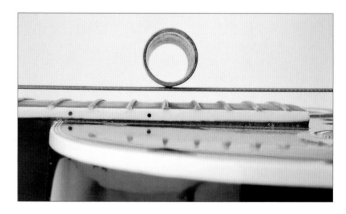

ABOVE: An acoustic guitar set up for slide. Note the high action.

Slide set-up

In fact, it is quite hard to play slide satisfactorily on a guitar set up for ordinary duties. Slide guitar generally requires a much higher action, which is achieved by raising the height of both the bridge and nut. It also calls for heavier strings. This is usually addressed by having a guitar specifically set up for slide playing. With this in mind, it might be worth considering investing in a second guitar if slide playing appeals to you. Inexpensive instruments often work very well for slide, as the usual considerations concerning a finely calibrated action, intonation and fret buzz do not apply, since the strings do not ordinarily come into contact with the fretboard.

EXERCISE 1

This exercise is a simple 12-bar blues melody in standard tuning. Where two notes are linked by a slur and a line, the second note should not be picked. Try to hit each note as accurately as possible; extra slides may be added according to taste. To play open strings, simply lift the slide momentarily.

EXERCISE 2

This exercise is in open G tuning, but since only the top three strings are used, only the top string need be re-tuned (to D).

(★ = fret notes at eighth fret
using first finger behind slide)

Classical guitar

The term 'classical guitar' describes not only a particular type of guitar, but also the range of music that is conventionally played on it. At its broadest, classical guitar music is 'serious' Western concert music played on a nylon-strung guitar. However, the instrument is Spanish in origin, and much of the standard repertoire has a correspondingly Mediterranean flavour.

A different instrument

Classical guitar is a style that really does require a specific instrument. To play it seriously, you need to have a classical guitar strung with nylon strings: a steel-string acoustic guitar will not make the right sound. That is not to say that acoustic players have nothing to learn from the classical tradition. It is still worth looking at exploring the music and techniques of the classical players, and perhaps borrowing a few ideas.

The strict rules of classical guitar

In classical guitar, the right hand always plays fingerstyle; plectrums and fingerpicks are never used by classical players. The rules governing the roles of both hands are considerably stricter than for general-purpose fingerstyle acoustic playing. The left-hand thumb is always positioned on an imaginary line running down the centre of the guitar's neck.

The strings are plucked with the fingernails of the right hand, which means that classical players have to take considerable care of their right-hand fingernails. They file and polish them to achieve the optimum shape as well as length – because even the slightest roughness can produce unwanted sounds and impede the exact control of volume and tone required from the guitar.

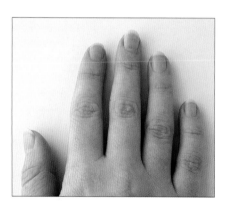

ABOVE: The thumb- and fingernails of the right hand should be filed so that they are a consistent length and shape.

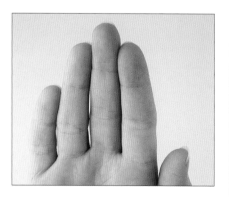

ABOVE: Right-hand fingernails should be just visible (1–2mm/less than ⅛in) when the hand is viewed with the palm to the front.

Posture

Classical teachers insist on a very specific posture. The guitar sits on the left thigh, with the neck pointing upwards at a slight angle. To facilitate this while maintaining a straight back, the left foot is placed on a footstool. Any kind will do – even a pile of books can be used – but the specifically designed guitarist's footstools are slightly angled so that the position of the foot is absolutely correct.

ABOVE: Classical guitar posture. The footstool ensures the guitar is at the correct angle to the body.

Basic technique

The fingers of the left hand usually only fret notes that are actually played – even when, from the point of view of an acoustic guitarist, these notes might seem to belong to a familiar and easily formed chord shape. This is one respect in which the formal approach of classical players is markedly different from that of other guitarists. The aim of a classical guitarist is to achieve a high level of 'finger independence' (see 'Further classical guitar techniques'), and fretting unused notes is seen as superfluous and counterproductive.

Classical guitar music is usually written using standard notation only. It is generally up to the guitarist to work out the fingering, but both right-hand (p i m a) and left-hand (0 1 2 3 4) fingerings may sometimes be shown.

In many situations, the right hand employs a technique similar to that used for fingerstyle folk playing: the thumb covers the three bass strings (E, A, D) while the fingers cover one treble string each (G:i, B:m, E:a). However, classical guitar often breaks this mould in a number of ways: consecutive notes on the same string are often played by alternating fingers, and the fingers, rather than the thumb, are often used to play melodies on the bass strings.

Recommended listening:
- Leo Brouwer: "Berceuse"
- Manuel de Falla: "Fisherman's Song" (from *El Amor Brujo*)
- Fernando Sor: "Variations on a Theme by Mozart"

EXERCISE OP. 35 BY FERNANDO SOR (1778–1839)

Try this simple piece, which is written entirely in C major in first position. If you are unsure, all of these notes may be located by consulting the C major scale (see 'The C major scale and first position'). Both left- and right-hand fingerings are given, but omitted where a note or figure is repeated. Bass notes (E, A and D strings) are always played with the thumb, but watch out for the open G in the first bar of the last line – this is also played with the thumb.

Further classical guitar techniques

Classical guitar demands more discipline than most other styles of guitar playing. This is because you need to have strength and flexibility in your left hand. At the same time, agility plus extremely fine control of volume and tone are important for the right hand. Here, we will explore in detail some ideas which can help you build these goals into your practice from the beginning.

Finger independence

One of the main technical aims of classical guitar study is to achieve a high level of finger independence in both the left and right hands. The left-hand fingers should be able to find any conceivable shape within a space of at least four frets and to move independently of each other; all combinations of right-hand fingers should be equally usable.

In particular, any left-hand finger should be able to sustain a note on one string while the other fingers are in use on other strings. This principle can be used to generate an almost infinite variety of practice exercises. For example, choose any pair of strings, such as the B string and the D string. Keep the left hand within first position (the first four frets), and only allow each finger to play notes at its 'own' fret. Begin by playing the B string, first fret with the first finger, then the remaining three frets on the D string without cutting off the note on the B string. Next, play the B string, second fret with the second finger, letting this note ring while the remaining fingers play frets 1, 3 and 4 on the D string, and so on.

It is important to make sure that all the fingers hover directly above the fretboard when not in use. The result will not be musical, but will be very useful for developing finger strength and independence. An example pattern using this approach is shown below.

Tremolando

Classical guitar achieves various interesting textures using specific techniques. One of these is tremolando, in which alternating fingers are employed to play rapid repeated notes. With sufficient speed and smoothness, the result is perceived not as individual notes but as a homogenous musical texture. This is usually combined with a moving bass line or counter-melody played by the thumb. Tremolando technique cannot be achieved in one step, however; speed must be increased slowly while taking care that the correct right-hand fingers are used throughout and as evenly as possible.

Tremolando playing usually uses the same right-hand fingering pattern repeatedly: p a m i (thumb, ring, middle, index), in which the thumb plays a bass note which is allowed to ring and the fingers then play a note on a higher string three times in quick succession.

ABOVE: The left hand in first position. Although only one note is being fretted, the remaining three fingers are hovering just above the fretboard.

EXERCISE FINGER INDEPENDENCE

This exercise is shown in TAB notation for ease of reading. Make sure that all notes on the upper string of each pair are allowed to ring over the lower string. To add value for the right hand, make sure you alternate strictly between the index finger (i) and middle finger (m); starting on either is equally valid.

Basic tremolando technique

This basic pattern uses only open strings, so that you may concentrate entirely on the right hand. For variety, you could also find an E major scale using just the E string.

1 Play the open bottom E string with the thumb (p). Let this bass note ring on underneath the next three.

2 Play the open top E string with the ring finger (a).

3 Play the open top E string with the middle finger (m).

4 Play the open top E string with the index finger (i).

EXERCISE "ALLEGRO" BY CARCASSI (EXCERPT)

This piece uses repeated notes that create the tremolando effect if played fast enough, but is also musically satisfying at a slower tempo. All the notes that are shown here can be found in first position except the very last note, which is found at the fifth fret. Follow both left- and right-hand fingerings exactly, and aim to play this piece fluently at 60 beats per minute before you start increasing the tempo of the piece.

Gypsy jazz

The gypsy-jazz style combines elements of the musette style of Parisian café entertainers with jazz-influenced compositions and improvisation. Gypsy jazz ensembles typically include a rhythm section consisting of double bass and several acoustic guitars, along with a selection of underpinning melody instruments including the violin, guitar and accordion.

Rhythm and melody styles

Drums are rarely heard in gypsy jazz, at least in its purest form. Instead, one or more guitars lay the rhythmic foundations using a forceful strumming style with a great deal of attack. As with all swing jazz, beats 2 and 4 are emphasized heavily. Chords on beats 2 and 4 should be played much louder than beats 1 and 3, and also more *staccato* (shorter). This is usually achieved by left-hand muting: play the chord, then quickly release finger pressure to stop it from ringing. Open strings should therefore be avoided.

Melodies should be played with as much attack as possible. Most serious players in this style use a particular type of acoustic guitar based on the Selmer-Macaferri model that was made famous by Django Reinhardt. However, the bright, almost nasal sound quality of this type of guitar can also be approximated by playing close to the bridge (although playing too close will result in loss of volume as well as carrying a greater risk of string breakage).

Some players deliberately vary the right-hand position between strums to help accent beats 2 and 4.

The harmonic minor scale

One of the identifying features of gypsy-jazz improvisation (and many of its original tunes) is the use of the harmonic minor scale. There are a few different types of minor scale, all of them related to the major scale. The harmonic minor scale is based on the same set of notes (starting a minor third lower, or on the sixth step of the major scale). However, the harmonic minor gains its unique flavour as a result of modifying one note: the seventh note is raised by a semitone.

For example, the A harmonic minor scale is based on the same notes as C major (no sharps or flats) but the seventh note (G) is raised to G$\sharp$. This means that one interval in the scale (from the sixth to the raised seventh, F to G$\sharp$ in A minor) is neither a tone nor a semitone, but an augmented second (three semitones). The diatonic chords of the minor key are obtained from harmonizing this scale.

ABOVE: Moving the right hand closer to the bridge can help achieve a sharp, cutting sound for melodic playing.

The Hot Club Quintet

Django Reinhardt and Stéphane Grappelli's seminal Hot Club Quintet recordings established a template which gypsy jazz has followed ever since. Two rhythm guitarists (including Django's brother Joseph) and double bass provided a good backdrop for Reinhardt and Grappelli's virtuosic melodies and free-wheeling improvisational interplay.

ABOVE: The Hot Club Quintet featuring Reinhardt and Grappelli.

Recommended listening:
- Boulou Ferré Quartet: *Relax and Enjoy*
- Django Reinhardt and Stéphane Grappelli: *Swing from Paris*
- Stochelo Rosenberg: *Ready'n Able*
- Trio Manouche: *The Nu Gypsy*

EXERCISE HARMONIC MINOR SCALE

This exercise consists of the A harmonic minor scale in second and then fifth position. Both positions require some stretches (see 'Practice patterns') performed by either the first or fourth finger, marked 'S' here. The other fingers stay in position. Once you can play this fluidly, try using it to improvise over the chord sequence in the exercise below.

EXERCISE GYPSY JAZZ MELODY

This melody mainly uses the notes of the A harmonic minor scale in both second and fifth position, as shown above. However, there are a few chromatic passing notes which occur between these scale notes. It may help to try recording yourself playing the chord sequence – use short, sharp strums on each beat, emphasizing beats 2 and 4.

Latin jazz

The term 'Latin' in its musical sense covers a range of styles, from Cuban salsa to Argentinean tango. When jazz musicians use the term, however, they are usually concerned with the various forms of *bossa nova*. This style of jazz evolved in Brazil in the 1950s, and it can be said to consist of rich jazz harmonies fused with the dance rhythms of Brazilian samba.

Bossa nova basics

The nylon-strung acoustic guitar usually plays an accompanying (but central) role in bossa nova music. Typical guitar patterns outline the harmony, bass line and the characteristic rhythms of the style. The bass line usually alternates between the root and fifth of each chord; the harmony makes almost constant use of extended chords (mainly ninths, whether major, minor or dominant). Latin-jazz guitarists usually stick to the conventions of jazz chord voicing and movement (see 'Introducing jazz chords'). Many patterns voice the tonic chord using a shape with the root on the fifth string so that the root and fifth of the bass line can be found at the same fret. Exercise 1 applies the 'signature' bossa nova guitar pattern (bass line and chords) to a typical Latin-jazz chord sequence.

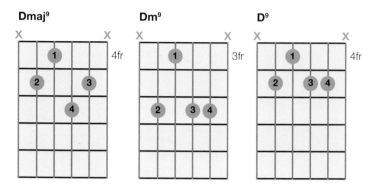

ABOVE: *Major, minor and dominant ninth chords in D. For all of these shapes, the second finger can shift to the bottom E string (at the same fret) to play the fifth in the bass.*

Antonio Carlos Jobim and João Gilberto

The bossa nova craze that swept America and the world in the early 1960s heralded the mass-market arrival of Latin jazz. Since then, the style has maintained its position at the more commercial end of the jazz spectrum. One man's legacy still looms larger than any other in this music: Brazilian composer, guitarist and pianist Antonio Carlos Jobim. Jobim wrote a staggering proportion of the songs that have become Latin standards, including "The Girl from Ipanema", "Desafinado"

and "Wave". His collaboration with Stan Getz and guitarist João Gilberto on the album *Getz/Gilberto* is a milestone and one of the best-selling records in jazz history; its infectious bossa nova rhythm is largely Gilberto's personal invention. The bossa nova is one of those styles that can be identified on hearing one instrument playing two bars of music. The instrument in question is the nylon-string guitar and the birth of the archetypal guitar pattern is documented in Gilberto's introduction to "Desafinado" on this album.

LEFT: *Between them, Jobim (far left) and Gilberto (left) played an enormous part in both the creation of the bossa nova style and subsequently its huge popularity in the USA and Europe.*

Montuno

This is another type of musical figure that is very common in Latin jazz. It usually describes a repetitive syncopated figure with a descending bass line used as a basis for improvisation. This technique originated in Cuban salsa, but is also often heard in a jazz context. Each repeated two-bar section may be played many times before continuing to the next.

Repetition is a key feature of montuno; playing each figure only once or twice would detract from the feeling of continuity, which is essential to this dance-derived style. One of the defining features of Latin jazz is that the quaver (eighth note) feel is not swung, unlike most modern jazz. A pair of quavers should be played exactly as written, with the offbeat falling precisely halfway between beats.

EXERCISE BOSSA NOVA SEQUENCE

This exercise is written using polyphonic notation: there are two independent sets of notes in each bar. One set of notes (tails down) represents the bass line, played with the thumb, while the other set (tails up) represents the rhythmic chords. This allows independent rhythms to be written while showing the full duration of each note or chord.

Tip

For some variety, try playing this bossa nova sequence using left-hand muting, which will produce much shorter, percussive chords.

EXERCISE MONTUNO VARIATIONS

This exercise consists of various montuno patterns, each of which should be played repeatedly before moving on to the next. For variety, each figure is transposed into a new key (a popular montuno device). All the chord shapes here use a partial barre across the top three strings; this should be played using the first finger for the first three shapes, shifting to the second finger for the fourth (m6) shape (allowing the first finger to play the bass note).

Flamenco

As well as being a living traditional style in its own right, the Spanish folk music known as flamenco has had a considerable influence on many composers' work for classical guitar. The musical flavour of flamenco is a product of an advanced repertoire of right-hand techniques that can be difficult to learn, but are well worth it since they are highly rewarding to play.

Components of the style

An important component of flamenco is the energetic rhythmic strumming technique known as *rasgueado*. The rasgueado technique is unusual in that, unlike plectrum strumming or general-purpose fingerstyle strumming, several right-hand fingers (and sometimes the thumb) are used separately. This makes it possible to play fast and complex rhythms. Proper rasgueado technique is not easy to learn, however, and can constitute a lifetime's study in itself. The exercises opposite are intended only as an introduction to the very basics of the technique.

Rapid rhythms are achieved in rasgueado by strumming with individual fingers. The basic motion of each finger is either an outward 'flick' (known as an out-stroke) in which the finger starts by being tucked into the palm of the hand and then rapidly extends, strumming as it goes, or the reverse of this (an in-stroke) in which the finger strums upwards before curling back into the palm.

To learn rasgueado technique, you should first get used to making the individual finger strokes that will then be combined in rhythmic patterns. As rasgueado is essentially a percussive technique, try to make each finger hit (rather than strum) the strings, but in order to avoid a bottom-heavy sound, focus on the top E string even when playing all the strings.

Practise individual out-strokes and in-strokes using each right-hand finger. Each stroke should be short and sharp; maintain focus on this aspect when putting together strokes into rhythmic patterns such as Exercise 1 (opposite). For greater focus, rasgueado patterns may be practised on open strings at first – or even without the guitar (you can flick against the left wrist).

ABOVE: Rasgueado out-stroke: the finger 'flicks' outwards until it is fully extended.

ABOVE: Rasgueado in-stroke: the finger curls back into the palm of the hand.

ABOVE: Spanish flamenco guitarist Paco de Lucia performs on stage in Madrid.

Rest stroke technique

The second major component in learning flamenco guitar is the execution of fast – often very fast – melodic playing using the 'rest stroke' technique. Rather than pulling away from the string after plucking it, as in arpeggio patterns, the fingertip moves downwards, coming to rest on the next lowest string. This produces a different tone and enables more precise control and faster playing. Rest-stroke passages are usually played by alternating the index (i) and middle (m) fingers. This technique is also common in advanced classical guitar.

Tip
To play flamenco using a standard classical guitar, a removable transparent scratchplate, called a *golpeador*, may be worth buying.

Recommended listening:
- Juan Martín: *Classic Flamenco*
- Paco de Lucia: *Dos guitarras flamencos en stereo*
- Paco Peña: *Fabulous Flamenco!*
- Manitas de Plata: *Feria Gitane*

Rest stroke on the top E string

1 Rest the tips of both the index and middle fingers on the B string, so that drawing either finger back will result in playing the string with the nail.

2 Play the top E string using the nail of the index finger, then bring the fingertip back to rest on the B string, allowing the E string to ring.

3 Play the top E string again, this time using the nail of the middle finger. Again, bring the tip of the finger back to rest on the B string.

EXERCISE BASIC RASGUEADO PATTERN

Each strum here is assigned both a finger and a direction: the downstroke symbol ⊓ is used for the out-stroke, and the up-stroke ∨ for the in-stroke. The pattern remains the same throughout the exercise and should be practised very slowly at first, gradually building up speed while making sure

you stick to the pattern exactly. Don't expect to get instant results in this style! Experienced performers interpret each strum themselves in long passages of music. While different guitarists play rasgueados with individual flair, the part of the rasgueado that is most important is the final strum.

EXERCISE SPANISH PHRYGIAN

This scale should be played using rest strokes throughout. Alternate strictly between fingers i and m (the index and middle fingers).

Don't expect to achieve instant fluency here; diligent practice at very gradually increasing tempos will ultimately give a greater reward.

The 12-string guitar

You may feel daunted by the idea of playing double the usual number of strings – but the good news is that if you can strum away on a six-string you will probably be able to get a decent sound out of a 12-string. There is no difference in the fundamental technique – the only aspect that is different is that the fingering is a little harder in some ways.

What is a 12-string guitar?

The 12 strings on a 12-string come in six pairs of two – six 'courses' to use the technical term. The pairs lie close together on the neck, so that each finger always frets both at once. This makes playing a bit more difficult than playing a single string, because rather more precision and pressure are required. Moreover, the neck of a 12-string is wider than the neck of a standard six-string acoustic – and this, too, takes some getting used to. All in all, playing a 12-string is physically more demanding than playing an ordinary guitar, but well within the reach of any competent player.

The chord shapes that you make are the same as the ones you are used to, because the tuning of a 12-string is the same as that of a six-string – in a manner of speaking. The top two pairs of strings (B and E) are tuned in unison (exactly the same note). The remaining four (E, A, D, G) are tuned an octave apart. Each pair consists of one string tuned to the same pitch as a six-string, and one string tuned an octave higher. Usually, the higher string of each pair is placed above the standard string, so that the higher string is struck first when strumming or picking downwards.

The sound

This doubling-up of the strings is reminiscent of the configuration of other guitar-like instruments, such as the mandolin. However, the 12-string guitar as we know it is a modern invention – undoubtedly American, and dating from around the turn of the 20th century. The effect of the double courses is to yield a very full, resonant sound when the guitar is strummed. This derives not only from the fact that you are playing twice as many notes at a time, but also from the chorus effect produced when two notes are very nearly, but not quite, the same pitch (or an octave apart). The tiny differences in pitch are not enough to make the guitar sound out of tune; instead they create a slow, shimmering effect that is extremely lush and pleasant to listen to.

> **Recommended listening:**
> - Joan Armatrading: "All the Way From America"
> - Boston: "More Than a Feeling"
> - Pink Floyd: "Wish You Were Here"
> - The Rolling Stones: "As Tears Go By"

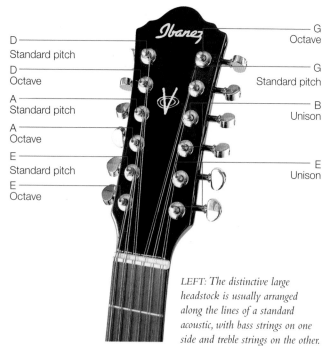

D — Standard pitch
D — Octave
A — Standard pitch
A — Octave
E — Standard pitch
E — Octave

G — Octave
G — Standard pitch
B — Unison
E — Unison

LEFT: The distinctive large headstock is usually arranged along the lines of a standard acoustic, with bass strings on one side and treble strings on the other.

ABOVE: Almost all 12-string guitars have a scratchplate to protect the top of the guitar from the vigorous strumming often associated with the instrument.

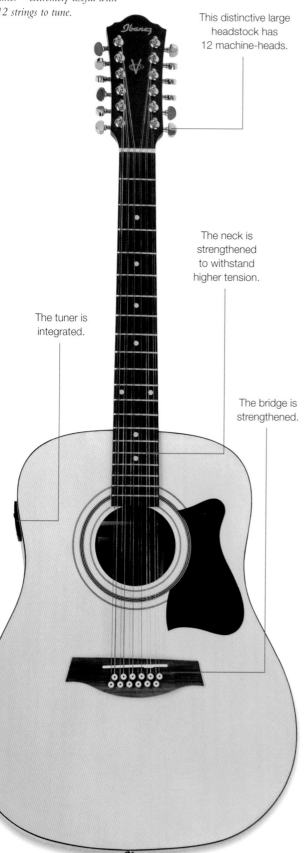

BELOW: *The 12-string shown here, although not an electro-acoustic model, has an integrated tuner – extremely useful with 12 strings to tune.*

This distinctive large headstock has 12 machine-heads.

The neck is strengthened to withstand higher tension.

The tuner is integrated.

The bridge is strengthened.

Leadbelly

Huddie Ledbetter, known as Leadbelly, described himself as 'the king of the 12-string guitar', and he undoubtedly played an important role in popularizing the instrument. Today, Leadbelly's recordings are also a vital bridge between the past and present. Born in 1888 in Louisiana, USA, Leadbelly was among the oldest of American folk musicians to make recordings in the 1930s and '40s. His originals, as well as the traditional songs he learnt as a labourer and during his many spells in prison, have found their way into the repertoire of artists as diverse as Bob Dylan, Led Zeppelin and Nirvana. Although often labelled a blues singer, Leadbelly drew on a far broader range of styles, and his best-known song "Goodnight Irene" is essentially a country ballad. In Leadbelly's original recordings, he accompanies himself on a variety of different instruments, including piano and accordion, but most often on a 12-string guitar, usually tuned a fourth below standard tuning (B E A D F♯ B), resulting in his powerful and sonorous 'roaring' signature guitar sound.

ABOVE: *Leadbelly playing the large Stella 12-string guitar with which he was most often seen.*

Tuning a 12-string guitar

The chorus effect is desirable, but this does not mean that a lazy approach can be taken to tuning: there are few sounds as grating as that of a badly tuned 12-string, and in any case, the chorus effect will be produced well within the limits of 'perfect' tuning. The usual approach is to get the lower string of each pair in tune first, and then to make sure the higher octave agrees exactly. This (along with changing strings) is a time-consuming process. However, the tuning arrangement is part of what gives this guitar its distinctive sound.

Chords are the guitarist's basic vocabulary,

the universal starting point for mastery

of the instrument's special language.

Chordfinder

To begin to play, you need to know just

a handful of chords, just as to speak another

language you need to know only a few words

at first. But to play eloquently on the guitar,

you must have a large lexicon at your disposal.

Introduction

This chordfinder is a kind of basic dictionary. It is not exhaustive, because there are many more obscure chords, and many more ways of playing the better-known chords than can be accommodated in one book or section of a book. However, if you master the chords on the following pages – or even half of them – then you will be reasonably well equipped to express yourself through your guitar.

Explore and experiment

Having access to a ready reference set of chord diagrams can be enormously useful. For example, whenever you encounter an unfamiliar chord in a songbook, it is likely you will be able to match it to a comparable chord shape in the finder. You may also wish to set off on a 'journey of discovery' to expand your knowledge of a certain chord type, key or tuning. Be aware, however, that there is a limit to the amount of new data that you can absorb in one session. The best way to learn a new chord is to find as many uses for it as you can, and experiment by combining it with other ones.

Reading the chord diagrams

Each chord is presented in three formats: as a chord diagram, in the standard musical notation that is common for all instruments, and in guitar tablature. A chord box (also known as a fret box) is a grid with six vertical lines representing the guitar's strings and horizontal lines representing the frets. Dots or circles are placed within this grid to show the position of the fingers. In this chordfinder, the finger dots are numbered (fingers 1–4) although many songbooks do not show these numbers.

There are certain graphic conventions connected with chord boxes. Where the highest horizontal line – that is, the top edge of the box – is drawn as a double line, this represents the 'nut' of the guitar. The nut is the raised ridge at the top of the neck. When the nut is not shown, the chord is fingered further up the fretboard. The number next to the chord tells you exactly where: 5fr indicates that the lowest active fret in this chord is the fifth fret. There are a few other symbols that you need to know: an O placed directly above the string indicates that the open string is part of the chord; an X shows that the string is not to be played. Two or more finger dots at the same fret may be joined by a curved line, indicating a full or partial barre – that is, the underside of the finger (usually the first finger) presses down on two or more strings at once.

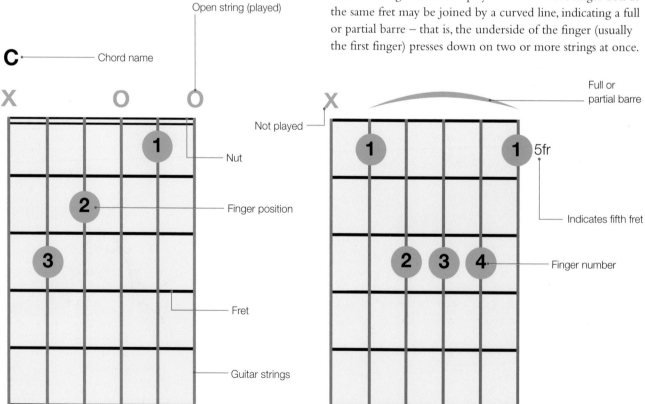

Notation and tab

Next to each chord box you will find two staves yoked together. Each of these staves represents a different way of representing the chord in question. The upper stave is standard musical notation: if you can read music, it tells you which notes are in the chord. The notation is universal in the sense that the chord shown in the notation could be played on any instrument that can play more than one note at a time (a piano, for example), or indeed on a group of instruments played by different individuals.

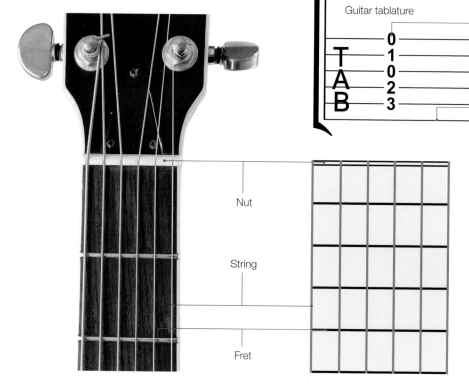

Standard musical notation and guitar tablature

Standard notation

Guitar tablature

Indicates fret to be played

Lowest string (E)

Nut

String

Fret

LEFT: *The chord box represents the frets and strings as seen face on: vertical lines represent the strings, while the frets are horizontal. When reading chord boxes, as with tablature, it is vital not to interpret the order of the strings in the wrong direction.*

The lower stave is guitar tablature ('TAB' for short). The lines, although superficially similar to the five-lined stave above, represent not the pitch of the note, but the six strings of the guitar. The bottom line stands for the lowest string, low E in standard tuning. The number on each line or string shows the fret that is to be played. Note that it does not show which finger to use, unlike the adjacent chord diagram. The numbers in TAB show which fret to play. The notes of the chord are arranged vertically, indicating that they are to be played together as a single chord.

X and O indications

In most of the first-position chords (and many other shapes further up the neck) the open-string notes must be able to sound clearly. If you concentrate only on producing the fretted notes, it is very easy to accidentally mute the 'O' notes. Try playing the strings one at a time to make sure that these are also sounding. Similarly, letting the 'X' strings sound will often result in a discordant effect.

A final note

For all the common chord families included in the following pages, at least one shape is shown per chord type for each step of the chromatic scale (the series of notes that rises and falls in semitones, or half notes).

All of the chords are in standard tuning (E, A, D, G, B and E) unless otherwise stated. However, some basic chord shapes for other tunings are also provided – and these are all clearly flagged in the introductory text on those pages. There are also some 'jazz voicings' that you can experiment with once you have mastered the basic shapes of the chords, as well as understand what their effect is.

Here and there, 'Try this' boxes are also included, which contain interesting and useful information about the construction of certain chord types. They also explain each type's sound and character, or their relationship to other members of the wide family of chords. Some suggestions for possible musical uses are detailed along with examples of songs that have used those chord types.

Major chords

The major chords consist of the root note plus the third and fifth notes of the major scale. In C, for example, those notes would be the root note C, plus E and G. In this section, you will find at least one way of playing the simple major chord for every step in the chromatic scale. Note that some notes can be expressed more than one way: D♭ is the same note as C♯, and B♭ is the same note as as A♯. The names used here are those most likely to be encountered. In Western music, major chords are often described as sounding 'happy'.

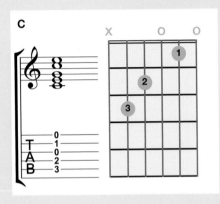

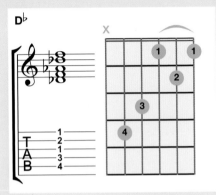

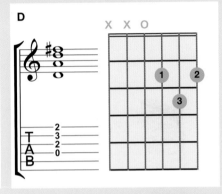

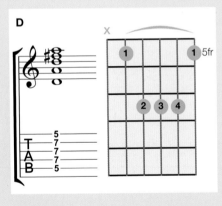

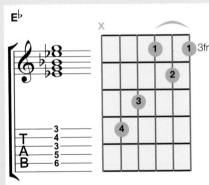

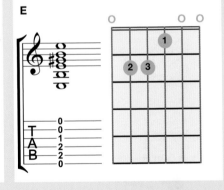

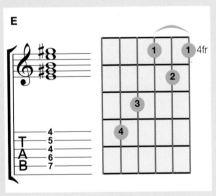

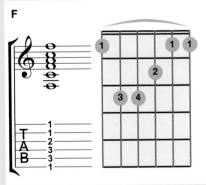

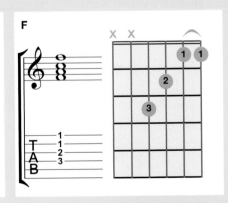

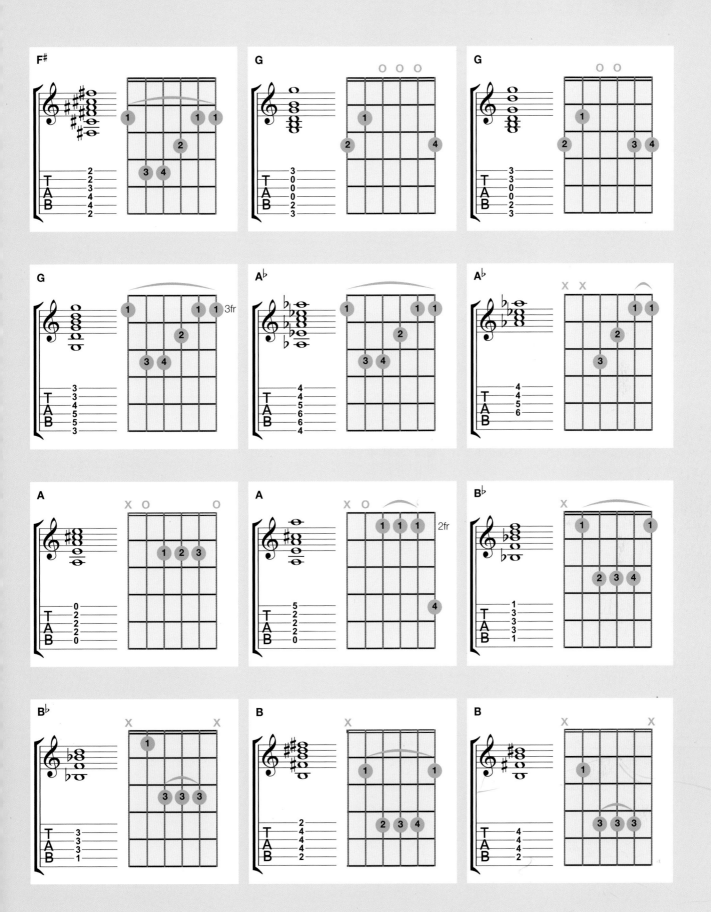

Minor chords

The minor chords consist of the first, third and fifth notes of the minor scale. The third note is flattened (lowered) in comparison with the major chord; it is a semitone lower. For the guitar player this means that many chord shapes can be changed from major to minor by changing one fretted note, or moving one finger. For example, E major becomes E minor by lifting the first finger from the first fret of the G string, thereby changing the major E-G#-B to the minor E-G-B. In Western music, minor chords are often characterized as having a sad sound.

Key

X = don't play

O = play open string

Cm

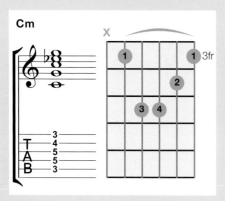

C#m

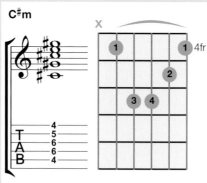

Dm

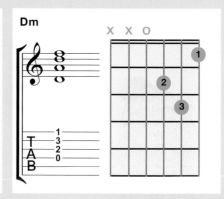

E♭m

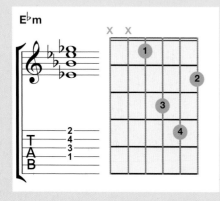

E♭m

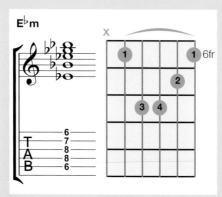

Em

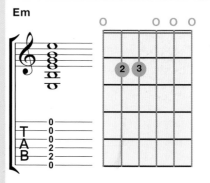

Fm

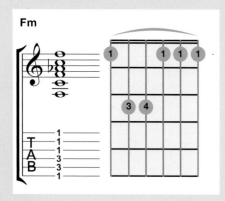

Fm

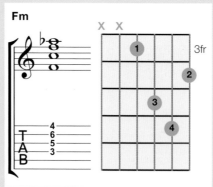

F#m

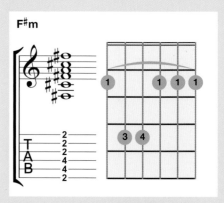

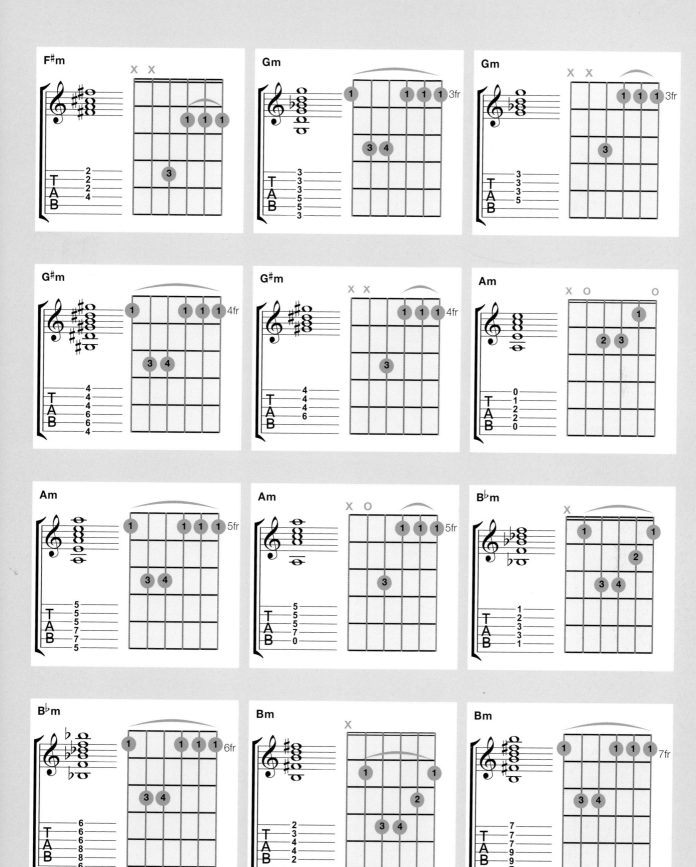

Seventh chords

The seventh, also known as the dominant seventh, is denoted by a number 7 after the root name. The chord consists of four notes: the root note, the major third, the perfect fifth, and the flattened seventh (a semitone below the seventh of the major scale, or one tone below the root note). The dominant seventh has an unresolved feel that makes it 'want' to resolve to a chord a perfect fourth above – an essential element of any guitarist's box of tricks, particularly when playing blues or derived styles including jazz and rock 'n' roll.

Key
X = don't play
O = play open string

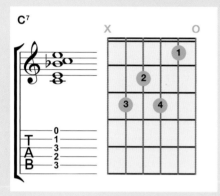

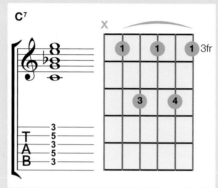

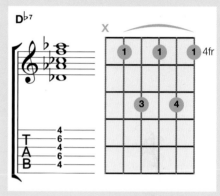

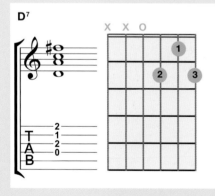

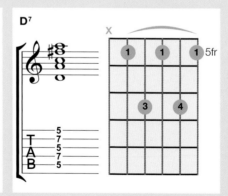

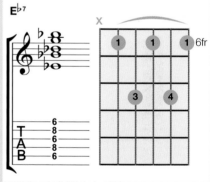

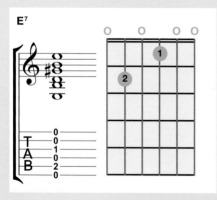

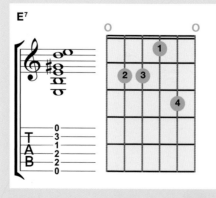

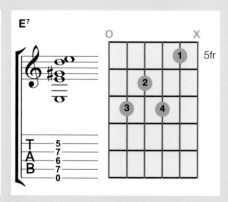

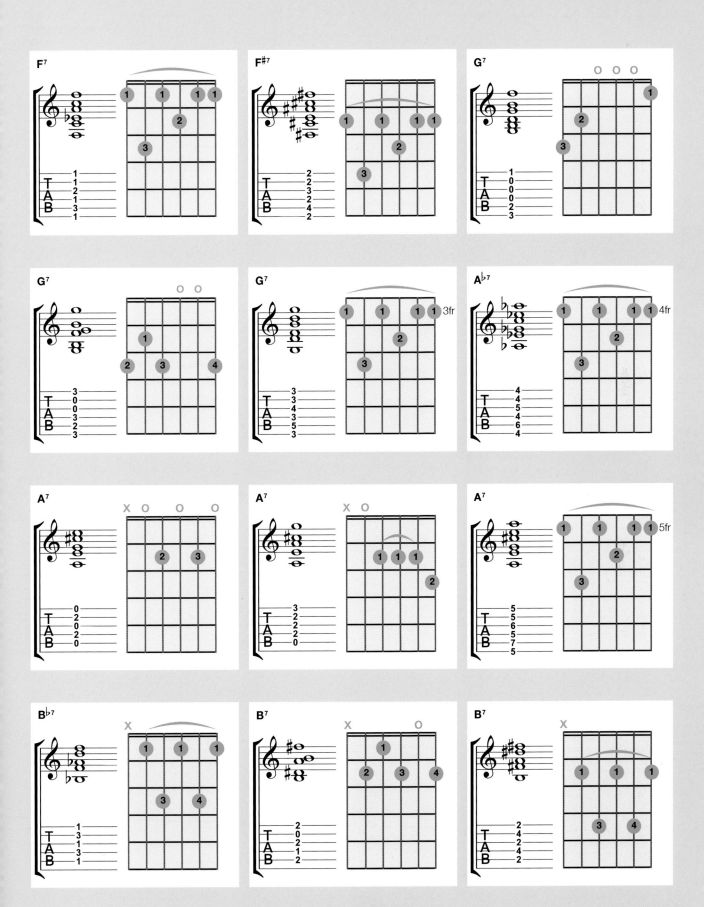

Minor seventh chords

The minor seventh chord is constructed by adding a fourth note to the minor triad – a minor seventh interval from, or a tone below, the root. This is the same note as the seventh in a dominant seventh chord. Minor seventh chords are denoted by m7, min7 or -7 after the root note. Like the dominant seventh, minor seventh chords often seem to 'want' to move to another chord: in their case, a dominant seventh chord a fourth above. This chord relationship is known as a II-V progression, and is crucial to modern jazz and many related styles, particularly Latin jazz.

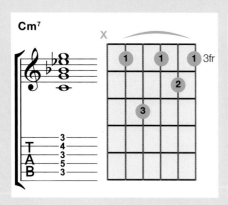

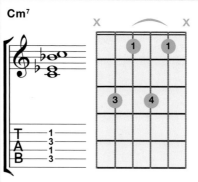

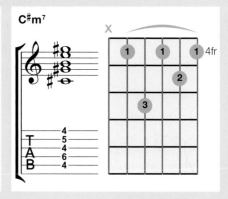

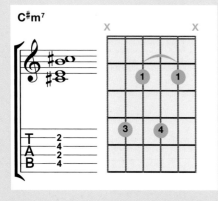

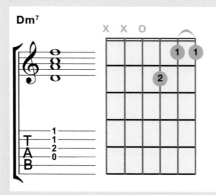

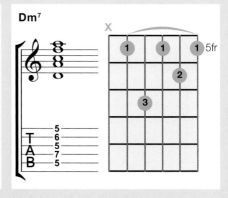

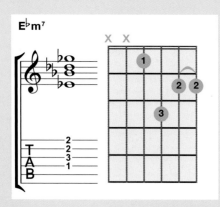

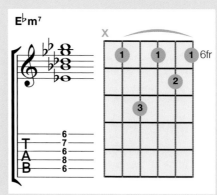

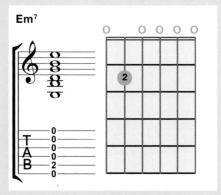

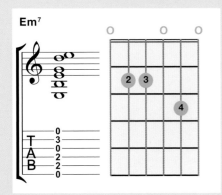

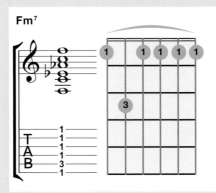

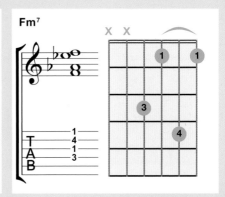

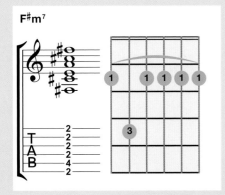

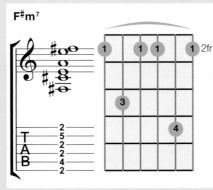

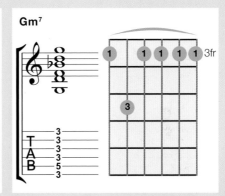

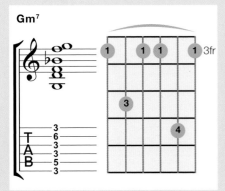

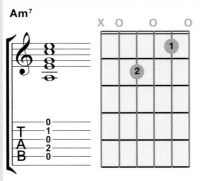

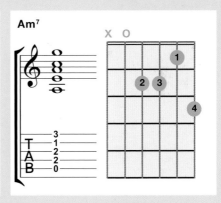

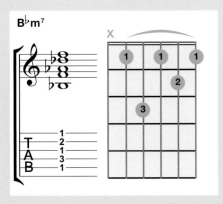

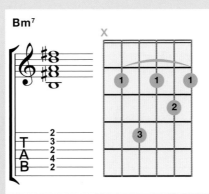

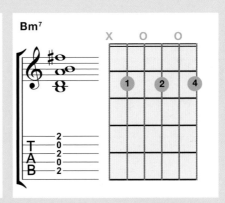

Major seventh chords

The major seventh is the archetypal sweet-sounding jazzy chord, and is constructed from four notes: the root, the major third, the perfect fifth, and the seventh note of the major scale (or to put it another way, a semitone below the root). The major seventh is usually denoted as maj7, but is occasionally indicated with a triangle thus: Δ or Δ⁷. The major seventh chord can often be used as chord I or chord IV in the major key (if a jazzy sound is desired), but beware of using it in any style where a bluesy effect is required.

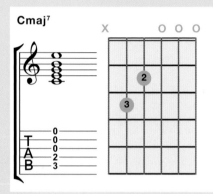

Cmaj⁷

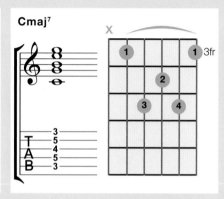

Cmaj⁷

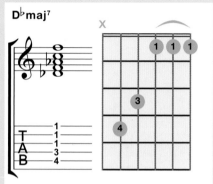

D♭maj⁷

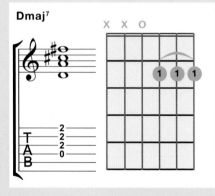

Dmaj⁷

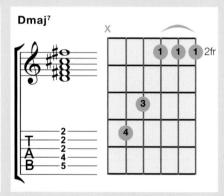

Dmaj⁷

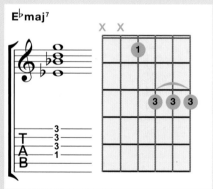

E♭maj⁷

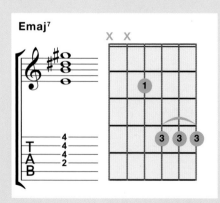

Emaj⁷

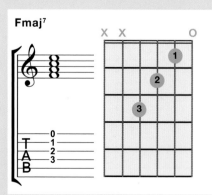

Fmaj⁷

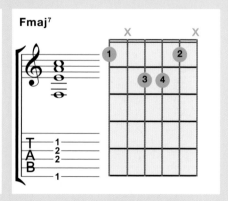

Fmaj⁷

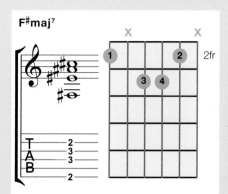

F♯maj7

2fr

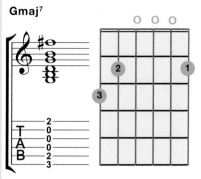

Gmaj7

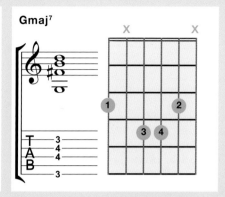

Gmaj7

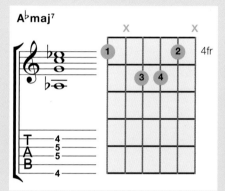

A♭maj7

4fr

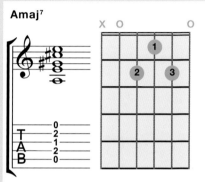

Amaj7

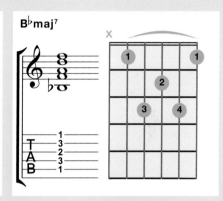

B♭maj7

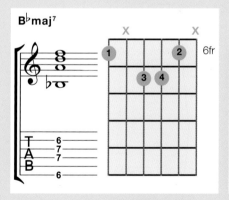

B♭maj7

6fr

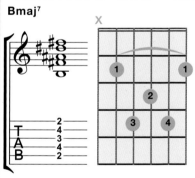

Bmaj7

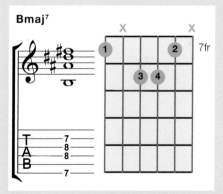

Bmaj7

7fr

Try this

The major seventh is found on steps I and IV in the major key. That is to say, if you play the first, third, fifth and seventh notes of the scale, or the fourth, sixth, eighth and tenth (going into the next octave), then the result is a major seventh. This means that the major seventh can often be played instead of the simple major chord at the fourth or fifth step. So in C, for example, try playing Cmaj7 or Fmaj7 instead of plain C or F. It won't always work (in particular, there may be some tension created if the melody contains the root note of the chord), but sometimes it will give an interestingly sophisticated sound.

ABOVE: *Listen to Wings' "Band on the Run".*

Diminished seventh chords

The diminished seventh is constructed from four minor thirds stacked on top of each other. This makes for a chord that can be described as spooky or jangly. For simplicity, some notes in diminished seventh chords may be re-spelled in notation. The top note of C diminished seventh, for example, is B♭♭ (B double flat) but it is often written as A, which is physically the same note. The symmetrical construction means that two diminished seventh chords a minor third apart (for example A and C) contain exactly the same notes, so can be freely substituted for each other.

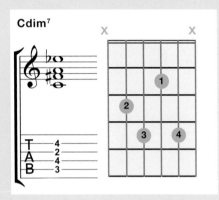

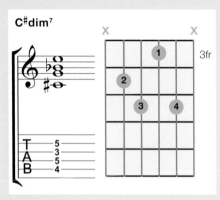

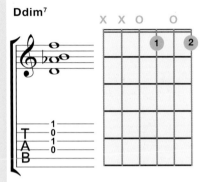

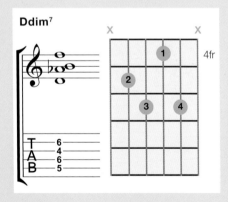

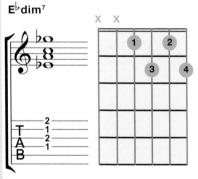

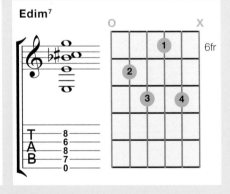

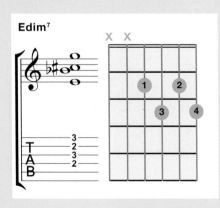

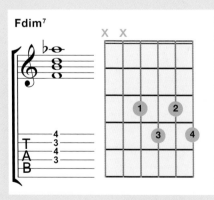

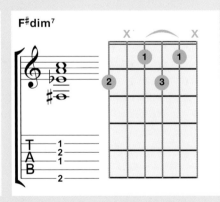

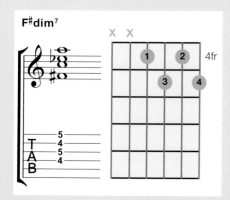

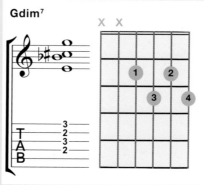

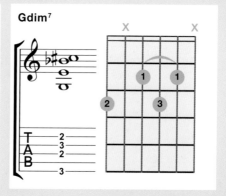

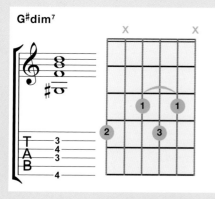

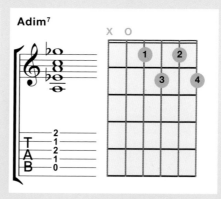

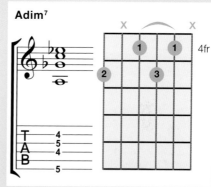

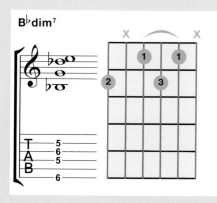

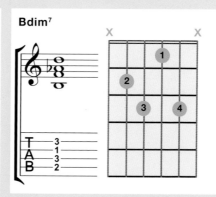

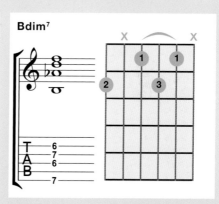

Try this

Diminished chords can be moved around the fretboard against a ringing open bass string. The open low E, A and D strings between them provide bass notes that will work against any diminished chord here. Try moving any shape up or down the fretboard in intervals of three frets at a time, perhaps arpeggiating the fretted notes with the right-hand fingers, while the open-string bass note (played by the thumb) is allowed to ring. This is one of those 'guitaristic' moves that is well worth incorporating as a stock-in-trade idea, though beware of over-using it as it can sound a little too much like horror-film music for some styles.

ABOVE: *Listen to James Taylor's "Don't Let Me Be Lonely Tonight"*.

m7♭5 chords

The m7♭5 chord consists of the root note, the minor third, the diminished fifth and the minor seventh. It is also known as 'half-diminished' because of its similarity to the diminished seventh. The only difference is that in m7♭5, the seventh note is a semitone higher. Although the half-diminished chord is found in the major key (chord VII), it is not encountered very often, and is most often used by players as a substitute for a dominant ninth chord a major third below – for example, Em7♭5 may be played when C9 is written.

Cm⁷♭⁵

Cm⁷♭⁵
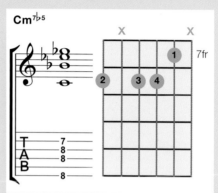

C#m⁷♭⁵
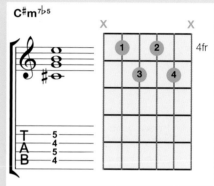

C#m⁷♭⁵
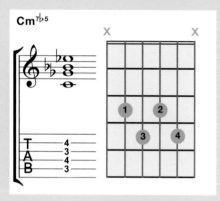

Dm⁷♭⁵
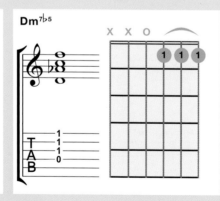

Dm⁷♭⁵
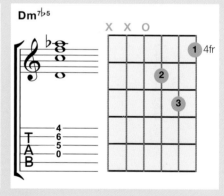

D#m⁷♭⁵
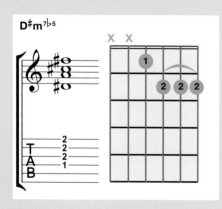

Em⁷♭⁵
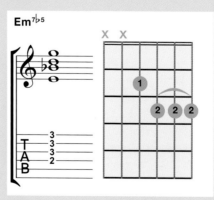

Em⁷♭⁵
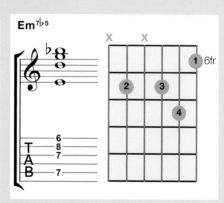

Fm⁷♭⁵
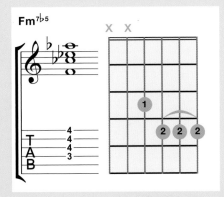

Fm⁷♭⁵
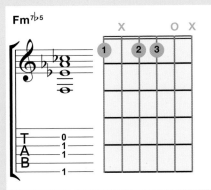

F#m⁷♭⁵
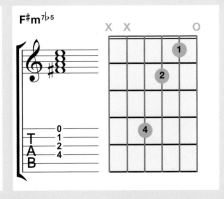

F#m⁷♭⁵
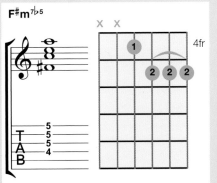

Gm⁷♭⁵
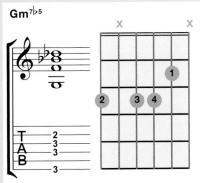

Gm⁷♭⁵
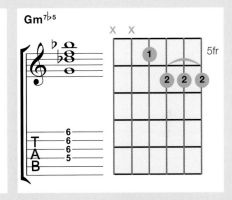

G#m⁷♭⁵
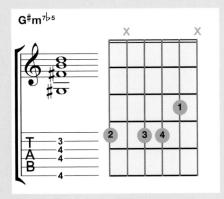

Am⁷♭⁵
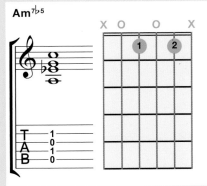

Am⁷♭⁵
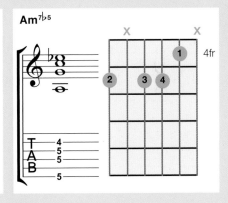

A#m⁷♭⁵
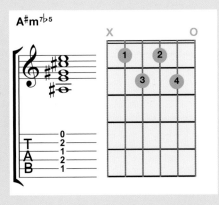

Bm⁷♭⁵
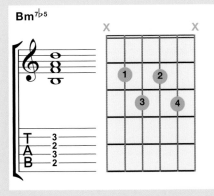

Bm⁷♭⁵
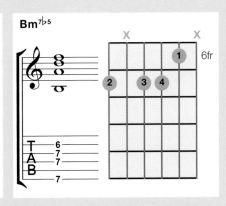

Dominant seventh jazz voicings

A voicing is an alternative way of stacking up the three or four notes that make up a chord. In these voicings of the dominant seventh, the fifth is omitted. This lends a sparse quality to the sound, and creates a kind of space which a singer's voice can explore. In the context of a band, a bass player might choose to omit the root note too – since this provides an opportunity for much greater finger movement, and also frees up fingers to add more advanced extended notes such as ninths and 13ths on the top two strings.

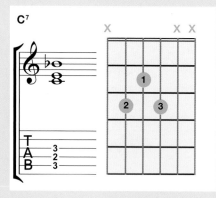

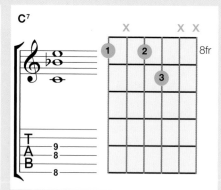

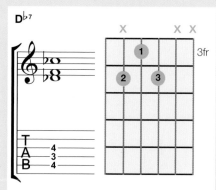

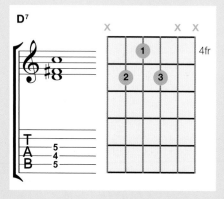

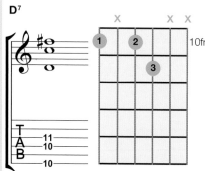

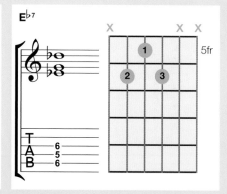

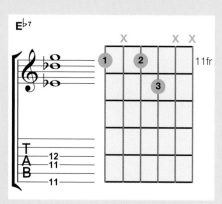

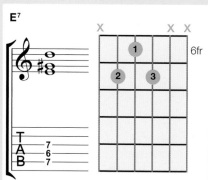

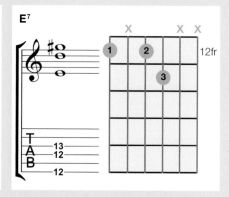

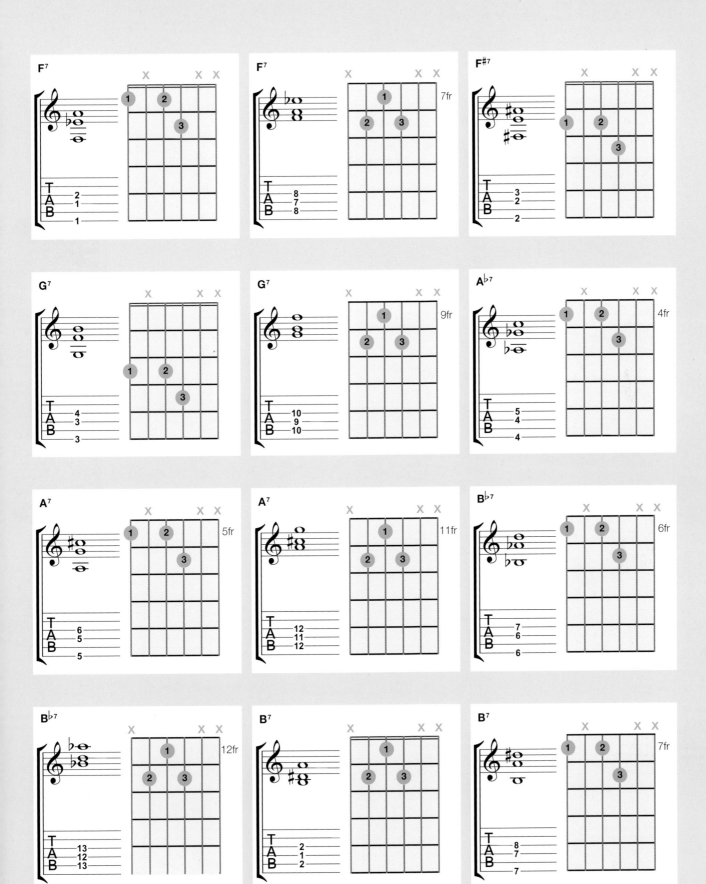

Minor seventh jazz voicings

The minor seventh jazz voicings, like the dominant seventh jazz voicings, omit the fifth. They often occur as chord II in a II–V progression. In this instance, the seventh note usually resolves downwards by a semitone to the third of the V chord. As the fifth is omitted, these shapes may also be used freely where m7♭5 is written. All the shapes here with the root on the A string can easily be turned into m9 (minor ninth) chords by re-assigning the fingers so that the fourth finger is free to play the B string at the same fret as the note on the G string – great for Latin jazz.

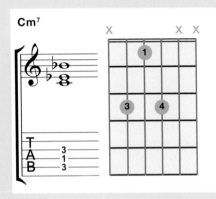

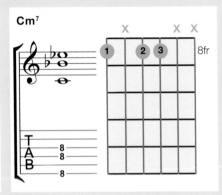

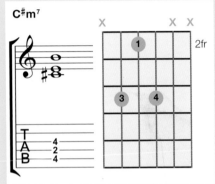

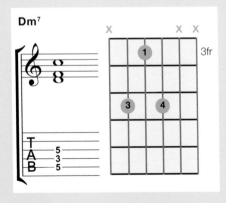

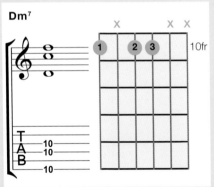

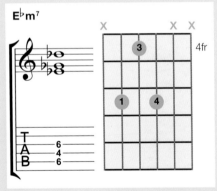

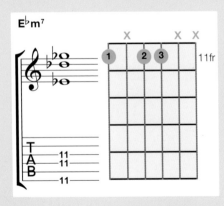

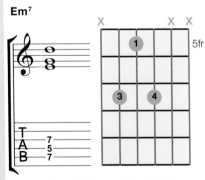

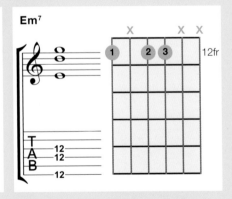

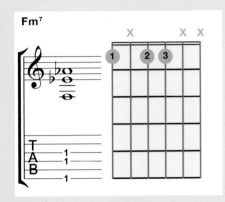

Fm⁷

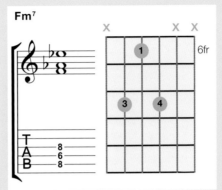

Fm⁷

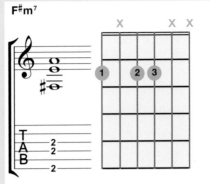

F♯m⁷

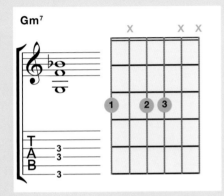

Gm⁷

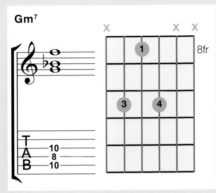

Gm⁷

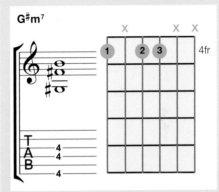

G♯m⁷

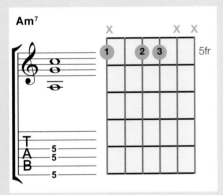

Am⁷

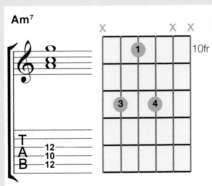

Am⁷

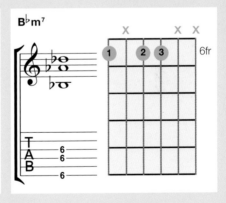

B♭m⁷

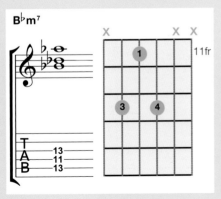

B♭m⁷

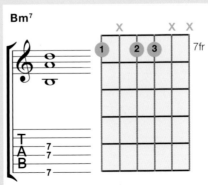

Bm⁷

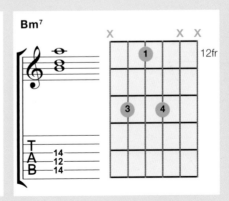

Bm⁷

Major seventh jazz voicings

This minimal jazz voicing, like those for the dominant seventh and minor seventh, omits the fifth of the chord, and so consists of the root, the major third and the major seventh. The major seventh chord is often found as chord I after a II–V progression; all three shapes should be chosen for minimal movement. If chords I and II are voiced with the root on the bottom string, chord V will be found with the root on the A string, and vice versa. The third of chord V will remain present in chord I (as the seventh), while the seventh of chord V falls by a semitone to become the third of chord I.

Cmaj⁷

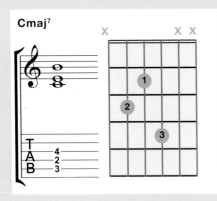

Cmaj⁷

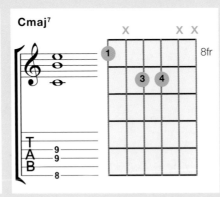

D♭maj⁷

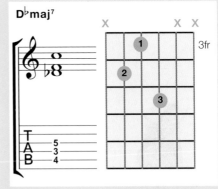

Dmaj⁷

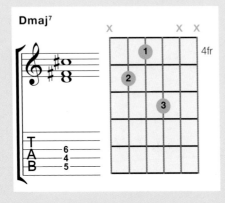

Dmaj⁷

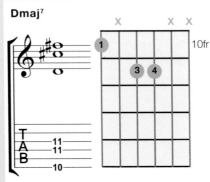

E♭maj⁷

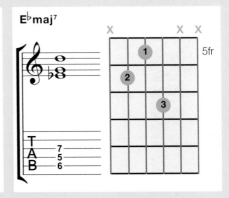

E♭m⁷

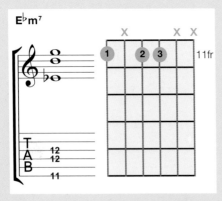

Emaj⁷

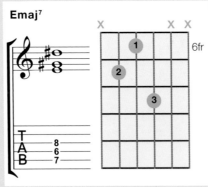

Emaj⁷

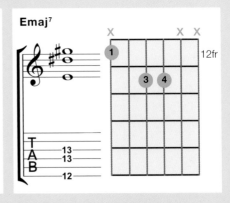

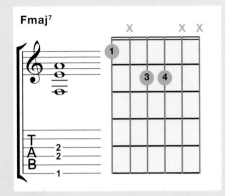

Fmaj7

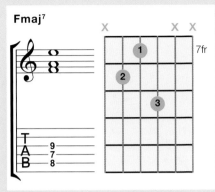

Fmaj7

7fr

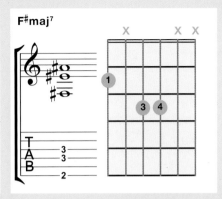

F♯maj7

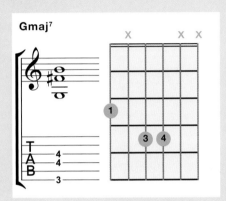

Gmaj7

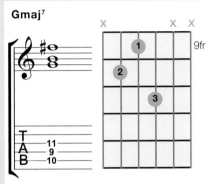

Gmaj7

9fr

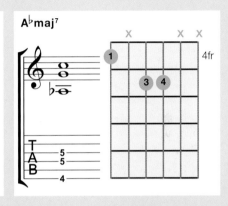

A♭maj7

4fr

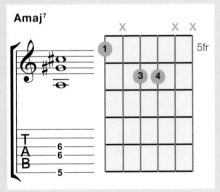

Amaj7

5fr

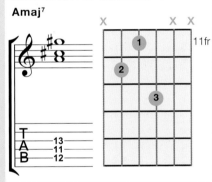

Amaj7

11fr

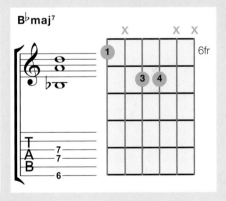

B♭maj7

6fr

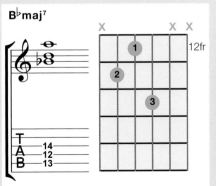

B♭maj7

12fr

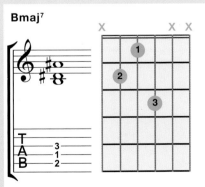

Bmaj7

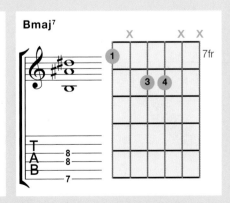

Bmaj7

7fr

Suspended fourth

A suspended fourth consists of the root, perfect fourth and perfect fifth of the scale. A suspension is created when one of the notes in a chord is replaced with another which sounds like it 'wants' to resolve to the note replaced. In popular music, this usually takes the form of raising the third in a major chord by one semitone. As this note is a perfect fourth above the root, the result is known as a suspended fourth chord (denoted as sus4). The same suspension works well with dominant sevenths, and is denoted as 7sus4. The Who's "Pinball Wizard" has suspensions in action.

Csus⁴
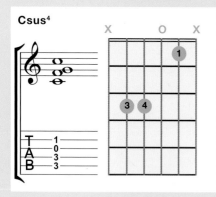

Csus⁴
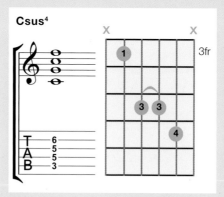

D♭sus⁴
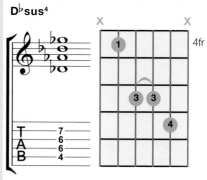

Dsus⁴
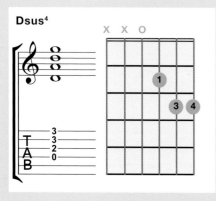

D⁷sus⁴
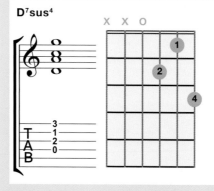

E♭sus⁴
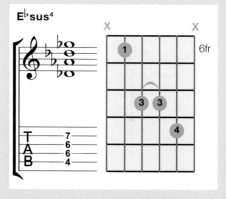

Esus⁴
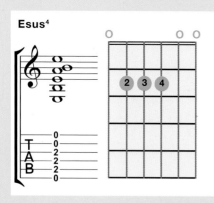

E⁷sus⁴
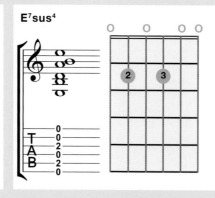

Fsus⁴
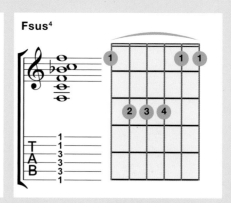

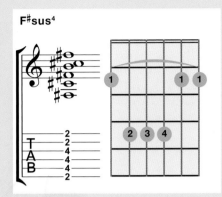

F#sus⁴

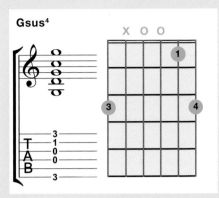

Gsus⁴

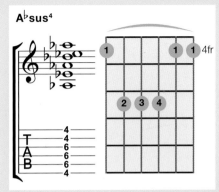

A♭sus⁴

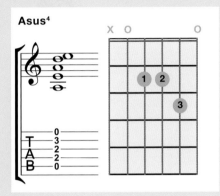

Asus⁴

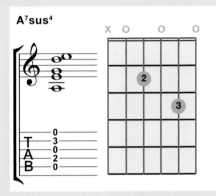

A⁷sus⁴

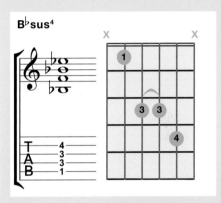

B♭sus⁴

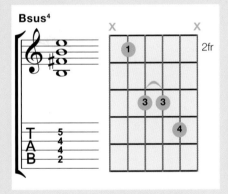

Bsus⁴

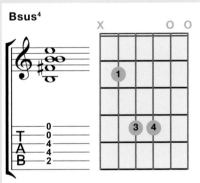

Bsus⁴

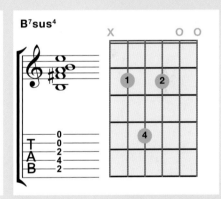

B⁷sus⁴

Try this

Although the suspended fourth is the most common suspension, a different one is heard in many acoustic guitar styles. This is the suspended second (sus2) chord. Here, the major third is replaced by the note one tone below (a second from the root), which also resolves to the third. Dsus2 and Asus2 are the most popular first-position sus2 chords as the suspension is created by removing a finger to leave one string open (the top E and B strings respectively in these chords). Try the sequence D – Dsus4 – D – Dsus2 – D: many famous songs have been written around this kind of figure, most famously James Taylor's "Country Road".

ABOVE: *Listen to James Taylor's "Country Road".*

Half-open chords

These chords all produce interesting sounds by moving familiar chords into unfamiliar positions, while one or more open strings remain unchanged. This creates tension, but there is a compensating 'drone' effect from the open strings. Extensive use of these chords is generally limited to keys that contain the notes of the open string or strings. This means E and B – in other words, sharp keys rather than flat keys, although this can of course also be used to created more dissonant sounds if that is the effect you want to create.

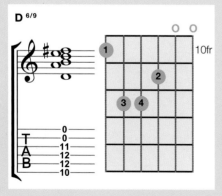

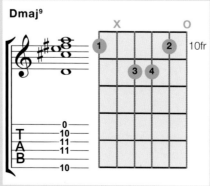

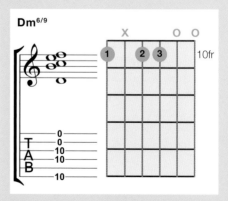

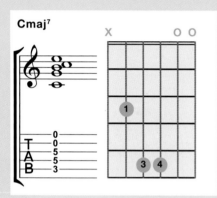

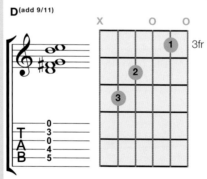

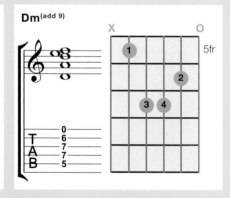

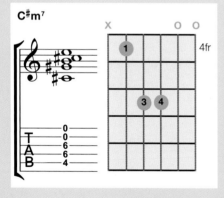

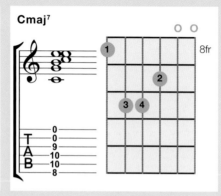

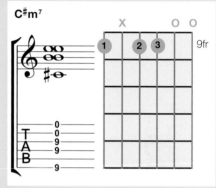

Em⁷

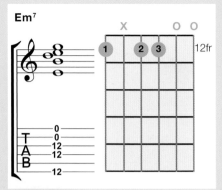

Fmaj⁷#¹¹

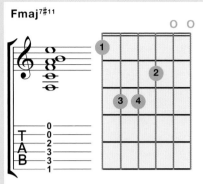

F#(add 11)

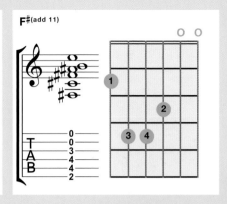

F#m⁷

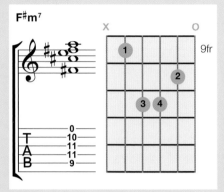

F#m¹¹

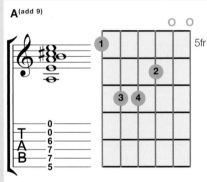

G⁶

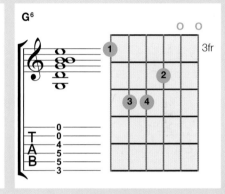

G#m⁷(♭13)

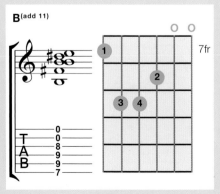

A(add 9)

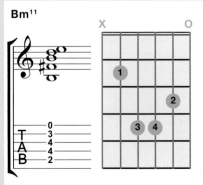

Am⁹

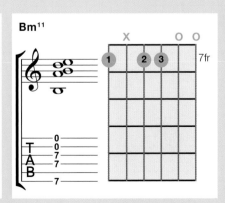

B(add 11)

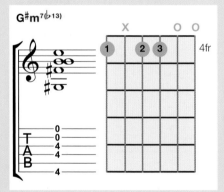

Bm¹¹

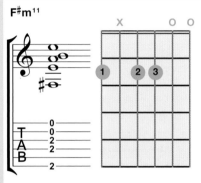

Bm¹¹

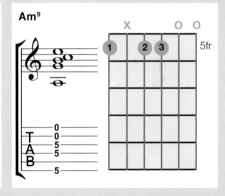

Essential chords in open G

In open G, the strings are tuned to DGDGBD. As with any open tuning, the point of playing in open G is to explore the tensions that can be created by moving fretted notes against open strings. This usually means that the notes D and G will be ringing. This will not directly contradict the harmony as long as you stick to the keys of G or G minor, and it can give interesting results in other keys that contain these notes. Chord shapes in open G can be viewed as variations on shapes found in standard tuning, as the tuning of the second, third and fourth strings is unchanged.

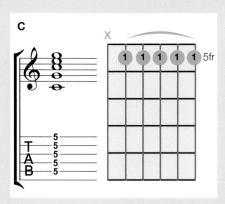

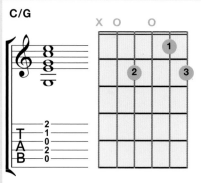

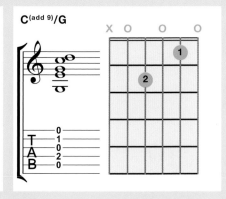

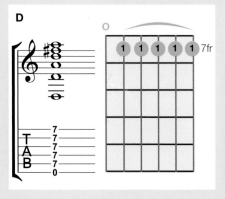

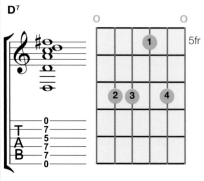

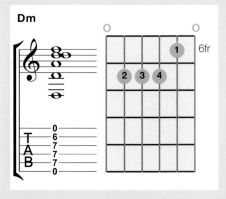

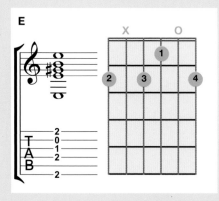

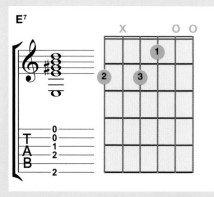

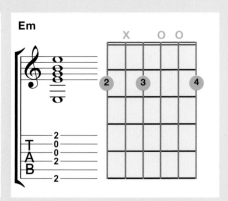

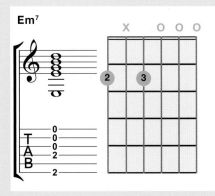

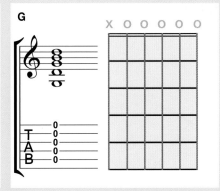

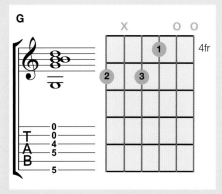

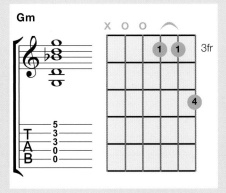

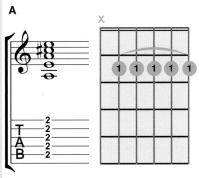

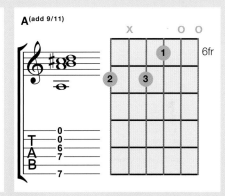

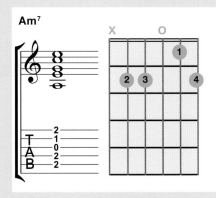

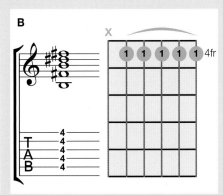

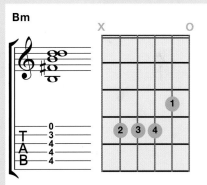

Try this

The capo is even more useful in open tunings than it is in standard tuning. For example, placing the capo at the second fret in open G is the best way to achieve open A tuning without the running the risk of breaking strings. Moreover, the sound and feel of the guitar can be changed radically by using the capo at higher frets, and many people find that this is frequently a better way to play in remote keys. The combination of using an open key along with the capo at a high fret can result in a sound that is significantly different from that created by standard tuning.

ABOVE: *Listen to Nanci Griffith's "Love at the Five and Dime".*

Essential chords in open D

In open D, the strings are tuned to DADF#AD. The character of most open tunings is defined by the string that is tuned to the third of the tonic chord. There is usually only one such string: the other five are generally tuned to the root or the fifth. Open D takes some getting used to, since the third (F#) is on the third string – not one of the top two, as is the case with many open tunings. As a result of the location of the third, some of the essential shapes in open D can be a little unwieldy, and some seemingly familiar shapes can result in very unusual sounds.

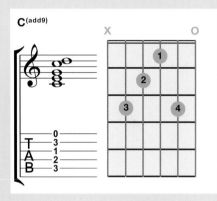

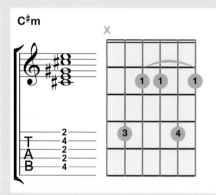

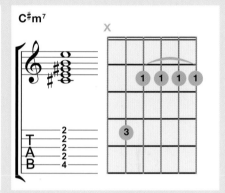

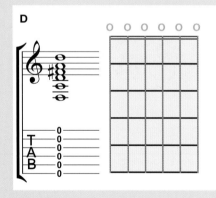

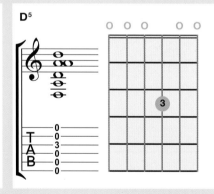

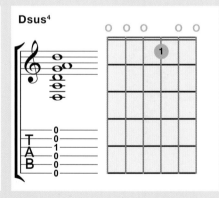

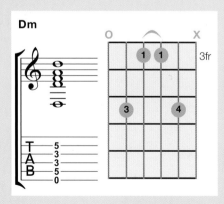

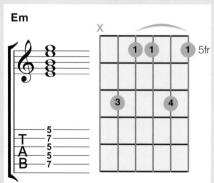

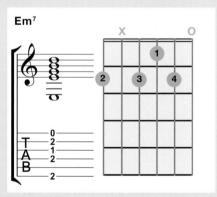

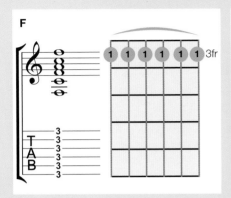

F
3fr
1 1 1 1 1 1

TAB
3
3
3
3
3
3

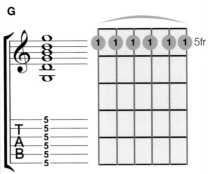

G
5fr
1 1 1 1 1 1

TAB
5
5
5
5
5
5

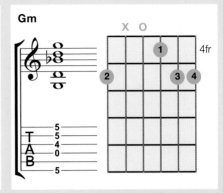

Gm
X O
4fr
1
2 3 4

TAB
5
5
4
0

5

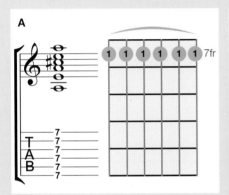

A
7fr
1 1 1 1 1 1

TAB
7
7
7
7
7

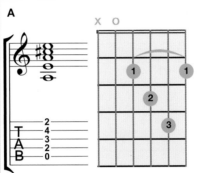

A
X O
1
1
2
3

TAB
2
4
3
2
0

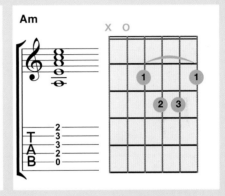

Am
X O
1
1
2 3

TAB
2
3
3
2
0

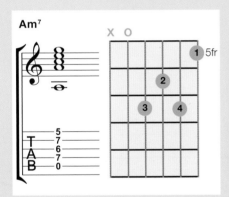

Am7
X O
5fr
1
2
3 4

TAB
5
7
6
7
0

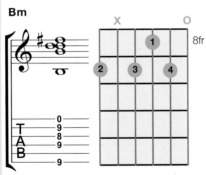

Bm
X O
8fr
1
2 3 4

TAB
0
9
8
9

9

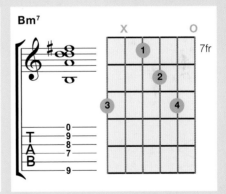

Bm7
X O
7fr
1
2
3
4

TAB
0
9
8
7

9

Try this

One way that you can maximize the possibilities of open D chords is to explore double-stopped sixths on the A and F# strings (that is, the second and fourth strings). The beauty of this idea is that where a shape creates tension, it can instantly be resolved by moving to an adjacent sixth shape. For some added spice, try sixths that contain notes from outside the key of D, or even moving chromatically (one fret at a time). If in doubt, lean heavily on the open bottom E string to provide a drone. This will give a sense of continuity even to shapes that are actually musically unrelated.

ABOVE: *Listen to Joni Mitchell performing "Chelsea Morning".*

Essential chords in DADGAD

DADGAD tuning is similar to open D tuning, but with a G instead of F#
on the third string, giving a Dsus4 chord on the open strings. The resulting
major second 'crunch' interval between the G and high A strings lends
DADGAD a more sophisticated sound than open tunings. But as with
many alternative tunings, interesting sounds can be obtained with minimal
finger movement. The D5 shown here is a favourite among DADGAD
players, and is often executed by first strumming or picking with the
G string open, and then adding the fretted note using a hammer-on.

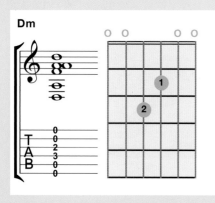

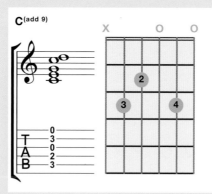

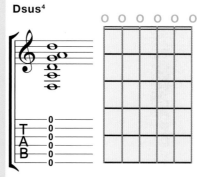

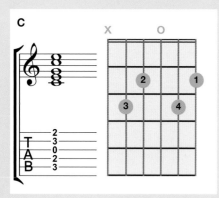

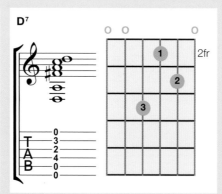

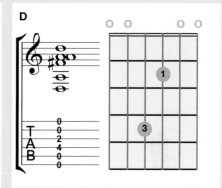

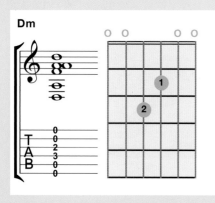

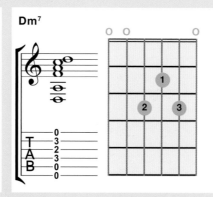

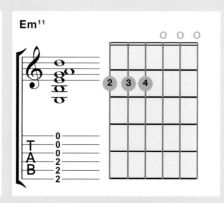

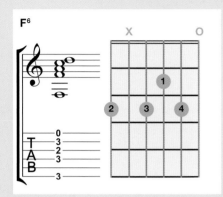

F⁶

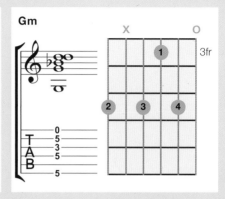

G

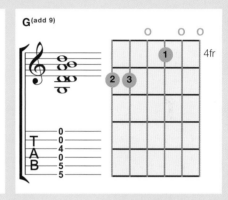

Gm

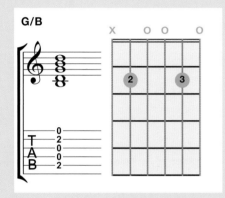

G/B

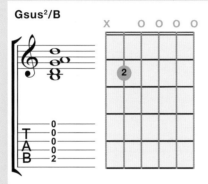

Gsus²/B

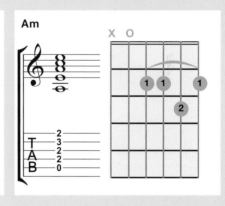

G⁽ᵃᵈᵈ ⁹⁾

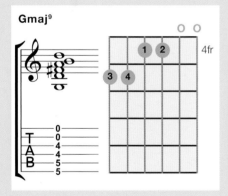

Gmaj⁹

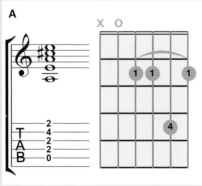

A

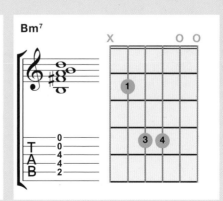

Am

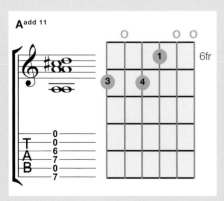

Aᵃᵈᵈ ¹¹

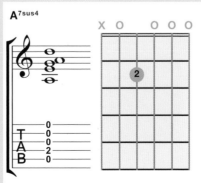

A⁷ˢᵘˢ⁴

Bm⁷

There is an extensive range of guitars available

nowadays, but they can all be traced back to

an ancestor around 3,000 years ago.

History of
the guitar

This chapter follows the development of the

guitar from the first plucked strings, through the

Baroque period to the classical guitar of the early

19th century and beyond, and looks at some of

the pioneering makers who together helped to

ensure the guitar is as popular today as ever.

Early ancestors of the guitar

Some of the earliest depictions of people playing stringed instruments – and therefore the distant ancestors of the modern guitar – are to be found in Babylonian reliefs dating from *c*.1800BC. While chordophones (as stringed instruments are called) may well have existed for many centuries before this, hard evidence of their development, and therefore that of the guitar, can only be traced from more recent times.

The first plucked strings

Because of the kinds of materials used in the construction of stringed instruments – generally wood and other degradable products – they do not survive the ravages of time, and, in consequence, unravelling the history of the guitar involves a fair amount of guesswork. There are bas-reliefs from early in the second millennium BC that show us that the Hittites of Anatolia, modern Turkey, played stringed instruments that were distinctly guitar-shaped. Much later depictions also survive from medieval Europe, including a 14th-century carving in Exeter Cathedral, UK, which shows an angel

playing a guitar-like instrument. However, any research into the metamorphosis of such instruments into the lute, vihuela or Baroque guitar is speculative, and it is perhaps in looking at the origins of the instruments' names that we can find more solid evidence for their history and development.

Early relatives

As the Roman Empire expanded, guitar-like chordophones such as the *pandura* (ancestor of the Greek bouzouki) and the *fidicula* were adopted far and wide. After the decline of Rome and the growth of the Muslim sphere of influence throughout the southern and eastern Mediterranean, the Middle Eastern *oud* was introduced into Europe by the invading Moors. This was an Arabic instrument dating back to at least the eighth century and originally called the *al 'ūd*, literally meaning 'the wood'. This instrument soon became the similarly named and shaped *lut*, or in English, the lute. By the 14th century, the lute-shaped *guitarra moresca* (Moorish guitar) and the guitar-shaped *guitarra latina* (Latin guitar) had both become common instruments in Spain, and eventually the distinction between them was abandoned, leaving simply the word *guitarra*, which is still the Spanish word for 'guitar'. This name has its origins ultimately in the Greek *kithara*, 'lyre', which in its turn may have come from the Persian *setar*, meaning 'three-stringed'.

The Renaissance

By the 16th century, the lute had become one of the most widely played musical instruments throughout Europe, although in Spain and Portugal the vihuela (possibly derived from the *fidicula* of Rome) was also very popular. Like the lute, the vihuela had 'courses' (pairs of strings) rather than single strings – six in the case of the vihuela, frequently a single top string that was used to play the melody while the courses provided the accompaniment. While the *vihuela de arco* (played with a bow) and the *vihuela de peñola* (with a plectrum) both appear in medieval sources, the *vihuela de mano* (played with the fingers and later abbreviated simply to 'vihuela') seems to have existed only since the 15th century.

LEFT: *A Babylonian terracotta relief plaque from the second millennium BC, depicting a man playing an early form of guitar. These instruments are commonly referred to as the Hittite guitars.*

From the Renaissance to the Baroque

The transformation of the guitar from courses to single strings was a gradual one, and many developments often took place in parallel. The model that emerged in the 16th century of having a single high string with paired courses was an interim development that took many forms over a number of centuries. One was the four-course guitar, an instrument for which the French lutenist and guitarist Guillaume Morlaye (*c*.1520–1577) composed, and he published a collection of these compositions in 1552. However, this was a short-lived design, and it was the five-course Baroque guitar that came to dominate the field. Infinitely more versatile than its ancestors, this new instrument went on to become a star performer in an age of musical virtuosity.

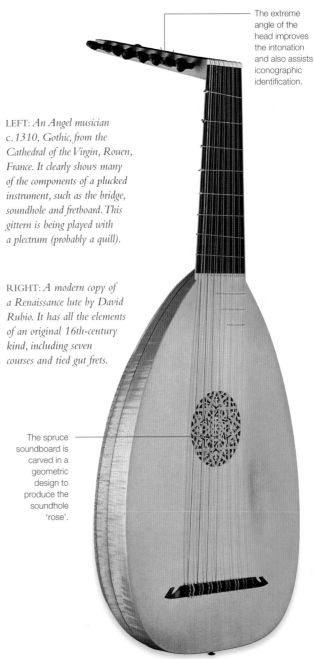

The extreme angle of the head improves the intonation and also assists iconographic identification.

LEFT: *An Angel musician c.1310, Gothic, from the Cathedral of the Virgin, Rouen, France. It clearly shows many of the components of a plucked instrument, such as the bridge, soundhole and fretboard. This gittern is being played with a plectrum (probably a quill).*

RIGHT: *A modern copy of a Renaissance lute by David Rubio. It has all the elements of an original 16th-century kind, including seven courses and tied gut frets.*

The spruce soundboard is carved in a geometric design to produce the soundhole 'rose'.

Like the Renaissance lute, the vihuela was tuned mainly in fourths – actually 44344 or GCFADG (low to high) – very close to the modern guitar's standard tuning of 44434 or EADGBE, albeit higher in pitch. The vihuela came in different sizes and therefore different keys, but maintained the same intervals between the strings – the various pitches were mentioned in 1538 in *Los Seys Libros del Delphín* by the Spanish lutenist and composer Luis Narváez (*c*.1500–*c*.1560), as well being evident from various contemporary pictures.

Seven-course variants also remained popular for a long time – there are surviving examples of such instruments made around 1760 in Seville by Francisco Sanguino (*c*.1705–1771) – and they are mentioned as late as 1799 in a guitar 'method' (instruction manual) called *Principios para Tocar la Guitarra de Seis Ordenes* by the Italian composer Federico Moretti (1760–1838), who wrote extensively for the guitar.

The five-course Baroque guitar

The closing years of the 16th century saw the earliest music written for the five-course guitar. At first this involved a simple chord-strumming technique for accompanying other musicians, and its very simplicity made it hugely popular. In Spain it began to replace the traditional vihuela and, elsewhere in Europe, the lute, which had by this time become an unwieldy, oversized instrument with anything up to 14 courses.

Early guitar music

It was in the Baroque period (roughly between 1600 and 1750) that the guitar acquired its own music. The celebrated Italian guitarist and guitar teacher Francesco Corbetta (c.1520–1577) was one of the first to develop the early five-course guitar's repertoire by writing attractive, melodic but uncomplicated music for amateurs to play. Since these amateurs included King Carlos II of Spain and Queen Anne of Great Britain, the place of the guitar in popular music making was secured. Many guitar methods were published all over Europe during this time. One of the most popular was *Instrucción de Música sobre la Guitarra Española* (*An Instruction in Music for the Spanish Guitar*) of 1674 by the Spanish composer Gaspar Sanz (1640–1710), whose music still forms an important part of the modern instrument's repertoire.

The five-course guitar's tuning was not unlike that of today's standard EADGBE (from low to high), Sanz specifying ADGBE for the five courses, rising from low A upwards. Musicians in Italy and France used a slight modification.

While instruments were also tuned to ADGBE, the 'bottom' A was pitched a fifth above the D string next to it. This system of the bottom strings being tuned higher than the ones above them, known as 're-entrant tuning', still survives in instruments such as the ukulele and the five-string banjo. Some Baroque guitar composers were attracted to the *campanelles* (bell-like sounds) that were produced by re-entrant tuning, and made effective use of it, notably Corbetta himself as well as the French lutenist and guitarist Robert de Visée (c.1655–c.1732), who worked at the court of Louis XIV. De Visée's music also gives the bass line a prominent role in the suites he composed.

BELOW: *Sanz's music using the Alfabeto system. An important advance in the 17th century was the shift from writing music out in tablature (similar to the way fingered chords are still written in popular guitar accompaniments) to notating it on the five-line stave like all other music then and now.*

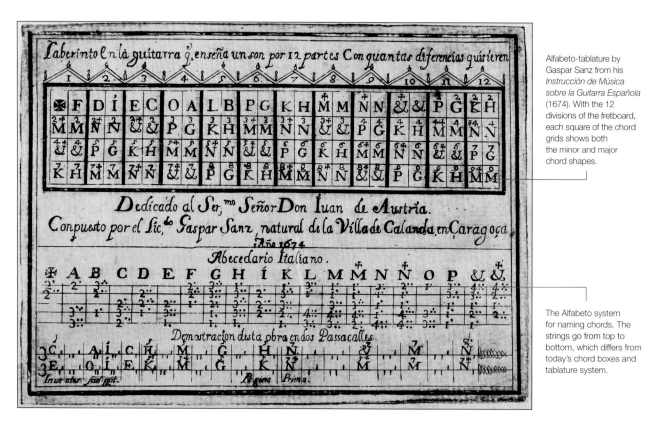

Alfabeto-tablature by Gaspar Sanz from his *Instrucción de Música sobre la Guitarra Española* (1674). With the 12 divisions of the fretboard, each square of the chord grids shows both the minor and major chord shapes.

The Alfabeto system for naming chords. The strings go from top to bottom, which differs from today's chord boxes and tablature system.

Changing tastes and decoration

Ever-changing musical tastes brought other instruments to the fore. In England in the 18th century, the Continental five-course guitar gave way to the English guitar (a cittern-shaped instrument usually with six courses tuned to CEGCEG, low to high). It also seems that the guitar-making trade was largely taken over by violin makers, especially in France. This is particularly evident in the changing range of materials used to construct the instruments, with ivory, ebony, tortoiseshell and cypress giving way to maple.

We cannot be entirely sure of the actual ratio of decorated guitars to plain ones because it is likely that the lavishly ornamented instruments stood a better chance of survival than plain models, which may have been less well looked after. The traditional decorative materials continued to be commonplace in instruments made for wealthy customers, although in many cases it is doubtful if the guitar makers themselves did the inlay work. It may be that the crafts guilds prohibited them from doing so, as there is some evidence that makers sometimes imported ready-made inlaid soundboards.

Another decorative feature that was typical of this time was the delicately carved grille covering the soundhole and known as a 'rose', which also served an acoustical purpose by lowering the bass resonances.

LEFT: *A rose in a late 18th-century five-course French guitar. Although there are ten tuning pegs, only nine are being used, the top 'course' remaining single. At the same time as this guitar was made, many other guitar makers were already constructing guitars with five single strings and without the decorative rose.*

Stradivari

One guitar maker who achieved great fame in a different field was Antonio Stradivari (1644–1737) of Cremona, probably the best-known violin maker of all time. Very few of his guitars have survived, perhaps because of their lack of decoration – his designs tended to be plain. It is intriguing to note that he designed roses that lay flush with the soundboard both inside and out, similar to those found in the soundholes of lutes, rather than the more typical roses of other makers that extended deep into the body of the instrument.

The involvement of such an inspired craftsman in guitar making was a sure sign of the instrument's increasing importance in the musical landscape, and that its continued use and development were assured.

BELOW: Two Ladies of the Lake Family *by Sir Peter Lely c.1660 features a lady playing a five-course Baroque guitar, complete with bridge moustachios and a sunken rose, both features of this period. The lady is holding the guitar in the position later favoured in the 19th century.*

RIGHT: *Stradivari made many guitars of all shapes and sizes, despite being more famous as a violin maker. Sadly only a few are known today, but from the surviving workshop templates it is known that many more were made, making him a renowned guitar maker of his time.*

The transitional guitar

As the Baroque style of music began to give way to simpler Classical forms in the mid-18th century, so the music written for the guitar was evolving into the less elaborate style of melody with accompaniment that characterizes this period. Perhaps symbolically, the delicately carved rose covering the soundhole of the guitar fell into disuse at this time, to be replaced with the plain, open soundhole so familiar today.

The different guitar forms

Towards the end of the 18th century, two dominant forms of guitar coexisted in Europe: the six-course guitar in Spain, and the five-course guitar, which was found elsewhere on the Continent. In England (and also Ireland and Scotland) in the middle of the 18th century, there was a vogue for an instrument that was called the 'guittar' or 'English guitar'. This resembled a traditional cittern but, unlike the cittern which was plucked with a plectrum, the English guitar was played with the fingers. When the 'regular', or classical, guitar was introduced to England at the beginning of the 19th century, the term 'Spanish guitar' was adopted to differentiate it from the English type.

The route to single strings

Changing the top double course, which would normally carry the tune, to a single string to make the melody ring out clearer, led eventually to the idea of using single strings throughout the guitar's range, and the five-course guitar with ten strings soon became one with five single strings. This change – perhaps as a result of the music for the instrument becoming more chord-based – appeared around 1785 in Naples, and all the surviving five-string instruments from this time are Neapolitan in origin. Contemporary examples from other parts of Europe of five-course guitars that were converted to single-string instruments do survive, although these all underwent later modification to six single strings.

ABOVE: *A portrait of Anne Ford posing with a wire-strung English guitar, by Thomas Gainsborough, 1760. Ford also played the gut-strung Spanish guitar, harp and viola da gamba (pictured in the background).*

ABOVE: Blind Man Playing the Guitar, *a painting by Francisco De Goya y Lucientes (1746–1828). Painted in 1778, it shows a five-course Spanish guitar, but many of his later sketches depict six-course guitars.*

New styles of playing and tuning

The Neapolitan five-string guitars show the instrument at its mid or transitional point. The earlier double-stringing had been abandoned. However, in Spain at the end of the 18th century, five-course guitars were still being played, although gradually being adapted for six-course playing, with the addition of extra strings.

In 1799, three works were published to teach this instrument to meet a growing public interest. Two of these guitar methods, by Fernando Ferandiere (*c.*1750–1816) and Federico Moretti (1760–1838), tell us much about the style of music written for the instrument, and how it was

RIGHT: The Lute Player, *a painting by Cesare Saccaggi c.1900. A young lady is 'playing' a French or Italian lyre-guitar (not lute, as the title suggests) although the instrument was actually in vogue a century earlier.*

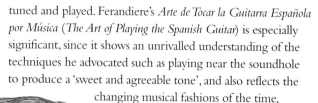

ABOVE: *Dionisio Aguado playing a guitar, painted by Etienne Laprevotte, taken from his method of 1843. His guitar is supported by his special invention, the so-called tripodium.*

tuned and played. Ferandiere's *Arte de Tocar la Guitarra Española por Música* (*The Art of Playing the Spanish Guitar*) is especially significant, since it shows an unrivalled understanding of the techniques he advocated such as playing near the soundhole to produce a 'sweet and agreeable tone', and also reflects the changing musical fashions of the time, although he was still using instruments with a mixture of paired courses and single strings.

In a significant move towards modern standard tuning, Ferandiere recommended that the guitar be tuned as E (coursed, but with one string an octave higher than the bass E), ADGB (unison paired courses), and ending on a single top E. The downwards extension of the pitch to a bass E was the end of the old-fashioned re-entrant tuning where the bottom course was pitched higher than the pair next to them, and Ferandiere's prescribed range and intervals have remained in use ever since.

Six single strings

The time when the six-course guitar fell out of use in Spain is impossible to pinpoint exactly. Many surviving double-course instruments of the period were later converted to be able to accommodate six single strings, and the celebrated Spanish composer-performer Dionisio Aguado (1784–1849) expresses his own preference for single strings in his method of 1825. However, there are surviving six-course guitars built around this time – such as one from 1822 by the Cadiz maker Joséf Pagés (1762–?) – so it seems fair to conclude that in Spain at least the paired six-course guitar was still very much in vogue in the early 19th century.

Towards the early modern guitar

We can see that there were two distinct, concurrent routes to the modern stringing of the classical guitar. The first, in Spain, moved from five to six courses to six single strings between the 1750s and 1820s, while in Italy and France (but not England) the trend went from five courses to five single strings in the 1780s, and then the sixth was added later. However, this probably happened in the same decade, i.e. the 1780s. It is from these developments and on through the 19th century that we see the guitar begin to evolve steadily towards the form we recognize today.

Early 19th-century guitars

By the early 19th century, with the addition of the sixth string and the adoption of EADGBE tuning as standard, the guitar was beginning to look recognizably modern. With these advancements guitar makers could increase the range of notes available and performers could extend their playing techniques, thus enabling composers to introduce new colours and ideas into their music.

New music for a new instrument

An age of elegant simplicity followed the intricacies of the Baroque era: the Classical period, from which we derive the term 'classical guitar'. Key composers for the instrument at the time – who also published methods, studies and other material designed to teach people to play – included the Neapolitan Ferdinando Carulli (1770–1841), and the Spaniards Fernando Sor (1778–1839) and Dionisio Aguado (1784–1849), and their works helped to keep the instrument's growth in popularity on track.

An important London-based luthier was the French-born Louis Panormo (1784–1862). Possibly under the influence of Fernando Sor, who spent several years in London, Panormo started making Spanish-style instruments, and by 1823, when Sor left London, Panormo was employing the Spanish technique of 'fanbracing', that is, reinforcing the soundboard inside with thin, fan-shaped struts of wood. This was unusual outside of Spain, since at this time most craftsmen were still using the transverse bracing system developed by the likes of Lacôte and the Fabricatores.

The new makers

Two of the earliest makers of the new six single-string guitar, Giovanni Battista Fabricatore (c.1750–c.1812) and Gaetano Vinaccia (c.1759–after 1831), were working in Naples at the turn of the 19th century, but there is one maker whose guitars were mentioned time and time again by the leading players of the day: René Lacôte of Paris (1785–c.1860). Lacôte's instruments seem to have been prized above all others, and they are still in great demand among today's players of historic guitars.

Lacôte's construction techniques and principles remained largely consistent throughout his career, although he did experiment and was sensitive to the needs of individual performers. He made guitars from different woods, and preferred to veneer the necks with the same material as the back and sides, to give the instruments a visual harmony. He also made some guitars with adjustable necks, adjustable frets and even some with double soundboards and two soundholes, as well as models with more than six strings.

By the second quarter of the 19th century, most countries in Europe had their own favoured master builders of these new guitars. Italy had the Fabricatores and Guadagninis, both large families of makers and active throughout the century, while Spain boasted many makers – including Joséf Pagés (1762–?), Antonio de Lorca and José Recio (1806–?) – all emerging from the tight control of the crafts guilds and all of them vying for supremacy.

ABOVE: *One of only a couple of known portraits of the Spanish composer Fernando Sor. This image is taken from a painting of 1815, the year he moved to London when he was 37 years old.*

BELOW: *Early fanbracing usually consisted of three splayed bars, which were increased to seven in the 1820s by Louis Panormo. This X-ray shows a typical example of Panormo's fanbracing.*

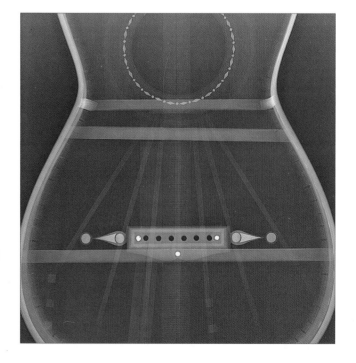

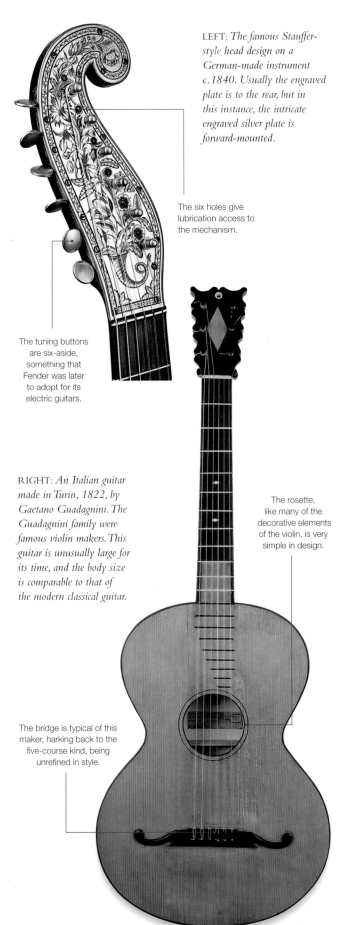

LEFT: *The famous Stauffer-style head design on a German-made instrument c.1840. Usually the engraved plate is to the rear, but in this instance, the intricate engraved silver plate is forward-mounted.*

The six holes give lubrication access to the mechanism.

The tuning buttons are six-aside, something that Fender was later to adopt for its electric guitars.

RIGHT: *An Italian guitar made in Turin, 1822, by Gaetano Guadagnini. The Guadagnini family were famous violin makers. This guitar is unusually large for its time, and the body size is comparable to that of the modern classical guitar.*

The rosette, like many of the decorative elements of the violin, is very simple in design.

The bridge is typical of this maker, harking back to the five-course kind, being unrefined in style.

ABOVE: Girl with a Guitar, *1897, by Pierre-Auguste Renoir, depicts a young female flamenco guitarist. Interestingly, another of his (French) paintings from the same year seemingly features a guitar with a split ebony/pearl fingerboard as the one above shows.*

To the New World

Another important manufacturer at the time was Johann Georg Stauffer (1778–1853), whose much sought-after instruments sometimes contained little or no bracing at all. Stauffer and his son Johann Anton were the leading makers in what had become the new musical capital of Europe, Vienna. It was here that a famous composer/maker relationship grew up between the builders in the Stauffer workshop and the celebrated virtuoso Luigi Legnani (1790–1877), giving rise to the renowned Legnani–Stauffer models, many of which featured adjustable necks and a twin-octave range in pitch.

It is thought that the influential German maker Christian Frederick Martin (1796–1873) may have been apprenticed in the Stauffer workshop. Martin eventually emigrated to the USA in 1833 and started the foundations of the seminal guitar company of C. F. Martin & Co. Martin's influential guitars were widely copied, both in the USA and in many German factories, and for nearly two centuries the firm has remained pivotal in maintaining the guitar's position, particularly with its role in the development of the steel-string guitar.

A steady decline

The second half of the 19th century saw the popularity of the instrument decline in many countries. By this time many of the top European makers, including Panormo, Stauffer and Fabricatore, had ceased their activities. The classical guitar was in danger if not of extinction, at least of being sidelined as a serious instrument. However, the flame was kept burning brightly in Spain, and developments were taking place in the USA that would bear fruit many years later.

Arcas, Torres, Tárrega and beyond

The second half of the 19th century witnessed the birth of the modern classical guitar as developed by Antonio de Torres (1817–1892). The high quality of his guitars and the influential performers who played them meant that the classical guitar, in Spain at least, continued to be celebrated rather than being forgotten, as had so many other once-popular instruments over the centuries.

Arcas, Torres and the Lioness

While the fashion for the guitar had begun to fade by the middle of the 19th century in many countries, in Spain, where guitar music was a national institution, and the USA, the instrument continued to hold its own. In Spain, interest was kept alive by the genius of some brilliant composer-performers, the first of whom was Julián Arcas (1832–1882). Early in his professional life as a travelling virtuoso he had met and befriended the instrument maker Antonio de Torres, whose own career was boosted enormously when Arcas began playing an instrument that he had lent to him in 1856 called 'La Leona' (the Lioness). Torres went on to become the maker of some of the finest guitars in the world, changing the way classical guitars have been built ever since.

Tárrega and the next generations of performers

Arcas was also a guiding influence upon another, younger composer-performer, Francisco Tárrega (1852–1909). Tárrega had played to him as a ten-year-old, and Arcas was so impressed that he invited the boy to study with him. Tárrega went on to become one of the greatest performers of his time, and he played at least three guitars made by Torres – two of maple and one of rosewood. Tárrega became a key figure in the development of the guitar's repertoire, a composer

ABOVE: *A photograph of Francisco Tárrega in 1901 playing an 1888 guitar by Antonio de Torres, which Tárrega's widow said was his favourite guitar. Most people will know at least four bars of Tárrega's music as the Nokia ringtone is taken from his* Gran Vals.

LEFT: *A drawing by the Spanish artist Ramon Cases, 1900, of Miguel Llobet, the Catalan guitarist and student of Tarrega. Llobet's famous Torres guitar of 1859 was the inspiration behind the guitars by Hermann Hauser.*

of many famous pieces for the instrument who laid the foundations of 20th-century classical-guitar playing through his own pupils, including Miguel Llobet (1878–1938) and Emilio Pujol (1886–1980). His transcriptions of works by Schumann, Chopin, Beethoven and others became hugely popular.

Equally important, though, were Tárrega's performing style and his understanding of what the guitar could do. After hearing Tárrega play transcriptions of some of his piano pieces, the great Spanish composer and pianist Isaac Albéniz (1860–1909) remarked that they were better than his originals.

Given Tárrega's influence, it is no surprise that the greatest classical guitarist of the 20th century, Andrés Segovia (1893–1987), began his professional career playing many of Tárrega's guitar transcriptions. Segovia inspired the best composers of the day to write for the guitar. He also did a great deal to encourage young instrument makers, although throughout his long career he mainly played guitars made by only four different makers: Santos Hernandez (1874–1943), Hermann Hauser (1882–1952), Ignacio Fleta (1897–1977) and José Ramírez III (1922–95). His two longstanding companions, the famous 1912 Santos Hernandez guitar (made in the workshop of Manuel Ramirez) and his 1937 Hauser I guitar, were bequeathed to the Metropolitan Museum of Art, but sadly with the proviso that no one is ever allowed to play them.

Torres' lasting influence

While experts continue to debate the specific contributions that Torres made to the design of the modern classical guitar, there is no doubt that his instruments represent a summit of achievement in guitar design, and his influence has continued into the 20th century and beyond. Even today there are makers who still follow his construction methods very closely, and no other luthier has had anything like the same influence on the refinement of the classical instrument. Just as many contemporary violin makers still base their instruments on the designs of Stradivari, since the 19th-century guitar makers have continued to follow the lead set by Antonio de Torres.

By the mid-20th century nearly every feature of the modern classical guitar was in place – its size and shape, woods used in its construction, and a host of other technical improvements. The final element was the switch from unreliable gut strings to nylon ones, pioneered by Segovia in the years after World War II, which has brought the design of the classical guitar to a state approaching perfection.

Guitar strings

Here are depicted some unused 100-year-old gut guitar strings, marketed by Viennese and English companies, but probably made in Naples. They were prone to breaking, especially when the tuning instructions were: "tuning the top string just before breaking point"; hence musicians bought them by the box. Before the 1940s, 'cat gut' (actually sheep or pig intestine) was the chosen material for Spanish guitar strings. With this material being in short supply during World War II, possibly exacerbated by its use in the stitching of wounded soldiers, it was clear that a new substance was needed. This coincided with the invention, just a decade earlier, of DuPont's nylon and, from 1947, nylon became the preferred material for classical guitar strings.

The flamenco guitar

Although the Spanish art form of flamenco today is inextricably linked with the guitar, its origins certainly pre-date the guitar as we know it. Flamenco guitar is as much a rhythm instrument as it is a melodic one, and one of its chief functions is to enhance the clapping and stamping that traditionally accompany the songs and dance, which are at the heart of flamenco.

Origins

The flamenco dance is popularly understood to be an Andalucian form, particularly associated with Romany communities, although its influences are far more diverse than this would suggest, bringing together many sources going back hundreds of years. When the guitar began to be used as an instrument to accompany flamenco is not recorded, but a flamenco-guitar rhythmic-strumming technique known as *rasgueado* began to be heard quite clearly in some Baroque guitar music from the 17th century, such as Gaspar Sanz's *Spagnolettas* and *Canarios* of the 1670s. From its outsider roots, flamenco's emergence as a serious art form owes much to the early 20th-century composer Manuel de Falla (1867–1936), who organized the first flamenco festival in Granada in 1922. It is now listed as one of UNESCO's "Masterpieces of the Oral and Intangible Heritage of Humanity".

BELOW: *Manuel de Falla, shown late in life. Although not a guitarist himself, de Falla captured the flamenco essence in his orchestral works, and also wrote the masterpiece for solo guitar,* Le Tombeau de Debussy.

ABOVE: El Jaleo *by John Singer Sargent was completed in 1882, but it is based on earlier contemporary sketches. It depicts the essence of the flamenco dance through clapping, tapping and guitar rhythms.*

Tools of the trade

Some of the earliest guitars made specifically to accompany a flamenco troupe came from the workshops of José and Manuel Ramírez, and the actual term 'flamenco guitar' appears in Manuel's workshop catalogue of *c*.1913. In an earlier Ramírez catalogue of *c*.1888, two different kinds of guitar are mentioned: *guitarras de concierto* (concert guitars) and *guitarras de sevillanas* (Sevillanas guitars). Despite the reference to the Andalucian dance, the Sevillana, and the distinction made between *guitarras de sevillanas* and concert instruments, these were not yet the flamenco guitar familiar to us today.

It may be that the first instruments specifically for flamenco resembled the '1916' model made in Manuel Ramírez's workshop by Santos Hernandez. Hernandez made flamenco guitars in both cypress (known as *blanca*, white) and rosewood (*negra*, black). These guitars have a pure, percussive sound, which makes them the ideal accompanying instrument for flamenco, since true flamenco guitars are constructed so that the sound decays quickly, unlike the sustained sonority required for a classical instrument.

Rámon Montoya

The father of the modern solo flamenco guitar is generally considered by today's aficionados to be Rámon Montoya (1880–1949). Other famous performers, some of whom are traditionalists while others have added new elements, include Rámon's nephew Carlos Montoya (1903–1993), Niño Ricardo (1904–1972), Sabicas (1912–1990), Paco Peña (b. 1942), Paco de Lucia (b. 1947) and Juan Martín (b. 1948).

Another way to achieve the necessary 'timbre' for flamenco comes from keeping the 'action' – that is, the height of the strings above the fingerboard – somewhat lower than on a classical guitar, thus producing a more raspy sound. With the strings nearer to the frets, the guitarist can play with greater virtuosity, which reduces left-hand fatigue during lengthy performances. Finally, flamenco instruments are often equipped with a distinctive tap-plate called a *golpeador*, which is today commonly made of transparent plastic and similar to a scratchplate on a steel-string or electric guitar. The purpose of this is to protect the guitar body from the guitarist's rhythmic finger taps, called *golpes*.

Flamenco guitar style

The rhythmic structure of flamenco music is called its *compas*, and some of its musical forms have a distinctive and recognizable 12-beat pattern. One musical scale used in flamenco – for voice and guitar – is known as the 'Phrygian' mode (based on ancient Greek scales) rather than standard Western scales, giving the characteristic sound.

Guitarists make use of *falsetas*, gaps between the singing where they can demonstrate their virtuosity, and this has led over time to the flamenco guitar being developed as a solo instrument as well.

The *cejilla*

Singing is a vital element of flamenco, and accompanying guitarists will need to be able to adjust their playing to the vocal ranges of each singer. To do this the guitarist sometimes is required to use a device called a *cejilla*, or capo. A fortuitous side-effect of using the *cejilla* is that it causes the instrument to sound more sharp and percussive, something that the guitar maker also strives to achieve in a flamenco instrument.

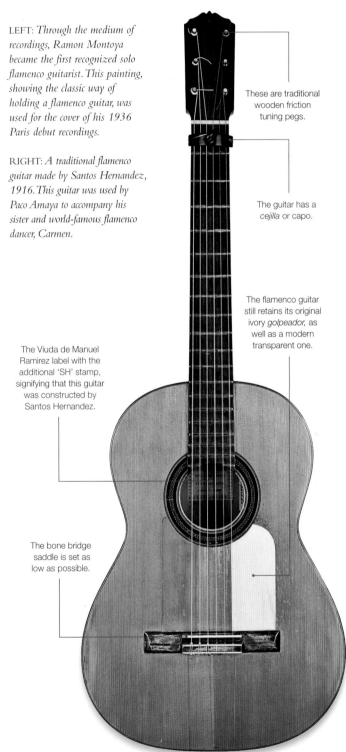

LEFT: *Through the medium of recordings, Ramon Montoya became the first recognized solo flamenco guitarist. This painting, showing the classic way of holding a flamenco guitar, was used for the cover of his 1936 Paris debut recordings.*

RIGHT: *A traditional flamenco guitar made by Santos Hernandez, 1916. This guitar was used by Paco Amaya to accompany his sister and world-famous flamenco dancer, Carmen.*

These are traditional wooden friction tuning pegs.

The guitar has a *cejilla* or capo.

The flamenco guitar still retains its original ivory *golpeador*, as well as a modern transparent one.

The Viuda de Manuel Ramirez label with the additional 'SH' stamp, signifying that this guitar was constructed by Santos Hernandez.

The bone bridge saddle is set as low as possible.

Pioneers of the steel-string guitar

Just as the classical guitar was being refined in Spain, the steel-string guitar was being developed in the USA towards the end of the 19th century. It was all about volume. Guitarists playing in traditional and folk groups needed to be able to compete with the much louder banjos, mandolins and fiddles, all of which had become metal-strung, and with the advent of jazz, a guitarist using a classical instrument would not have been able to compete in volume against the brass.

An earlier idea

The use of metal strings on musical instruments goes back to at least the Italian *battente* guitars of the 17th century. Likewise, the English 'guittar' had metal strings, and this instrument was very popular in North America between around 1760 and 1810. However, one must assume they were long forgotten before the idea of using metal strings on regular guitars was proposed, although it may not have been much later

ABOVE: *A photograph of Christian Frederick Martin, the most famous name in American guitar history.*

that the first US guitars were fitted with steel strings. Certainly by the second half of the 19th century, various references can be found – for instance, in advertisements – to suggest that the idea of equipping guitars with steel strings was in place.

C. F. Martin & Co.

The guitar-making lineage of C. F. Martin goes way back to the 1830s, when Christian Frederick Martin emigrated to New York from Germany. Although perhaps not the only

company making steel-string instruments in the early 20th century, C. F. Martin was pioneering in this regard and remains the best known of the early manufacturers. It is also very likely that today's steel-string guitars incorporate many innovations that Martin brought with him from Johann Georg Stauffer's Vienna workshop, including the pin-bridge design and the jazz guitar, with its floating fingerboard.

In 1916, Martin introduced the popular Dreadnought model, which, with its enlarged soundbox and its loud, resonant, bassy tone, has become a template for the steel-string acoustic guitar ever since. Steel-string Martin instruments are still highly prized, and early examples can now change hands at auction for huge sums of money.

Flat-tops and archtops

The Dreadnought and its ilk are what are known as 'flat-top' instruments, in that, like the classical guitar from which they derive, the front and back of the body are relatively flat and braced internally to strengthen the body. However, in 1902, Orville Gibson's (1856–1918) Gibson Mandolin-Guitar Manufacturing Co. Ltd (now the Gibson Guitar Corporation) patented an 'archtop' design for a mandolin that also covered its guitars. The front of the soundbox – mandolin or guitar – is distinguished by its carved, arched top (and often back), which meant that internal bracing could be eliminated by using a stronger body, so creating a clearer-sounding instrument without any internal structures interfering with the tone.

While Gibson was not the first to produce an archtop, following the patent, the company exploited the method in its instruments, initially using it for mandolins.

When the guitar maker Lloyd Loar (1886–1943) joined the firm in 1919, he introduced the idea of f-shaped

LEFT: *Hampton Institute, Hampton VA, c.1898. Guitar, mandolin and banjo orchestras were all the rage at the turn of the 19th century, and they were actively promoted by the major musical instrument manufacturers.*

soundholes to the archtop designs that are now so common. Gibson's first model in the new shape, the Gibson L5, was introduced in 1922 and quickly became the brand leader for use in the rhythm sections of big bands as well as for jazz and blues players, both rhythm and lead.

Gibson also introduced flat-top models, such as the smaller 00, which bears a significant resemblance to a classical instrument, and the larger Grand Auditorium, or 000, similar in style to the 00 but larger and more powerful. All these flat-tops needed a higher degree of reinforcement than a classical instrument because of the greater strain imposed upon them by the tension of the steel strings. A primitive form of bracing was used in early Martin guitars by the 1840s, and this led eventually to the development of the system that was known as 'x-bracing'.

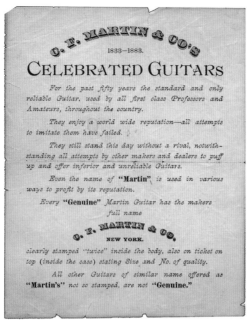

Other makers

Martin and Gibson were by no means the only guitar makers in the USA. Others included the Chicago-based instrument manufacturer Lyon and Healy, makers of the Washburn brand from the 1880s, which they sold in vast numbers. They mostly produced budget guitars, but also made lavishly inlaid ones that won a considerable number of awards.

Another important maker was Joseph Bohmann (1848–1928), who arrived in Chicago from Europe in 1873. He was soon at the head of a highly successful company that made steel-string guitars with stronger 'double-x-bracing'. Bohmann also made mandolins and harp guitars, curious crossbreeds which featured, in addition to the standard set of six strings, a row of unfretted harp-like strings that could be individually plucked. These unusual instruments continue to find a niche market even today.

Worldwide popularity

After World War II, and particularly following the 'folk revival' and the global reach of rock 'n' roll from the 1950s onwards, the guitar in all its forms has become ubiquitous across the world. Besides the individual luthiers worldwide who produce high-quality handmade instruments, the sustained popularity of the steel-string acoustic guitar now means that relatively affordable factory-made models of all levels are now produced in many countries, notably China, Korea and Japan, and not just in the guitar manufacturing heartland of the USA. The majority of guitars produced still bear close family resemblances to those pioneering models made by Martin, Gibson and their contemporaries.

LEFT: *The 50-year anniversary (1833–83) advertisement cites Martin as being in New York, but the guitars were actually made in Pennsylvania. Others tried to copy its guitars, some even using the name of 'Martin'.*

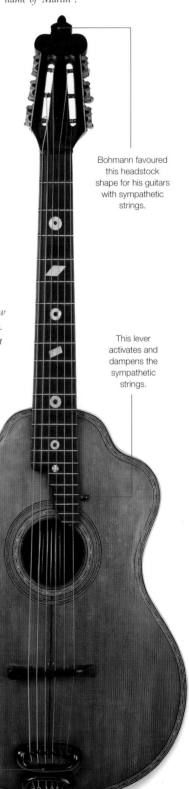

Bohmann favoured this headstock shape for his guitars with sympathetic strings.

This lever activates and dampens the sympathetic strings.

RIGHT: *This guitar by Joseph Bohmann, c.1915, exemplifies how individual he was with respect to his design. The head, body and fingerboard shape, as well as the position markers, show little influence from other makers. Bohmann was careful to take out patents for this design, not that many other makers were likely to have copied his design.*

The Bohmann guitar incorporates a unique style of tailpiece.

The guitar today

The acoustic guitar market today is so large and diverse that there is room for a seemingly endless array of instruments at all price levels and with numerous different designs. Bespoke instruments, skilfully hand-crafted by luthiers, and factory-made guitars both have their place, and guitar making is an expanding industry in many countries throughout the world.

Independent specialisms

Most of the big companies make a range of instruments – classical, steel-string and all the sub-categories of these. However, today's independent acoustic-guitar makers often tend to specialize in making either nylon or steel-string instruments – after all, to build a strong reputation for making a particular style of guitar makes good business sense. Within the broader nylon or steel-string categories, each can be further subdivided – for example, nylon-strung classical, flamenco or historical guitars, or steel-strung flat-top or archtop instruments, and many additional variants, including resonator, lap-steel, harp or gypsy guitars (for more details on makers, see the Directory section).

RIGHT: *A modern harp-guitar by English luthier Stephen Sedgwick. It covers a staggering five-octave range, which in the hands of a professional, sounds like a miniature orchestra.*

Makers of both classical and steel-string guitars can be split into traditionalists and experimenters – although even traditionalists probably experiment at some point. This might seem like reinventing the wheel – the advice might be, 'don't mess with a successful formula' – but for luthiers it can represent a move forward or serve to justify why they build in a particular way and distinguish them from the competition.

Innovation versus tradition

As the history of guitar making shows, 19th-century craftsmen in particular were very quick to adapt to new ideas, and many of today's 'innovations' were actually first tried out at various points over the last couple of centuries – for example, London-based D. and A. Roudhloff used x-bracing in their guitars in the 1840s, and some makers in the early 19th century constructed guitars with arched tops. All these changes help to create a healthy, buoyant market as well as preventing makers from becoming stale and players becoming complacent. Whether it be Thomas Humphrey's raised fingerboards, Robert Ruck's soundports (holes drilled into the side of an instrument for increased sonority), Greg Smallman's carbon fibre-lattice soundboard bracing or Ovation's fibreglass bowl backs, these and countless other innovations in recent decades can all help to meet the demands of increasingly exacting players.

Trends and fashions come and go, and many ideas and forms disappear, only to reappear at some point in the future. For example, many players today feel that 'oversized' guitars,

ABOVE: *Modern luthier Martin Woodhouse is carving the braces which support and strengthen the soundboard against the pull of the strings. The resulting flexibility of the soundboard is one of the most important factors that determine the final sound of a guitar.*

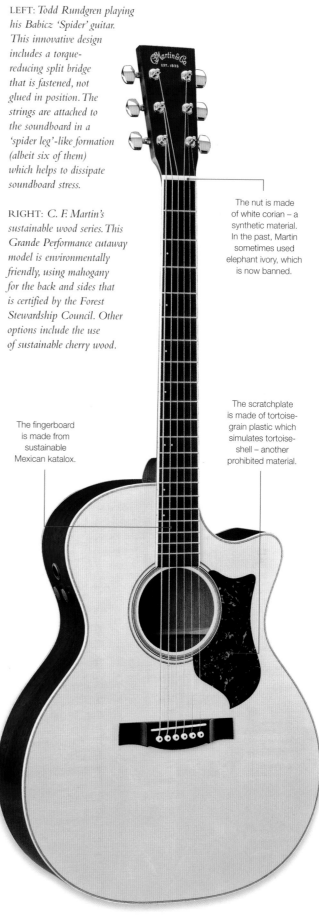

LEFT: *Todd Rundgren playing his Babicz 'Spider' guitar. This innovative design includes a torque-reducing split bridge that is fastened, not glued in position. The strings are attached to the soundboard in a 'spider leg'-like formation (albeit six of them) which helps to dissipate soundboard stress.*

RIGHT: *C. F. Martin's sustainable wood series. This Grande Performance cutaway model is environmentally friendly, using mahogany for the back and sides that is certified by the Forest Stewardship Council. Other options include the use of sustainable cherry wood.*

The nut is made of white corian – a synthetic material. In the past, Martin sometimes used elephant ivory, which is now banned.

The scratchplate is made of tortoise-grain plastic which simulates tortoise-shell – another prohibited material.

The fingerboard is made from sustainable Mexican katalox.

once considered indispensable – such as the large-bodied Martin Dreadnought steel-string and the 664mm (26.1in) scale Ramírez classical guitars – are less essential today due to readily available amplification. Instead, players are returning to smaller instruments with a clearly defined sound, sometimes even to copies of Lacôte- or Panormo-style guitars. The once-popular late 19th-century small parlour guitar is also enjoying a revival, and makers respond to this by producing modern copies – although older originals are often no more expensive to buy (even if you might then need to spend a small fortune restoring an antique instrument).

The green guitar

Today, makers have to be aware of the CITES ('Convention on International Trade in Endangered Species of Wild Fauna and Flora') Act and how it affects the supply of materials traditionally used to build musical instruments. The preferred wood used to make the back and sides of a guitar has long been Brazilian rosewood; not only is it beautiful, but many believe that a guitar made from this wood sounds better as well as making their instrument a cannier investment.

Since the material comes from the tropical rainforests of Brazil, there is now a ban on exporting new guitars made of certain woods unless the instrument is accompanied by a certificate stating that the wood was logged prior to the date that is stated in the CITES Act. Fortunately, guitar makers and their customers are slowly accepting that there are plenty of perfectly good alternatives to Brazilian rosewood, such as Indian rosewood.

The future

It's been a long road from the *kithara* to the modern acoustic guitar, and many once-popular instruments have fallen by the wayside, but on current evidence it looks like the guitar – as near a perfect tool for the job in hand as you will find – is going to be around in a recognizable form for some considerable amount of time yet.

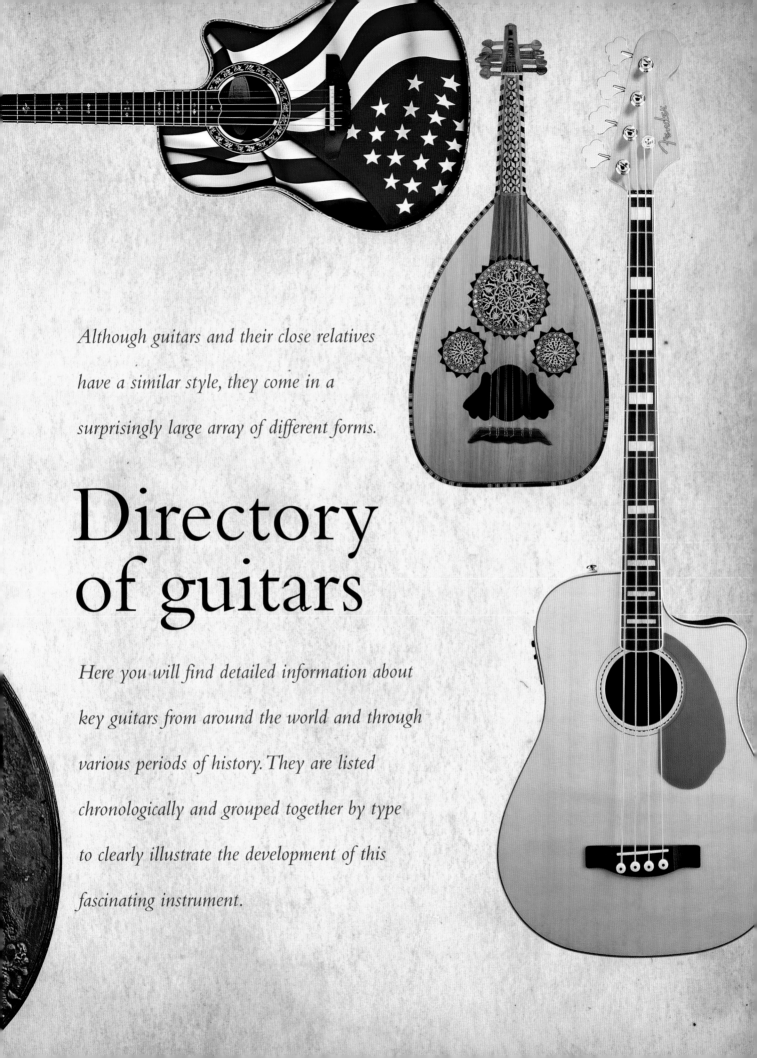

Although guitars and their close relatives

have a similar style, they come in a

surprisingly large array of different forms.

Directory
of guitars

Here you will find detailed information about

key guitars from around the world and through

various periods of history. They are listed

chronologically and grouped together by type

to clearly illustrate the development of this

fascinating instrument.

Early guitar-related instruments

The oud, which dates back to at least the eighth century, came from North Africa and the Middle East. It originally had frets, but these were dropped from the instrument by about 1300, which was quite late in the history of the oud. The European version of this instrument became known as the lute, which retained the frets.

Oud, c.1990

This modern oud has 11 strings and, unlike its relatives seen elsewhere in this section, it is fretless. Another distinguishing feature is that the neck is much narrower than that of the lute, for example. The three rosettes of this modern copy have a Moorish design, and the body is constructed of alternating dark- and light-wood staves. The five double courses of strings and single bass string – the latter an unusual feature – terminate at a moustache-shaped tie-bridge.

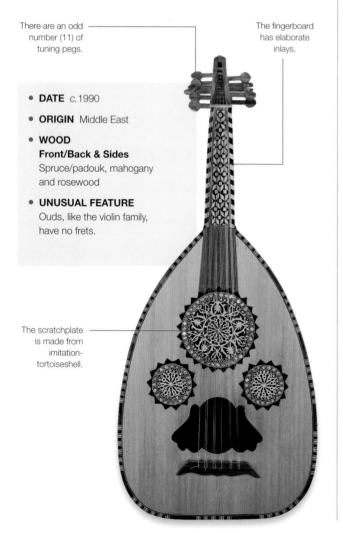

There are an odd number (11) of tuning pegs.

The fingerboard has elaborate inlays.

- **DATE** c.1990
- **ORIGIN** Middle East
- **WOOD**
  Front/Back & Sides
  Spruce/padouk, mahogany and rosewood
- **UNUSUAL FEATURE**
  Ouds, like the violin family, have no frets.

The scratchplate is made from imitation-tortoiseshell.

Wendelio Venere: theorbo, 1600s

The German master luthier Wendelio Venere worked in Padua, Italy, between around 1570 and the 1630s. The spruce soundboard has three roses, reminiscent of an oud. The back is made of 11 ribs of maple with black-and-white stringing. This instrument has six short double courses with eight long single bases. Currently it is in chitarrone tuning. It was mainly used as an accompanying *basso continuo* instrument for opera.

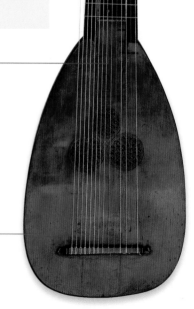

The length of this instrument makes it difficult to manoeuvre and transport.

- **DATE** 1600s
- **ORIGIN** Italy
- **WOOD**
  Front/Back & Sides
  Spruce/maple
- **UNUSUAL FEATURE**
  Save for a pipe organ, a theorbo is the longest musical instrument.

The neck is wide compared with that of a guitar but still not wide enough to accommodate all of the strings.

Notice the oud-shaped body.

Joachim Tielke: Baroque lute, 1707

The most decorative of all Baroque string instruments came from the workshop of Joachim Tielke (1641–1719). Tielke built many guitars and lutes in Hamburg between around 1672 and 1718. Many have ivory backs and ivory inlaid decorations on ebony-veneered necks. The Baroque lute has two pegboxes, the second on a curved extension of the neck, a style sometimes referred to as a 'swan neck'. It has 12 courses, seven over the neck, which are fretted, and another five that are played open.

The curved shape here is sometimes described as a 'swan neck'.

The tuning pegs are staggered to make the access easier when turning them.

- **DATE** 1707
- **ORIGIN** Germany
- **WOOD**
  Front/Back & Sides
  Spruce/ivory and ebony
- **UNUSUAL FEATURE**
  The twin pegboxes must seem strange to today's guitarist.

Lutes rarely had any binding, which made it easier to remove the soundboard for repairs.

The glue holding the narrow bridge to the soundboard is very strong to withstand the pull of so many strings.

John Dowland and the Renaissance lute

One of England's finest composers for, and players of, the lute was John Dowland (1563–1626). It is perhaps fitting that the finest 20th-century British work written for the guitar, Benjamin Britten's *Nocturnal After John Dowland*, is a set of variations on a theme by Dowland, "Come Heavy Sleep", from his *First Booke of Songs or Ayres*. Britten composed this with Julian Bream, himself a keen lutenist, in mind. Bream had many lutes made for him, and a favoured maker was David Rubio, whom he first commissioned to make an 'Elizabethan' lute in 1965. The lute here is a 1973 Rubio Renaissance lute.

Note the steep angle of the head.

The instrument has eight courses.

ABOVE: *The frontispiece of John Dowland's* First Booke of Songs or Ayres of Foure Parts, With Tableture for the Lute. *The four volumes were published individually between 1598 and 1612, and are today a major source for the repertoire of the eight-course lute.*

RIGHT: *A traditional Renaissance lute from the workshop of David Rubio. Some of Rubio's lutes from this period are more guitar-like, with fixed wooden frets. This one has tied gut frets and the soundboard is bound with parchment, making it easier to remove when it needed replacing or re-bracing.*

Early guitar-related instruments: citterns

Although the cittern reached the height of its popularity in France, Germany and Britain during the 18th century, it can be traced back a number of centuries prior to this. The 18th-century instruments were deeper-bodied than earlier models, and, although many varieties were produced, the most common type had a pear-shaped body, a floating (not fixed) bridge and metal strings that were played with the fingers.

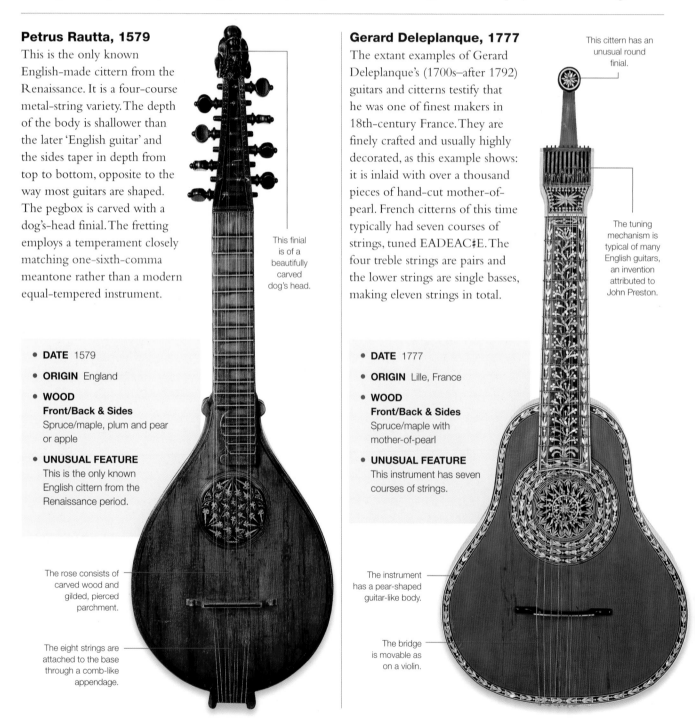

Petrus Rautta, 1579

This is the only known English-made cittern from the Renaissance. It is a four-course metal-string variety. The depth of the body is shallower than the later 'English guitar' and the sides taper in depth from top to bottom, opposite to the way most guitars are shaped. The pegbox is carved with a dog's-head finial. The fretting employs a temperament closely matching one-sixth-comma meantone rather than a modern equal-tempered instrument.

This finial is of a beautifully carved dog's head.

- **DATE** 1579
- **ORIGIN** England
- **WOOD**
  Front/Back & Sides
  Spruce/maple, plum and pear or apple
- **UNUSUAL FEATURE**
  This is the only known English cittern from the Renaissance period.

The rose consists of carved wood and gilded, pierced parchment.

The eight strings are attached to the base through a comb-like appendage.

Gerard Deleplanque, 1777

The extant examples of Gerard Deleplanque's (1700s–after 1792) guitars and citterns testify that he was one of finest makers in 18th-century France. They are finely crafted and usually highly decorated, as this example shows: it is inlaid with over a thousand pieces of hand-cut mother-of-pearl. French citterns of this time typically had seven courses of strings, tuned EADEAC♯E. The four treble strings are pairs and the lower strings are single basses, making eleven strings in total.

This cittern has an unusual round finial.

The tuning mechanism is typical of many English guitars, an invention attributed to John Preston.

- **DATE** 1777
- **ORIGIN** Lille, France
- **WOOD**
  Front/Back & Sides
  Spruce/maple with mother-of-pearl
- **UNUSUAL FEATURE**
  This instrument has seven courses of strings.

The instrument has a pear-shaped guitar-like body.

The bridge is movable as on a violin.

German cittern (anonymous), *c.*1780s

This *waldzither* was made in Saxo-Thuringia in the late 18th century; the stepped body shape was common for citterns from this part of Germany. The fretting employs a temperament closely matching one-sixth-comma meantone (similar to the fifth-comma) rather than a modern equal-tempered instrument. Many cittern tablatures for dances and songs survive from this period, and the main application was chord-based song accompaniment; many different tunings were used. The strings are attached to the base of the cittern via little pins.

The head terminates in a male angel with wings.

- **DATE** *c.*1780s

- **ORIGIN** Eastern Germany

- **WOOD**
  Front/Back & Sides
  Spruce/maple

- **UNUSUAL FEATURE**
  Frets are positioned in the fifth-comma-meantone temperament position.

Notice the irregularly spaced frets.

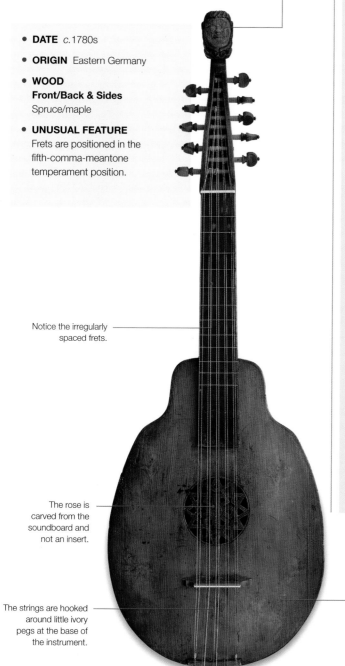

The rose is carved from the soundboard and not an insert.

The strings are hooked around little ivory pegs at the base of the instrument.

John Preston: keyed cittern, *c.*1790

In the 18th century, John Preston (1727–98) was the most prolific maker of English guitars. He started making English guitars around 1765 which were just known as 'guittars' at the time. There are two main kinds of citterns with added keyboards: those with an internal mechanism, such as those by Christian Claus, and those by Preston in which a removable keyboard is mounted to a regular instrument. The strings are hit rather than plucked, producing a tone similar to that of a hammer-dulcimer. The right-hand technique employed is similar to the standard guitar. Preston is attributed with inventing the watch-key tuning mechanism seen here, as an alternative to wooden tuning pegs.

The finial here is purely decorative.

The string-ends are looped and attached to a 'rider' which, when moved, tightens or loosens the string.

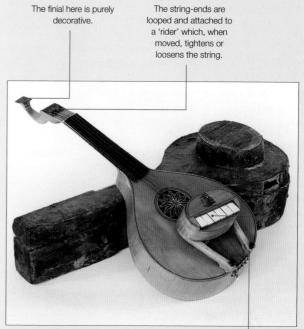

ABOVE: *The finial and fingerboard are inlaid with tortoiseshell, which is underlaid with a red substance producing a beautiful red and brown mottled effect. The strings are tuned with the use of a pocket-watch key. This particular example has the earlier wooden rose rather than the more commonly seen later removable metal design. It has its original and very rare wooden 'coffin' case.*

There are six ivory piano-like keys, one for each course.

The body shape is typical of citterns from Saxo-Thuringia.

Early guitar-related instruments: the mandolin family

As a plucked gut-string chordophone with frets, the Baroque mandolin was closely related to both guitar and lute, and luthiers such as Stradivari made all three instruments. Around 1800 the mandolin went its separate way, now having wire strings and being played with a plectrum rather than the fingers, and its standard tuning being the same as that of the violin: GDAE.

Stradivari: choral mandolino, 1680

This *mandolino* is one of only two known surviving examples thought to be by Antonio Stradivari (1644–1737). The back is made of seven maple ribs. Notice that the soundboard is not 'cant', or bent, at the bridge as in the modern form. The head was reconstructed according to Stradivari's original templates, which have survived. It has five courses of strings, and the tuning would have been the same as a modern mandolin (EADG, probably in unison pairs) with octave Bs added to the bass.

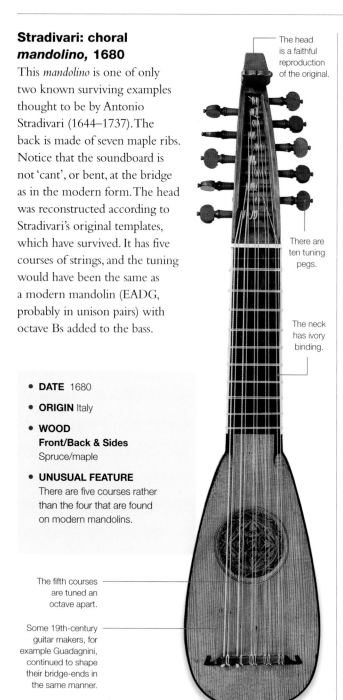

The head is a faithful reproduction of the original.

There are ten tuning pegs.

The neck has ivory binding.

- **DATE** 1680
- **ORIGIN** Italy
- **WOOD**
  Front/Back & Sides
  Spruce/maple
- **UNUSUAL FEATURE**
  There are five courses rather than the four that are found on modern mandolins.

The fifth courses are tuned an octave apart.

Some 19th-century guitar makers, for example Guadagnini, continued to shape their bridge-ends in the same manner.

Antonio Vinaccia, 1772

The Vinaccia family were famous Neapolitan instrument makers. Antonio Vinaccia (active 1750s–1790s) was the son of Gennaro Vinaccia. Other family members included Giovanni, Vincenzo, Gaetano and Pasquale (said to be the inventor of steel strings). Notice the 'cant', or bent, soundboard, which is a feature of another wire-string instrument, the *chitarra battente*. The back is made of 20 scalloped maple ribs interspersed with ebony and ivory stringing. The decoration features tortoiseshell and is lavishly inlaid with mother-of-pearl.

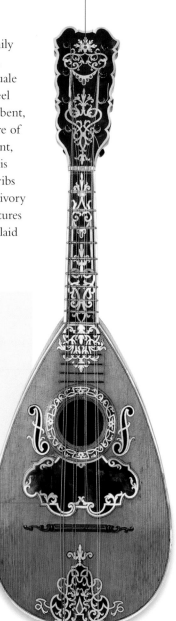

The head is decorated with tortoiseshell and mother-of-pearl.

- **DATE** 1772
- **ORIGIN** Italy
- **WOOD**
  Front/Back & Sides
  Spruce/maple with ebony and ivory stringing
- **UNUSUAL FEATURE**
  The instrument has fanciful f-holes.

The scratchplate is inlaid.

This instrument has a cant, or bent, soundboard.

Raffaele Calace: mando-lyre, 1913

Like Antonio Vinaccia, Raffaele Calace (1863–1934) came from a leading Neapolitan family of instrument makers. He was also a mandolinist and prolific composer for the instrument. Apart from its lyre shape, this example is no different from a regular mandolin. However, the back is more rounded than the traditional kind. The two arms are hollow, which purportedly enhances the sound. The strings are attached to the bottom of the body and are covered by an engraved metal cover.

- **DATE** 1913
- **ORIGIN** Italy
- **WOOD**
  Front/Back & Sides
  Spruce/rosewood
- **UNUSUAL FEATURE**
  The two arms give it
  a lyre-like appearance.

The arms have small ornamental finials.

A traditional oval-shaped soundhole is used.

This instrument has a metal string-guard.

Luigi Embergher: Type-B study model, 1924

The Rome workshops of Luigi Embergher (1856–1943) produced some of the finest mandolins ever made. However, their superb workmanship and exceptional quality are not their only appeal; the sound they make also ensures there is a high demand for these instruments. Embergher's mandolins were commonly made in different sizes for ensemble playing. This model was first created *c.*1907 to satisfy demand for high-quality but moderately priced models for both beginners and more experienced players.

- **DATE** 1924
- **ORIGIN** Italy
- **WOOD**
  Front/Back & Sides
  Spruce/rosewood
- **UNUSUAL FEATURE**
  This model is almost austere
  when compared with other
  mandolins.

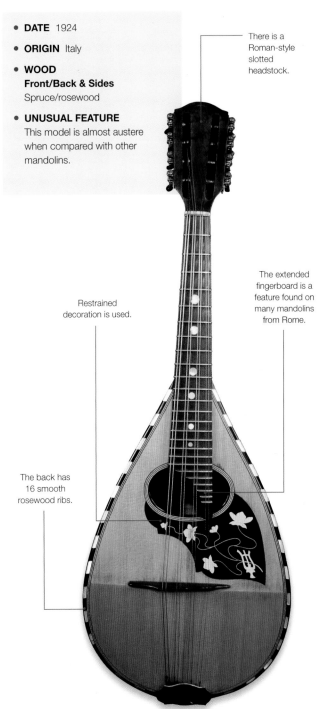

There is a Roman-style slotted headstock.

Restrained decoration is used.

The extended fingerboard is a feature found on many mandolins from Rome.

The back has 16 smooth rosewood ribs.

16th- to 18th-century guitars: the Renaissance and the Baroque

Surviving written documentation and pictorial evidence show that the four-course guitar was popular during the Renaissance. The Baroque guitar was favoured in Spain and Italy during the early 17th century, catching on later in France. Each country generated important centres of instrument manufacture, with names such as the Sellas family in Venice, Stradivari in Cremona and Voboam in Paris becoming celebrated.

Matteo Sellas (attributed): Baroque guitar, c.1640

Matteo Sellas (c.1600–1654) established his workshop in Venice in the 1620s where his son Domenico also worked. This guitar has a vaulted back in which the strips of ebony are also fluted. The rose is unusual, being constructed of four layers of parchment, paper and leather that have been cut and pierced and then either left natural, stained red or gilded. This example still has its original string length; most instruments were altered over time as fashions changed.

- **DATE** c.1640
- **ORIGIN** Italy
- **WOOD**
  Front/Back & Sides
  Spruce/fluted ebony
  with ivory stringing
- **UNUSUAL FEATURE**
  This is a rare example as it has its original string length still intact.

'Matteo Sellas 1638' is engraved into the head.

Engraved details of rural scenes are shown on ivory plaques.

The rose has four tiers.

The soundboard is inlaid with ivory and ebony.

Alexandre Voboam: Baroque guitar, 1670

René, Jean, Nicolas Alexandre and Alexandre Voboam (d. c.1679) all made guitars in Paris during the 17th century. This one has ten tied gut frets and two inlaid wooden frets and is edged with ebony and ivory in a diagonal pattern. Although it is unusual for guitars to have the back and sides made of different woods (here dark ebony sides with a light juniper back) it was less uncommon in this period. It has two ivory buttons on the back and bottom to secure a strap.

- **DATE** 1670
- **ORIGIN** France
- **WOOD**
  Front/Back & Sides
  Spruce/ebony with ivory
  (sides); juniper with ebony
  and ivory (back)
- **UNUSUAL FEATURE**
  The maker used different woods for the back and sides.

The guitar is signed and dated on the head.

The instrument has ten tied gut frets and two wooden ones.

The barber-pole decoration is typical of Parisian instruments.

Antonio Stradivari: Baroque guitar, 1700

Although Antonio Stradivari (1644–1737) is probably the most famous name in the world of bowed-instrument making, fewer people know about the harps, lutes, *mandolinos* and guitars that also carry his name. There are two known extant *mandolinos* and four surviving guitars (dated 1679, 1680 [or 1688], 1681 and this one from 1700) and the remains of a neck and head (1675). Stradivari's guitars differ from others of the period in that the bodies are generally bigger and the string lengths longer.

- **DATE** 1700

- **ORIGIN** Italy

- **WOOD**
  Front/Back & Sides
  Spruce/maple

- **UNUSUAL FEATURE**
  This guitar has fixed frets rather than tied gut frets.

This guitar would originally have had tied gut frets.

The rosette around the hole is similar in design to that which Louis Panormo adopted the following century.

The instrument has a lute-like linear rose that is glued into place.

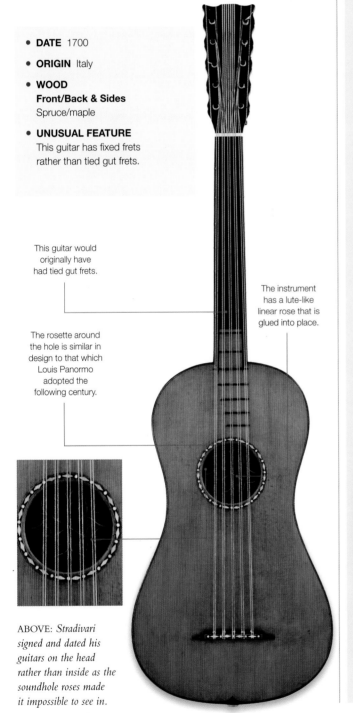

ABOVE: *Stradivari signed and dated his guitars on the head rather than inside as the soundhole roses made it impossible to see in.*

Evidence for the four-course Renaissance guitar

The four-course Renaissance guitar was small in comparison with the later five-course Baroque instrument. It was tuned in intervals of fourth–third–fourth, for example GCEA, with the fourth (bass) course tuned an octave apart. In Spain it coexisted alongside the vihuela, and Alonso Mudarra's famous *Tres Libros de Música en Cifra para Vihuela*, published in Seville in 1546, included music for both vihuela and four-course guitar. The instrument also enjoyed some popularity in Italy, England and, especially, France. A picture on the title page of Guillaume Morlaye's *Le Premier Livre*, published in Paris in 1552 – and backed up by many other contemporary illustrations – shows that this guitar was commonly strung with paired strings but with the top 'melody' string left single. This idea was later to take the five- and six-course double-strung guitar towards the single-stringed instruments (both five- and six-stringed) that ultimately led to the modern guitar.

ABOVE: *In the absence of any original surviving four-course guitars from the Renaissance period, iconographic and written evidence such as this French engraving from 1570 is vitally important to help guitar historians and organologists understand more about how these instruments worked.*

16th- to 18th-century guitars: the vihuela and chitarra battente

There are very few existing early (that is, pre-mid-17th-century) guitar-related instruments that have survived the ravages of time or conversion (and often inappropriate reconversion) as fashions changed. In fact, only three original vihuelas still exist. Consequently, the instruments here are exceedingly rare and valuable examples of a particular period in the development of the modern guitar.

Belchior Dias (attributed): Baroque guitar, c.1590

This is an extremely important early guitar, one of the world's oldest surviving examples of a Baroque instrument. Although there is no label, it is attributed to the Portuguese maker Belchior Dias, as its decoration is similar to a 1581 example by Dias housed at the Royal College of Music, London. The instrument has a replacement soundboard.

A five-course Baroque guitar has ten tuning pegs.

The interlaced marquetry pattern is in the style of Dias.

- **DATE** c.1590

- **ORIGIN** Portugal

- **WOOD**
  Front/Back & Sides
  Spruce (originally)/rosewood

- **UNUSUAL FEATURE**
  There is no maker's identification label on the instrument.

The instrument has a flat rose.

The applied mustachios complement the inlays to the upper soundboard.

Chitarra battente conversion from a Baroque guitar, 1626

This instrument probably started out as an Italian-made five-course Baroque guitar but was converted, as many were, to a chitarra battente. This was done by shortening the neck, changing the sides to accommodate a 'cant' mandolin-like soundboard, removing five tuning pegs and altering the bridge to allow for the use of wire strings. One later transformation took place to convert it to a six-string guitar, once again in keeping with the fashion of the day.

This guitar originally had ten tuning pegs, but only six are currently being used.

- **DATE** 1626

- **ORIGIN** Italy

- **WOOD**
  Front/Back & Sides
  Spruce/ebony and ivory

- **UNUSUAL FEATURE**
  The heads of converted guitars were usually cut down – this one has survived intact.

The fingerboard and pegbox feature ivory panels showing hunting scenes and Orpheus charming the beasts.

The bridge is modified for a reduced number of strings.

Chitarra battente, *c.*1690

In Italian, the words 'chitarra battente' literally mean 'beating guitar'. The soundboard has a 'cant' (bend) below the bridge that gives the instrument the greater strength needed from the pull of wire strings. These instruments usually had a rounded back, as this example does. The number of strings varied and were sometimes arranged in triple rather than double courses. They were played with a plectrum and used for accompaniment. This particular instrument has typical Italian-style soundboard inlays with a layered soundhole rose.

This guitar has 14 tuning pegs, thus indicating some sort of triple stringing.

The ebony head facing is beautifully inlaid with ivory.

- **DATE** *c.*1690

- **ORIGIN** Italy

- **WOOD**
  Front/Back & Sides
  Spruce/yew

- **UNUSUAL FEATURE**
  This chitarra battente has 14 tuning pegs.

LEFT: *Like most chitarra battentes, the back is rounded and the sides are angled to accommodate the bend in the soundboard.*

The strings pass through the bridge and are anchored to the base of the guitar.

Vihuela de mano

ABOVE: *The 'Chambure' vihuela. The conservation policies of many museums mean that this instrument will likely remain with its soundboard detached. From an organological perspective, this is a priceless opportunity to study how instruments were made in the past.*

There were at least three forms of vihuela in the 16th century, the *vihuela de arco* (bowed), the *vihuela de peñola* (plucked with a plectrum) and the *vihuela de mano* (plucked with the fingers), the latter becoming simply known as the vihuela. It is thought that Spain adopted the vihuela because the other popular instrument of the day throughout Europe, the lute, was too similar to the oud, which had connotations with Moorish Spain and was thus out of favour following the Reconquista. Of the only three known surviving vihuelas, one is in the Iglesia de la Compañia de Jesús de Quito in Ecuador and the others – the 'Guadalupe' instrument and the recently rediscovered 'Chambure' vihuela – are both in Paris, at the Musée Jacquemart-Andrée and the Cité de la Musique respectively. The 'Chambure' vihuela (pictured above) has a seven-piece, deeply fluted back of jujube wood, and the head accommodates 12 tuning pegs for strings arranged in six paired courses. The outline of the bridge can be seen.

18th- and early 19th-century transitional guitars: part one

The move towards the modern guitar took in many developments. In Spain, a direct line can be drawn from the 16th-century vihuela through the six-course guitar (mid-18th to mid-19th centuries). However, other countries, notably France, adopted the six-string lyre-guitar – tuned as a modern guitar – and a great deal of music was written for this instrument, mostly simple accompaniments to songs.

Francisco Sanguino: seven-course guitar, c.1759

Francisco Sanguino (c.1705–1771) was one of the first makers to use simple fanbracing to support the soundboard against the tension of 14 strings – and thus avoid what earlier lutenists had to be prepared to do in regularly disassembling and rebracing their soundboards. The exact tuning is unknown, as is the type of music it was used for, but the Spanish composer Federico Moretti mentions in his 1799 method *Principios Para Tocar la Guitarra de Seis Orderes* that he preferred guitars with this string arrangement.

The long head accommodates 14 tuning pegs.

Although it has a short neck, it has a longer-than-average string length of 663mm (26⅛in).

- **DATE** c.1759
- **ORIGIN** Spain
- **WOOD**
  Front/Back & Sides
  Spruce/cypress
- **UNUSUAL FEATURE**
  A seven-course guitar, this has 14 strings, which are tuned in pairs.

The intricate soundboard decoration was probably inlaid by an expert rather than the instrument maker.

(Anonymous) lyre-guitar, c.1815

With Classicism in vogue, lyres in the form of a guitar started to appear in the 1780s – mainly in Paris, but examples from Italy, Germany and Spain also survive. A substantial amount of music was written for the lyre-guitar, principally by Italian composers in Paris, including Matteo Carcassi (1792–1853), Ferdinando Carulli (1770–1841) and Francois Molino (1775–1847). Unlike the harp-guitar of today, however, the lyre-guitar was played upright.

The head is reminiscent of Napoleon's hat, and the arms end in decorative brass finials.

There are six wooden tuning pegs, and the ivory studs help guide the outer strings towards the neck.

- **DATE** c.1815
- **ORIGIN** France
- **WOOD**
  Front/Back & Sides
  Spruce/maple
- **UNUSUAL FEATURE**
  The soundhole roses resemble those that are found on lutes.

Juan Pagés: six-course guitar, 1802

Surviving guitars by Juan Pagés (1741–1821), one of the foremost makers in Cadiz, are exceptional. This is a six-course instrument, tuned as a modern 12-string. The scale length is 654mm (25⅜in), similar to standard guitars today, rather than the more usual 630mm (24¾in) of a 19th-century guitar. Many surviving six-course guitars underwent brutal modifications during the rise of the classical guitar, having their heads truncated and oversized bridges added to convert for playing with six single strings. This one was lucky.

Joseph Pagés: six-course guitar, 1822

Made by Joseph, or Joséf, Pagés (1762–?), who was the son of Juan Pagés, this guitar was brought to Gibraltar by 1822, where it ended up being owned by the Galliano banking family in Gibraltar. It is a very late example of the Spanish six-course guitar, made at a time when the rest of the guitar-playing world had switched to six single strings. With its squared-off head and minimal soundboard decoration – so much plainer than his father's 1802 example – the advent of the classical guitar seems not far off.

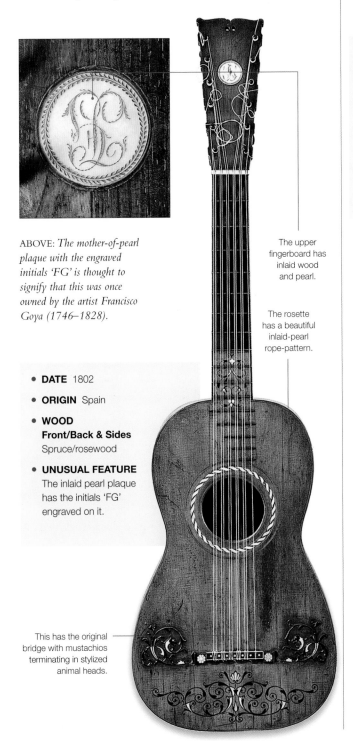

ABOVE: *The mother-of-pearl plaque with the engraved initials 'FG' is thought to signify that this was once owned by the artist Francisco Goya (1746–1828).*

- **DATE** 1802
- **ORIGIN** Spain
- **WOOD**
  Front/Back & Sides
  Spruce/rosewood
- **UNUSUAL FEATURE**
  The inlaid pearl plaque has the initials 'FG' engraved on it.

The upper fingerboard has inlaid wood and pearl.

The rosette has a beautiful inlaid-pearl rope-pattern.

This has the original bridge with mustachios terminating in stylized animal heads.

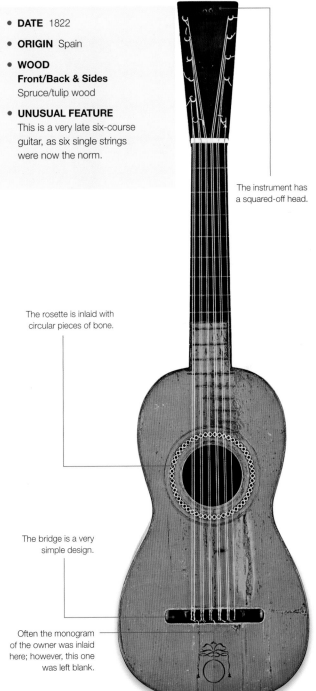

- **DATE** 1822
- **ORIGIN** Spain
- **WOOD**
  Front/Back & Sides
  Spruce/tulip wood
- **UNUSUAL FEATURE**
  This is a very late six-course guitar, as six single strings were now the norm.

The instrument has a squared-off head.

The rosette is inlaid with circular pieces of bone.

The bridge is a very simple design.

Often the monogram of the owner was inlaid here; however, this one was left blank.

18th- and early 19th-century transitional guitars: part two

By the late 18th century, the five-course guitar was moving away from its earlier Baroque style. In France, guitars were becoming plainer, and the move to six single strings had begun. These guitars exemplify this, with the sunken rose, double stringing and tied frets all on their way out. One feature that survived was the extension of the soundboard over part of the neck, but this went when raised fingerboards came in.

George Cousineau, c.1770

In Paris, George Cousineau (1733–1800) made violins and harps as well as guitars. This guitar has sloping sides, meaning that the back is much smaller than the front, which was thought to enhance sound projection. Although Cousineau was of the last generation to fit guitars with a sunken rose, compared with earlier five-course guitars this – apart from the rose itself and bridge mustachios – is very plain, which was not only the fashion but made a better sound.

LEFT: *Here we can see that the sides are not parallel. Instead, they are angled inwards, thus resulting in a much smaller back compared to the front.*

The hole in the top of the head was to tie a ribbon, either for decoration or to use as a guitar strap.

This guitar has tied gut frets.

This instrument has a rose of layered parchment.

- **DATE** *c.*1770
- **ORIGIN** France
- **WOOD**
  Front/Back & Sides
  Spruce/maple
- **UNUSUAL FEATURE**
  The sides are sloping.

Villaume and Giron, c.1790

Alexis Villaume and Claude Giron worked in Troyes, France, from *c.*1789 into the 1830s. This guitar must have been one of the last made with ten tuning pegs, and it was probably played – as it is today – with nine strings, the top course being single. It it is very similar in appearance to the Cousineau guitar, except that the Baroque feature, the sunken rose, has now gone, in this case leaving it with a rather small soundhole.

There are ten tuning pegs.

Although it has ten tuning pegs, this guitar uses only nine strings, the top course being single.

- **DATE** *c.*1790
- **ORIGIN** France
- **WOOD**
  Front/Back & Sides
  Spruce/maple
- **UNUSUAL FEATURE**
  The soundhole is very small.

There is an open soundhole instead of a sunken rose.

Many French-made guitars have alternating ebony and ivory edging.

Five-string guitar, c.1780

There are few surviving five-string guitars – this, of course, being the next evolutionary step towards the modern instrument. This guitar was probably made by either Giovanni Battista Fabricatore (c.1750–c.1812) or one of the Vinaccia family. Mother-of-pearl is inlaid in brown-coloured shellac and is flanked by tortoiseshell on the head. Although this guitar has much pearl decoration, it is roughly shaped and crudely placed into position. The back and sides are also of a cheap pine painted to imitate rosewood. These are all features which are lacking the finesse of Baroque instruments.

- **DATE** *c.*1780
- **ORIGIN** Italy
- **WOOD**
  Front/Back & Sides
  Spruce/pine
- **UNUSUAL FEATURE**
  The back is of cheap pine, painted to look like expensive rosewood.

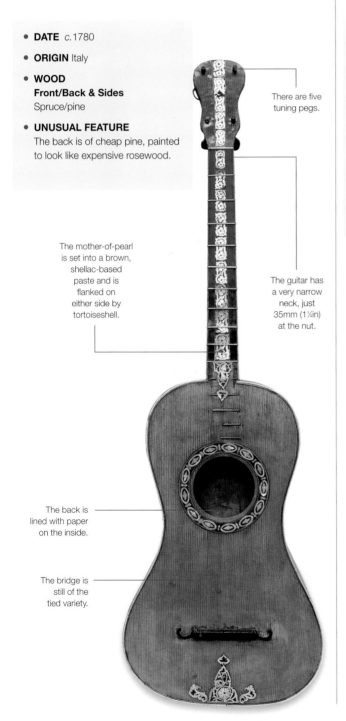

There are five tuning pegs.

The mother-of-pearl is set into a brown, shellac-based paste and is flanked on either side by tortoiseshell.

The guitar has a very narrow neck, just 35mm (1¼in) at the nut.

The back is lined with paper on the inside.

The bridge is still of the tied variety.

Converted five-course guitar, c.1770

This guitar was made originally as a five-course instrument, then a few years later it was converted to a five-single-string guitar. This was done by truncating the head and adding a five-pin bridge to the instrument. It does, however, still have its original nut, complete with ten grooves. It is actually a miracle that it was not converted again for six-string playing. Dendrochronology dates the soundboard to around 1757, so with time allowed for the curing of the wood, and also taking into account its stylistic features, its original date of manufacture is likely to be *c.*1770.

- **DATE** *c.*1770
- **ORIGIN** Italy or France
- **WOOD**
  Front/Back & Sides
  Spruce/maple
- **UNUSUAL FEATURE**
  This modified form of guitar would not have existed for very long, due to the making of five-stringed guitars and the almost immediate invention of the six-string guitar.

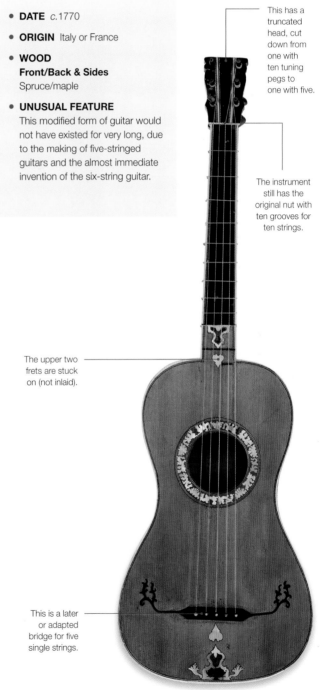

This has a truncated head, cut down from one with ten tuning pegs to one with five.

The instrument still has the original nut with ten grooves for ten strings.

The upper two frets are stuck on (not inlaid).

This is a later or adapted bridge for five single strings.

18th- and early 19th-century six-string guitars: Mediterranean

After the adoption of six single strings, the art of guitar making rose in the first half of the 19th century to a high not seen since the Baroque. The four makers whose instruments are shown here all used a similar concept for soundboard bracing, with diagonally placed bars being used to strengthen the boards against the tension of the strings, as distinct from the more usual Spanish use of fan-shaped bracing.

Giovanni Battista Fabricatore, c.1785

Giovanni Battista Fabricatore (c.1750–c.1812) is responsible for making the earliest known six-single-string guitars, of which this is one. This guitar is of a very simple construction with no back linings – instead, paper is used to help keep the back glued to the sides. Many of his later guitars, like his mandolins, were adorned with pearl and ivory, but this one just has ivory stripes to the back of the neck.

Notice that the frets diminish in length in the upper register.

- **DATE** c.1785
- **ORIGIN** Naples, Italy
- **WOOD**
  Front/Back & Sides
  Spruce/maple
- **UNUSUAL FEATURE**
  This guitar is paper-lined, like many Italian mandolins.

The bridge is tied.

The ornamentation is kept to a minimum with just these bridge extensions.

Gennaro Fabricatore, 1830

It is thought that there were two Gennaro Fabricatores making guitars – Gennaro I (c.1770–c.1844) and Gennaro II (1800–1853) – and it is not certain which one made this instrument. It has double linings to make it stronger, and there is also a very large nail supporting the neck-to-body join. The lavishly inlaid pearl decoration extends to the back of the body and neck, indicating this guitar was clearly made for someone very important, possibly royalty.

Note the Stauffer-style head with all six tuners on one side.

- **DATE** 1830
- **ORIGIN** Naples, Italy
- **WOOD**
  Front/Back & Sides
  Spruce/ebony
- **UNUSUAL FEATURE**
  The sides are solid ebony.

There are nearly a thousand pieces of individually hand-cut inlaid pearl.

The applied ebony decoration is in the form of oak and laurel leaves.

René Lacôte, 1830

Throughout the 'golden' period in the middle of the 19th century, René Lacôte (1785–c.1860) made guitars, which were played by Fernando Sor, Dionisio Aguado, Matteo Carrassi and Napoleon Coste, to name but a few. This one was made for Aguado, or at least one of his students, having signs that a tripodison (a type of guitar stand that Aguado endorsed) was once fitted. It must have been very much an experimental guitar, having an adjustable neck – one of only two known to have been made by Lacôte – and because it has two soundboards.

- **DATE** 1830

- **ORIGIN** Paris, France

- **WOOD**
  Front/Back & Sides
  Spruce/satinwood

- **UNUSUAL FEATURE**
  This has two soundboards with a second soundhole at the back.

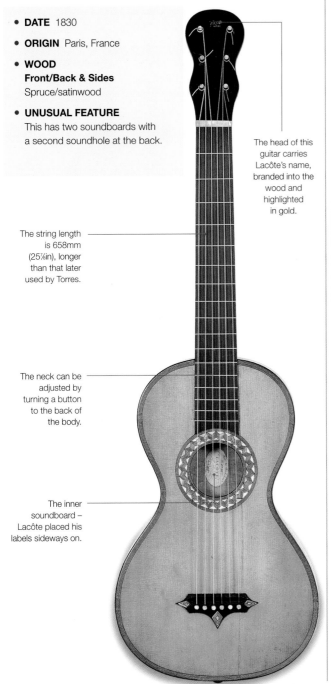

The head of this guitar carries Lacôte's name, branded into the wood and highlighted in gold.

The string length is 658mm (25⅞in), longer than that later used by Torres.

The neck can be adjusted by turning a button to the back of the body.

The inner soundboard – Lacôte placed his labels sideways on.

Agustín Altimíra, 1840s

The reason why this guitar is made in a French style remains a bit of a mystery as the maker, Agustin Altimíra (1805–82), lived and worked for his whole life in Barcelona, and died there. This example could easily pass as a French import, were it not for the fact that the head-to-neck joint, although executed in a French manner, retains a Spanish character. On closer inspection, it can be seen that the joint has a 'fake' Spanish-style carved 'dart'. An inlaid portrait on the back uses many exotic materials to give it depth and colour.

- **DATE** 1840s

- **ORIGIN** Barcelona, Spain

- **WOOD**
  Front/Back & Sides
  Spruce/burred walnut

- **UNUSUAL FEATURE**
  The elements are in a French style.

Note the enclosed French Lacôte-style tuning machines usually reserved for Lacôte's finest instruments.

The rosette features a hunting scene.

ABOVE: *The back is inlaid and painted beautifully using ivory and coloured shells depicting a scene of a Spanish soldier and the lady he loves playing the guitar.*

Two angels either side of the bridge are made from mother-of-pearl.

18th- and early 19th-century guitars: English

London was an exciting place to be in the 1800s. For the many foreign makers there it was a place to seek fame and fortune – for some it was also a refuge from political unrest. There were many forms of guitar in England, including the guittar and the many variants of harp-guitars. These all gave way to the Spanish guitar, and by the 1830s London-based makers were looking to French and Spanish makers for inspiration.

Early London-made guitar, c. 1810

This was made at a time when the classical guitar was becoming popular and was one of the first six-string guitars made in London. Its overall appearance and style are that of the Baroque guitar, and it was built before the London makers had established their own style. It has ivory frets, both inlaid and painted purflings and grand mustachios radiating from the bridge. This example has no bracing below the soundhole bars.

There are six wooden tuning pegs.

There are 11 ivory frets to the neck.

- **DATE** *c.*1810
- **ORIGIN** London, England
- **WOOD**
  Front/Back & Sides
  Maple
- **UNUSUAL FEATURE**
  The painted-on decoration is found on some violins but no other guitars.

The bridge decoration is in a Spanish style.

Edward Light Dital-Harp, c. 1816

The 'British harp-lute' – or 'dital-harp' – was patented by Edward Light (*c.*1727–1832) in 1816. Its selling point was its portability, compared with a regular harp, and there were many variants, some six-stringed tuned like the guittar, others, such as this, with many strings. It was taken up as an alternative to the waning English cittern and new Spanish guitar, but was short-lived, as the British people soon adopted the regular guitar.

The decoration is lavish gold-leaf and wood turning.

- **DATE** *c.*1816
- **ORIGIN** London, England
- **WOOD**
  Front/Back & Sides
  Spruce/maple
- **UNUSUAL FEATURE**
  The lower-string pitch is changed by pressing a button.

It has a fretboard for the upper register – perhaps another reason why it is classed as a harp-guitar rather than a harp.

It has 19 strings, of which 14 can be shortened by using stops, thus increasing the range of the instrument.

Louis Panormo: Madame Pratten's guitar, 1831

Louis Panormo (1784–1862) was born in Paris and died in Auckland, New Zealand but was best known as a key figure in London. He and other family members built guitars at a time when the guitar was at its mid-Victorian height. The most famous guitarist and guitar teacher of the day was Madame Sidney Pratten (1821–95). She played many guitars throughout her long career – this example not only has her name stamped into the head, but also a red wax seal with her initials 'SP'. It is a very typical Panormo instrument, built, as the label suggests, "in the Spanish Style".

The head follows the distinctive Panormo-style.

- **DATE** 1831
- **ORIGIN** London, England
- **WOOD**
  Front/Back & Sides
  Spruce/rosewood
- **UNUSUAL FEATURE**
  Panormo's guitars were always dated and had serial numbers.

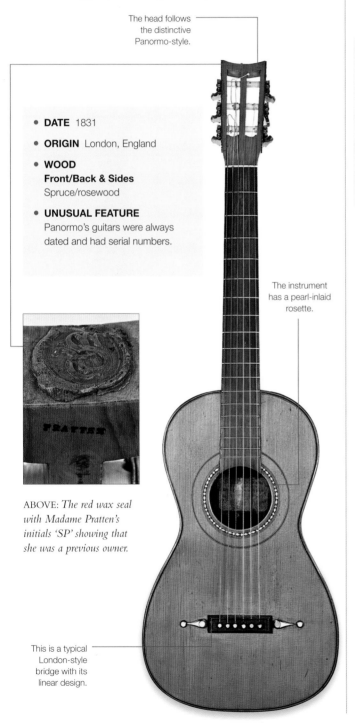

ABOVE: *The red wax seal with Madame Pratten's initials 'SP' showing that she was a previous owner.*

The instrument has a pearl-inlaid rosette.

This is a typical London-style bridge with its linear design.

Dominic and Arnould Roudhloff, 1840s

The Roudhloff brothers came to London from Mirecourt, an area of France well-known for its instrument makers, in the 1830s. They made some guitars in the French style and others, such as this example, which they called the 'melophonic guitar'. This was radically different: it was larger than the French instruments, the bridge saddle was angled and the internal soundboard used what later became known as x-bracing (something further developed by the American company C. F. Martin & Co.). The Roudhloff brothers also made many eight-string instruments.

- **DATE** 1840s
- **ORIGIN** London, England
- **WOOD**
  Front/Back & Sides
  Spruce/rosewood on mahogany
- **UNUSUAL FEATURE**
  This is a large instrument for the period.

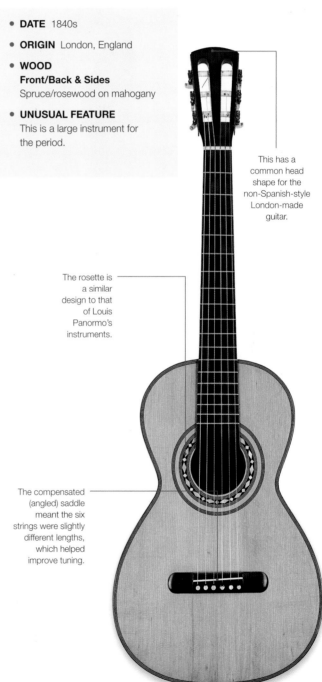

This has a common head shape for the non-Spanish-style London-made guitar.

The rosette is a similar design to that of Louis Panormo's instruments.

The compensated (angled) saddle meant the six strings were slightly different lengths, which helped improve tuning.

19th-century guitars:
Germanic and Russian

Early Viennese makers tended to follow Italian styles, later establishing their own school, which in turn influenced Germany and Russia. All three guitars here have adjustable necks – neck angle and thus string height can be altered. String lengths tended to be shorter than other European schools; this, coupled with generally narrower necks, mean players can use techniques such as fretting the bass string with the thumb.

Johann Stauffer: Legnani Terz model, c. 1830

Johann Anton Stauffer (c.1805–1851) was the son of Johann Georg Stauffer (1778–1853). Stauffer guitars from this period tend to have a rounded 'figure-of-eight' shape, and many had adjustable necks with raised fingerboards and a higher compass of notes, some ranging three octaves. This guitar is tuned a minor third higher than standard, in Terz tuning.

The head shape was adopted by Leo Fender in the 1940s for his electric instruments.

- **DATE** c.1830
- **ORIGIN** Vienna, Austria
- **WOOD**
  Front/Back & Sides
  Spruce/maple
- **UNUSUAL FEATURE**
  The string length is very short, being only 560mm (22in).

The instrument has extra frets that go up to high F (in Terz tuning).

The bridge is made of liquorice wood, as were many cheaper violin fingerboards at the time.

Mortz Gläsel guitar, c. 1870

A highly regarded luthier, Mortz Gläsel (1829–1917) worked in Markneukirchen, Saxony – also C. F. Martin's hometown. The unusual shape of this guitar – that of an early 17th-century viola da gamba – probably came from the fact that he was a connoisseur of ancient instruments. Many German-made guitars are unlabelled, so the makers' identities are unknown, but this one had Gläsel's label hidden in the lining of the original case.

The neck is inlaid with ivory and abalone.

- **DATE** c.1870
- **ORIGIN** Saxony, Germany
- **WOOD**
  Front/Back & Sides
  Spruce/burred walnut
- **UNUSUAL FEATURE**
  The body shape is that of a viola da gamba.

The instrument has a unique body shape similar to a viola da gamba.

The bridge is ornate and rather heavy.

Russian seven-string guitar, *c.*1880

Guitar music in Russia (also in Poland and Bohemia) called for seven-string instruments tuned to DGBDGBD, the open chordal tuning possibly influenced by the English guitar's CEGCEG. Like many Viennese and German guitars the neck is adjustable, although here it is to allow the musician to manipulate the neck while playing, thus raising and lowering the pitch. The label here reads: "Trading House of Musical Instruments/Founded in 1879 by Kulakov", suggesting he was a wholesaler. The German stylistic features make it clear that this was a German-made guitar that was exported to Russia.

- **DATE** *c.*1880

- **ORIGIN** Russia

- **WOOD**
  Front/Back & Sides
  Spruce/rosewood

- **UNUSUAL FEATURE**
  There are specially adapted tuning machines for seven strings.

Note the seven metal barrels.

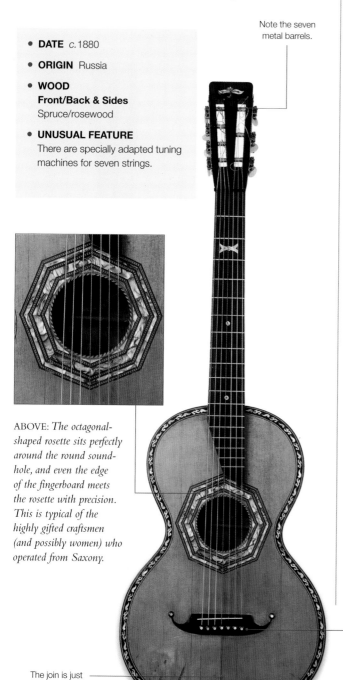

ABOVE: *The octagonal-shaped rosette sits perfectly around the round sound-hole, and even the edge of the fingerboard meets the rosette with precision. This is typical of the highly gifted craftsmen (and possibly women) who operated from Saxony.*

The join is just visible between the two halves of the soundboard.

Luigi Legnani

ABOVE: *A Stauffer label from 1827, which reads:* "Nach dem Modell" *(translated:* "After the design")/ "des Luigi Legnani 3347/von Johann Anton Stauffer & Co. in Wien." *It carries Stauffer's red wax seal featuring the double-headed eagle of the House of Habsburg.*

Luigi Legnani (1790–1877) was a guitar virtuoso as well as an amateur violin and guitar maker who helped both Stauffer companies (those of Johann Georg and his son Johann Anton) to design and develop their guitars. This is perhaps the most long-standing of all player–maker relationships, and the collaboration between Legnani and the Stauffers was probably more than simply an endorsement on Legnani's part. In 1822, J. G. Stauffer and his compatriot the violin maker Johann Ertl (1776–1828) received a 'privilege' for five years, extended in 1828, to 'improve' guitars. This privilege was probably a patent filed through the strict guilds, which at that time in Vienna controlled not only the right to make instruments but also whom one trained and even the prices one could charge. Some of their improvements included the raised fingerboard, a screw mechanism for neck adjustment and a new metal alloy for longer-lasting frets. These features appear on the Legnani models, but were most certainly a feature on regular Stauffer guitars as well.

There are seven bridge pins.

19th-century guitars: American

This section features two guitars by the New York-based maker C. F. Martin, the most famous of all American flat-top makers, plus guitars by the less well-known James Ashborn and John Haynes. All three makers are equally important, though, when considering the development of the American guitar, along with Elias Howe, the Larson Brothers and Robert Maurer.

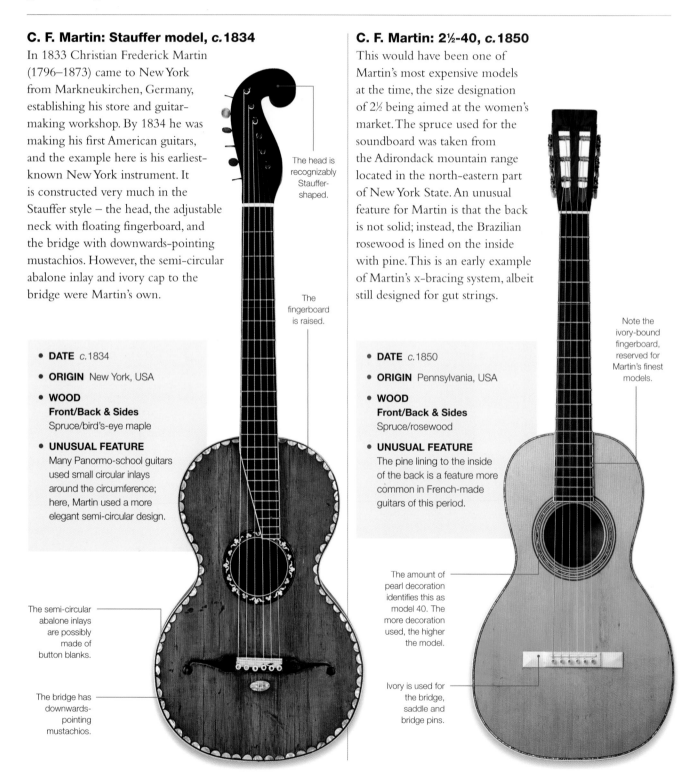

C. F. Martin: Stauffer model, c.1834

In 1833 Christian Frederick Martin (1796–1873) came to New York from Markneukirchen, Germany, establishing his store and guitar-making workshop. By 1834 he was making his first American guitars, and the example here is his earliest-known New York instrument. It is constructed very much in the Stauffer style – the head, the adjustable neck with floating fingerboard, and the bridge with downwards-pointing mustachios. However, the semi-circular abalone inlay and ivory cap to the bridge were Martin's own.

The head is recognizably Stauffer-shaped.

The fingerboard is raised.

- **DATE** c.1834
- **ORIGIN** New York, USA
- **WOOD**
  Front/Back & Sides
  Spruce/bird's-eye maple
- **UNUSUAL FEATURE**
  Many Panormo-school guitars used small circular inlays around the circumference; here, Martin used a more elegant semi-circular design.

The semi-circular abalone inlays are possibly made of button blanks.

The bridge has downwards-pointing mustachios.

C. F. Martin: 2½-40, c.1850

This would have been one of Martin's most expensive models at the time, the size designation of 2½ being aimed at the women's market. The spruce used for the soundboard was taken from the Adirondack mountain range located in the north-eastern part of New York State. An unusual feature for Martin is that the back is not solid; instead, the Brazilian rosewood is lined on the inside with pine. This is an early example of Martin's x-bracing system, albeit still designed for gut strings.

Note the ivory-bound fingerboard, reserved for Martin's finest models.

- **DATE** c.1850
- **ORIGIN** Pennsylvania, USA
- **WOOD**
  Front/Back & Sides
  Spruce/rosewood
- **UNUSUAL FEATURE**
  The pine lining to the inside of the back is a feature more common in French-made guitars of this period.

The amount of pearl decoration identifies this as model 40. The more decoration used, the higher the model.

Ivory is used for the bridge, saddle and bridge pins.

James Ashborn: Style 1, 1855

Probably a British engineer, James Ashborn (*c.*1810–?) is thought to have emigrated to the USA and started making guitars in Connecticut. He seems to have had some Spanish influence while producing guitars of a very individual nature. This is not immediately apparent until one looks more closely at the constructional features of his instruments, as many have parquet inlays and French-style veneered necks. They are very carefully and cleanly made, rivalling those of C. F. Martin in craftsmanship, although the materials and decorative elements are not of such high quality. Many of his guitars were distributed through the Hall and Firth companies.

The squared-off head is a traditional American style.

These are unusually long string-relief ramps.

- **DATE** 1855
- **ORIGIN** Connecticut, USA
- **WOOD**
  Front/Back & Sides
  Spruce/rosewood
- **UNUSUAL FEATURE**
  The veneered neck is a rare feature on American-made guitars.

The plain rosette identifies it as a 'style 1'.

The instrument has a two-piece bridge.

John Haynes: Tilton model, 1870

William B. Tilton was a New York maker who licensed his designs to other manufacturers, and this instrument was made by John Haynes in Boston to a Tilton design. Tilton patented his improvement – reducing the mass of the neck and bottom blocks to give the soundboard more area to vibrate and adding a wooden dowel to compensate for the less-rigid structure – for this design in the 1850s. The patent included the addition of a tailpiece to relieve string tension, so allowing for lighter x-bracing.

- **DATE** 1870
- **ORIGIN** Massachusetts, USA
- **WOOD**
  Front/Back & Sides
  Spruce/rosewood
- **UNUSUAL FEATURE**
  The guitar has a tailpiece and wooden dowel stick.

ABOVE: *The wooden banjo-type dowel stick has a metallic patent disc by Tilton.*

The head shape is not very American, and is therefore presumed to be a replacement.

The guitar has an elaborately engraved tailpiece.

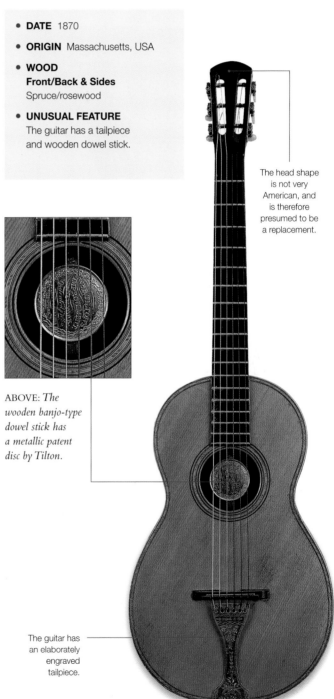

19th-century guitars: unusual varieties

There are very few innovations and designs in modern guitars that were not already tried and tested during the 19th century – including ways to make instruments louder, have a broader range, play more in tune, have a better tone, and be easier to play or transport. Some of these are still in use now, but the majority fall into the class of odd-ball fantasies that have had their time and been discarded.

Mauchant Frères archtop, c.1820

Many 19th-century French luthiers learnt their trade from violin makers and often produced both types of instruments. Little is known about the Mauchants, but clearly they designed this early archtop guitar with the cello in mind, as the internal bracing has a double cello-style bass bar running either side of the round soundhole. A guitar similar to this is pictured in Francisco Molino's famous *Grande Méthode Complète* of 1823.

- **DATE** *c.*1820
- **ORIGIN** Mirecourt, France
- **WOOD**
  Front/Back & Sides
  Spruce/maple
- **UNUSUAL FEATURE**
  This the earliest guitar with an arched top.

This two-dimensional scroll-shaped head is the reverse of the Stauffer head or today's Fender design.

This guitar has two cello-style c-holes, as well as the traditional round soundhole.

The bridge is floating rather than being fixed, as with instruments of the violin family.

It also has a traditional guitar-pin bridge.

C. F. Bauer double soundhole, c.1850

C. F. Bauer worked near Markneukirchen in Germany. Like Martin he had worked with Stauffer in Vienna, and some of his guitars show this influence. Inside, Bauer's name is stamped rather than using a label, something Martin continues today. The extended bass accounts for the extra soundhole and the off-kilter neck, which is mounted so as to centre the bridge on the body.

- **DATE** *c.*1850
- **ORIGIN** Klingenthal, Saxony, Germany
- **WOOD**
  Front/Back & Sides
  Maple
- **UNUSUAL FEATURE**
  This guitar has two soundholes, which allows the ten strings to resonate more.

There are four extra tuning machines to accommodate the sub-bass strings.

The neck is fixed at an angle to the body.

The two soundholes feature Stauffer-style rosettes.

The body is very large for a guitar of this period.

Unlabelled, probably Viennese: "Painted Scene", c.1850–60

Although it was fashionable for some French guitars to have painted scenes, usually to the back of the instrument, this guitar is certainly Germanic in origin. The decoration separating the Biedermeier scene from the many cherubs and two songbirds 'standing' on the bridge mustachios is executed with three-dimensional relief paintwork. Apart from the decoration, the guitar is an ordinary mid-19th-century Austrian guitar with a rosette that is quite typical of the instruments from the Stauffer workshop.

ABOVE: *The decoration features a typical Biedermeier scene with a lady playing guitar.*

The frets diminish in size towards the upper register.

The head is painted, with imitation gold leaf.

- **DATE** c.1850–60
- **ORIGIN** Germany or Austria
- **WOOD**
  Front/Back & Sides
  Maple
- **UNUSUAL FEATURE**
  It is rare to find a painted soundboard on a guitar (other examples have the paintings to the rear).

The upwards-facing bridge extensions complement the main painting.

George Lewis Panormo (attributed): Bambina Guitar, 1874

G. L. Panormo (1815–77) – not to be confused with his father George Panormo or his uncle Louis Panormo – continued the family business, and towards the end of his career made these small instruments, an early form of travel guitar, for the Victorian guitarist and guitar teacher Madame Pratten and her students. Confusingly, they were labelled 'Bambina', which means 'child', and hence they are often thought to be a children's model. The Bambina measures just 536mm (21⅛in) total length with a string length of 336mm (13¼in) – this was around half the length of a regular guitar of the time.

- **DATE** 1874
- **ORIGIN** London, England
- **WOOD**
  Front/Back & Sides
  Spruce/coromandel
- **UNUSUAL FEATURE**
  Its diminutive size made this a 19th-century forerunner to today's travel instruments.

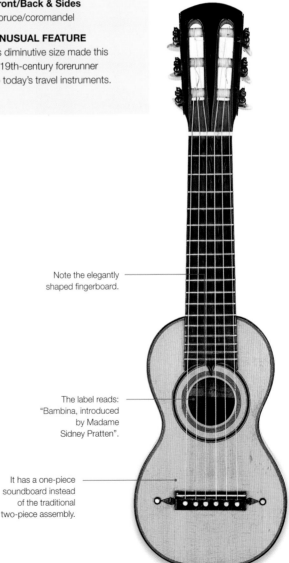

Note the elegantly shaped fingerboard.

The label reads: "Bambina, introduced by Madame Sidney Pratten".

It has a one-piece soundboard instead of the traditional two-piece assembly.

19th-century classical guitar makers: Antonio de Torres

Antonio de Torres (1817–92) is the father of the modern classical guitar, his instruments representing the summit of 19th-century design. His soundboard bracing and his synthesizing of what had gone before earned him this title, and no maker since has had such influence. He had two making periods; in between he ran a china shop. Of the 320 or so guitars he is thought to have made, around 100 are known today.

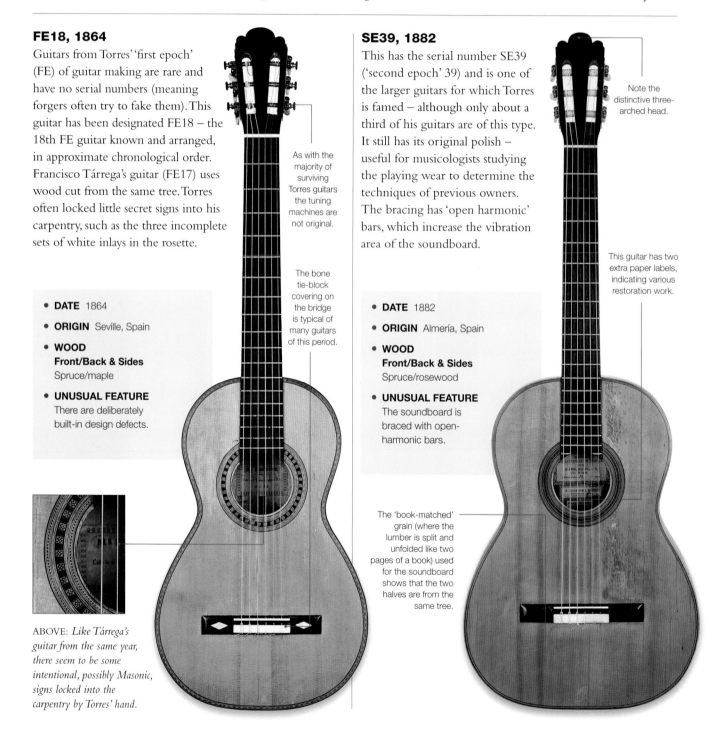

FE18, 1864

Guitars from Torres' 'first epoch' (FE) of guitar making are rare and have no serial numbers (meaning forgers often try to fake them). This guitar has been designated FE18 – the 18th FE guitar known and arranged, in approximate chronological order. Francisco Tárrega's guitar (FE17) uses wood cut from the same tree. Torres often locked little secret signs into his carpentry, such as the three incomplete sets of white inlays in the rosette.

- **DATE** 1864
- **ORIGIN** Seville, Spain
- **WOOD**
  Front/Back & Sides
  Spruce/maple
- **UNUSUAL FEATURE**
  There are deliberately built-in design defects.

ABOVE: *Like Tárrega's guitar from the same year, there seem to be some intentional, possibly Masonic, signs locked into the carpentry by Torres' hand.*

As with the majority of surviving Torres guitars the tuning machines are not original.

The bone tie-block covering on the bridge is typical of many guitars of this period.

SE39, 1882

This has the serial number SE39 ('second epoch' 39) and is one of the larger guitars for which Torres is famed – although only about a third of his guitars are of this type. It still has its original polish – useful for musicologists studying the playing wear to determine the techniques of previous owners. The bracing has 'open harmonic' bars, which increase the vibration area of the soundboard.

- **DATE** 1882
- **ORIGIN** Almería, Spain
- **WOOD**
  Front/Back & Sides
  Spruce/rosewood
- **UNUSUAL FEATURE**
  The soundboard is braced with open-harmonic bars.

Note the distinctive three-arched head.

This guitar has two extra paper labels, indicating various restoration work.

The 'book-matched' grain (where the lumber is split and unfolded like two pages of a book) used for the soundboard shows that the two halves are from the same tree.

SE127, 1889

This guitar belonged to the Spanish poet, novelist and literary editor Carlos Barral. Although the use of three pieces of wood to make up the back was common in Spanish lutherie, Torres also used three separate pieces – mahogany/walnut/mahogany – to make the sides of the body. The rosette is made up of 27 concentric circles of various inlaid woods. This guitar's scale length, which also determines where the metal frets are positioned, is 648mm (25½in), which is very close to today's standard of 650mm (25⅝in) string length.

This guitar has French tuning machines made by Eon et Fils.

- **DATE** 1889
- **ORIGIN** Almería, Spain
- **WOOD**
  Front/Back & Sides
  Pine or spruce/mahogany and walnut
- **UNUSUAL FEATURE**
  The sides, like the back, are made of three strips, two of mahogany and one of walnut.

The soundboard thickness ranges from 1.8mm (⅟₁₆in) to 2.3mm (⅛in).

Although this guitar sounds exceptional, the low quality of the materials used to construct it would not be used by luthiers today.

SE142, 1890

This is one of the last guitars that was made by Torres. Although the back and sides are constructed from cypress, which is now associated with the flamenco guitar, it is thought that in Torres' day there was no distinction. Instead, this guitar was probably built for the local amateur musician. Unfortunately, because Torres took the thinness of his soundboards down to absolute limits, many of his guitars have not survived intact. This one still maintains its original soundboard and thicknesses, albeit with some restorations.

This guitar originally had wooden tuning pegs but was later fitted with metal tuning machines.

- **DATE** 1890
- **ORIGIN** Almería, Spain
- **WOOD**
  Front/Back & Sides
  Spruce/cypress
- **UNUSUAL FEATURE**
  The soundboard is made of three pieces.

The soundboard is made of three pieces of spruce instead of the more traditional two pieces.

Even for a relatively modest Torres guitar, this one is highly prized by both players and collectors.

19th- and early 20th-century classical guitar makers

Early guitars by Vicente Arias (1833–1914) and Enrique Garcia (1868–1922) were much like those of Torres. Later, they developed their own styles, as did Manuel Ramírez and Francisco Simplicio, with guitars by all these makers tending to become more heavily constructed. Although Francisco Tárrega played guitars by Torres, there are photographs where he is clearly posing with guitars by Arias and Garcia.

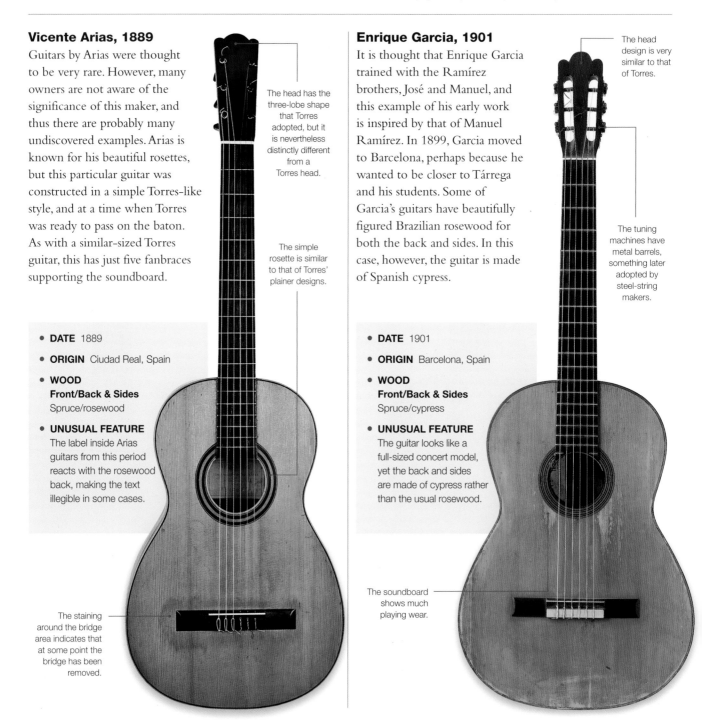

Vicente Arias, 1889

Guitars by Arias were thought to be very rare. However, many owners are not aware of the significance of this maker, and thus there are probably many undiscovered examples. Arias is known for his beautiful rosettes, but this particular guitar was constructed in a simple Torres-like style, and at a time when Torres was ready to pass on the baton. As with a similar-sized Torres guitar, this has just five fanbraces supporting the soundboard.

The head has the three-lobe shape that Torres adopted, but it is nevertheless distinctly different from a Torres head.

The simple rosette is similar to that of Torres' plainer designs.

- **DATE** 1889
- **ORIGIN** Ciudad Real, Spain
- **WOOD**
  Front/Back & Sides
  Spruce/rosewood
- **UNUSUAL FEATURE**
  The label inside Arias guitars from this period reacts with the rosewood back, making the text illegible in some cases.

The staining around the bridge area indicates that at some point the bridge has been removed.

Enrique Garcia, 1901

It is thought that Enrique Garcia trained with the Ramírez brothers, José and Manuel, and this example of his early work is inspired by that of Manuel Ramírez. In 1899, Garcia moved to Barcelona, perhaps because he wanted to be closer to Tárrega and his students. Some of Garcia's guitars have beautifully figured Brazilian rosewood for both the back and sides. In this case, however, the guitar is made of Spanish cypress.

The head design is very similar to that of Torres.

The tuning machines have metal barrels, something later adopted by steel-string makers.

- **DATE** 1901
- **ORIGIN** Barcelona, Spain
- **WOOD**
  Front/Back & Sides
  Spruce/cypress
- **UNUSUAL FEATURE**
  The guitar looks like a full-sized concert model, yet the back and sides are made of cypress rather than the usual rosewood.

The soundboard shows much playing wear.

Manuel Ramírez, 1911

The younger brother of José Ramírez I, Manuel Ramírez initially worked with his brother before they opened separate workshops. This guitar, with its wooden tuning pegs and ivoroid (fake ivory) tap-plate, has the appearance of a flamenco guitar. However, the back and sides are of rosewood, more commonly linked with classical instruments. This guitar was constructed just a year before Manuel Ramírez presented one to the youthful Andrés Segovia (1893–1987).

Many guitars from this period have had their wooden tuning pegs converted to tuning machines; this one retains its original pegs.

- **DATE** 1911
- **ORIGIN** Madrid, Spain
- **WOOD**
  Front/Back & Sides
  Spruce/rosewood
- **UNUSUAL FEATURE**
  Today, instruments featuring wooden tuning pegs, a tap-plate and with the back and sides of rosewood would be called *flamenca negra* guitars.

The pearl shapes used for the rosette were probably brought in by the maker.

The ivoroid tap-plate is used to protect the soft soundboard from nail wear.

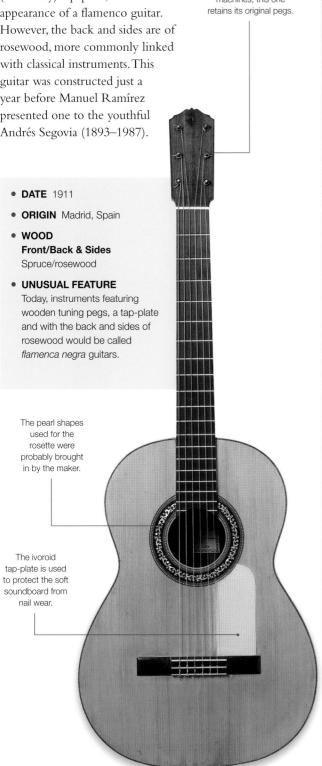

LEFT: *The beautifully carved rosewood head was reserved for their finest instruments. The tuning machines have solid mother-of-pearl buttons and the strings are attached by tying them around a small protruding knob.*

Francisco Simplicio, 1929

Enrique Garcia was Francisco Simplicio's teacher. This guitar has a metal *tornavoz* inside the soundhole, a device thought to have been first employed by Torres to help deepen the bass sound. The head is beautifully carved, a feature that became standard with many of the Argentinian makers, although it is also seen on some earlier German-made guitars. The bridge tie-block is enclosed by mother-of-pearl, which is also used for the tuning buttons.

- **DATE** 1929
- **ORIGIN** Barcelona, Spain
- **WOOD**
  Front/Back & Sides
  Spruce/rosewood
- **UNUSUAL FEATURE**
  This guitar has a bass-enhancing metal cylinder, a *tornavoz*, inside the soundhole.

The wooden marquetry of the rosette and the circumference of the body is exceptionally intricate.

The bridge has mother-of-pearl edging.

20th-century classical guitar makers: the Ramírez dynasty

From the time of José Ramírez I (1858–1923), founder of the Madrid school, the Ramírez family's business spans around 130 years. Their famous patrons have included Agustín Barrios, Narciso Yepes, George Harrison and Andrés Segovia. Only C. F. Martin & Co. has a longer history. The family also trained many luthiers who became established in their own right, including Paulino Bernabe and Felix Manzanero.

José Ramírez I, 1902

The Ramírez workshop has always catered for both the professional and the student, and this instrument would have been one of the more expensive models, with the tight-grain spruce top and the intricate inlays to the edging. However, being a smaller model with a string length of just 615mm (24⅛in), it was perhaps made for a young up-and-coming professional. Although it has wooden tuning pegs, it is not a flamenco guitar. Wooden pegs are lighter than mechanical tuners and, being used in this small guitar, make for a better balance.

The pointed central lobe to the head has been a Ramírez trademark throughout.

The name 'Carmen' is inscribed to the top of the head; perhaps this is the name of the woman for whom it was made.

- **DATE** 1902
- **ORIGIN** Madrid, Spain
- **WOOD**
  Front/Back & Sides
  Spruce/rosewood
- **UNUSUAL FEATURE**
  The guitar has a French-style, mother-of-pearl floral rosette.

It has an atypical, pretty floral rosette, perhaps in honour of Carmen.

José Ramírez II, 1946

Ramírez always employed other artisans to assist with production, and this guitar, although made in the workshop of José II (1885–1957) was, in fact, made by José Ramírez III. Again, this is one of the more expensive models offered by the Ramírez workshop. It has many unique and special touches. For example, although this is obviously a concert-standard instrument, the back and sides are of maple rather than the more traditional rosewood.

Note the book-matched spruce soundboard, clearly identified by the patterns in the tree rings.

The design and writing style of 'Jose Ramirez' on the paper label are still the same.

- **DATE** 1946
- **ORIGIN** Madrid, Spain
- **WOOD**
  Front/Back & Sides
  Spruce/maple
- **UNUSUAL FEATURE**
  The use of maple for the back and sides is not usual for the Ramírez family.

The bridge tie-block is edged with bone. This strengthens the points where the strings would dig into the wood.

José Ramírez III, 1960

This guitar was selected by Andrés Segovia to be one of his concert instruments. It bears the initials 'PB' inside, which indicates that in fact it was constructed by the Ramírez foreman Paulino Bernabé. José Ramírez III (1922–95) is famous for introducing the use of cedar as a soundboard material in the mid-1960s. This one was made just before that period and thus uses the more traditional spruce. Another innovation was the introduction of the longer string length of 664mm (26⅛in), perhaps to suit Segovia's large hands.

- **DATE** 1960
- **ORIGIN** Madrid, Spain
- **WOOD**
  Front/Back & Sides
  Spruce/rosewood
- **UNUSUAL FEATURE**
  This instrument has a long string length of 664mm (26⅛in).

Classical guitars were fitted with tuning machines as standard by 1960.

José Ramírez III chose to lacquer his guitars rather than French-polish them.

This was one of the last guitars Ramírez III made with a spruce soundboard, cedar becoming his preferred material.

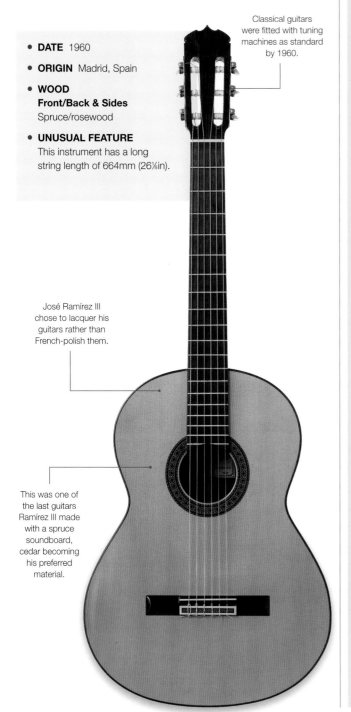

Amalia Ramírez

ABOVE: *Amalia Ramírez's hands-on approach in running the Ramirez guitar-making dynasty. Besides supervising the other artisans in her workshop and giving their guitars her final approval, she has also has designed some new and more affordable models.*

RIGHT: *This guitar was made by Amalia herself and, like Ramírez's time-honoured tradition of her predecessors, it meets the highest of standards. The back is of rosewood and the soundboard is made from spruce/rosewood. The paper label inside the soundhole is extended and carries the date of manufacture (1997), the serial and model number and Amalia's signature.*

The fingerboard is of ebony, the preferred hard-wearing material.

Note the trademark Ramírez head shape.

The central motif for the rosette is of red roses.

José Ramírez IV died at the young age of 47, leaving his sister Amalia (b. 1955) in charge of the business. Unlike many factory owners, she is actually hands-on, producing this beautifully handcrafted instrument herself. The classic José Ramírez head shape with its central peak is still observed, even after five changes of leadership. With many players struggling to manage the difficult left-hand stretches needed to play the Ramírez 664mm (26⅛in) string length, Amalia Ramírez has returned to the 650mm (25⅝in) option.

20th-century classical guitar makers: the Paris School

Classical guitar making in Paris began with the Spaniard Julian Gómez Ramírez (1879–*c*.1943), who was influenced by Torres and Manuel Ramírez. In turn, Robert Bouchet (1898–1986) learnt from J. G. Ramírez. Following on, Daniel Friederich (b. 1932) experimented more, while Dominique Field (b. 1954) keeps the tradition alive. These examples show how little body shape has changed over the four generations.

Julian Gómez Ramírez, 1939

In 1934, J. G. Ramírez repaired the Torres guitar SE39, which undoubtedly influenced his own making. He built guitars for many people – including the guitar maker Robert Bouchet, the maker and player Mauro Maccaferri and the husband-and-wife duo Ida Presti and Alexandre Lagoya – and he would write a dedication to them on a paper label. This guitar is undedicated and has the handwritten statement "Comme modèle" (literally translated 'Like other models').

- **DATE** 1939
- **ORIGIN** Paris, France
- **WOOD**
  Front/Back & Sides
  Spruce/rosewood
- **UNUSUAL FEATURE**
  The tuning machines are archaic in design, with butterfly-shaped buttons.

The tuning machines are 19th-century in style.

The rosette is a simple Torres-like design.

This is a Torres-style bone tie-block cap.

Robert Bouchet, 1962

This guitar belonged to the leading Austrian guitarist and musicologist Karl Scheit (1909–93). Robert Bouchet was an artist and art teacher in Paris and only a part-time guitar maker, yet he managed to make more than 150 guitars, including instruments for many prominent players, such as the British guitarist Julian Bream (b. 1933) who, until it was stolen, had an instrument from the same period as this one.

- **DATE** 1962
- **ORIGIN** Paris, France
- **WOOD**
  Front/Back & Sides
  Spruce/rosewood
- **UNUSUAL FEATURE**
  The tuning machines are in a typical 19th-century style.

The head shape is similar in style to some 19th-century French guitars.

The tuning machines are said to have been made or adapted by Bouchet.

Being an artist, Bouchet's paper labels were beautifully designed.

Daniel Friederich:
Serial No. 184, 1967

This is an early example of one of Friederich's concert models. However, many of the characteristics of his later instruments are already present, including the relief carving on the rosewood head and an early version of his much-admired rosettes. These features make it distinguishable from the student models that he made around this time, as does the superb craftsmanship and choice of materials and the inclusion of a serial number on the label. Like most classical guitars from this period, it has a spruce soundboard, although Friederich later became known for using cedar soundboards on slightly heavier instruments.

- **DATE** 1967
- **ORIGIN** Paris, France
- **WOOD**
  Front/Back & Sides
  Spruce/rosewood
- **UNUSUAL FEATURE**
  Friederich was not concerned with meeting the public demand of using figured Brazilian rosewood. In fact, he often used a different species of rosewood, coincidentally also from Brazil.

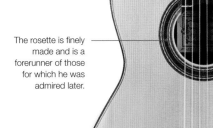

The head has a relief carving of a 'dart', which is a common feature on Friederich's guitars.

The rosette is finely made and is a forerunner of those for which he was admired later.

The tie-block uses the same central motif as the rosette decoration.

Dominique Field, 1998

Although he started out as a serious classical guitarist, Dominique Field became interested in making instruments in the 1970s, and he was lucky enough to be able to assist Robert Bouchet with the maintenance of several of Bouchet's guitars. He has subsequently had great success as a maker himself – to date he has made over 200 guitars and has a waiting list of around 15 years. This guitar is made of the finest woods, and the standard of his workmanship has helped earn Paris a world-class reputation as a centre for guitar makers.

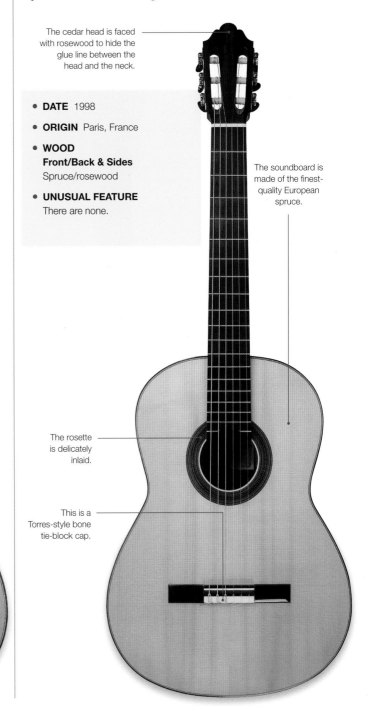

The cedar head is faced with rosewood to hide the glue line between the head and the neck.

- **DATE** 1998
- **ORIGIN** Paris, France
- **WOOD**
  Front/Back & Sides
  Spruce/rosewood
- **UNUSUAL FEATURE**
  There are none.

The soundboard is made of the finest-quality European spruce.

The rosette is delicately inlaid.

This is a Torres-style bone tie-block cap.

20th-century classical guitar makers: the Hauser family

The Hauser tradition of instrument building goes back to Josef Hauser (1854–1939), who started making instruments (mainly zithers) in the 1870s. However, it wasn't until the 1920s that his son Hermann Hauser I started building the guitars that we still recognize today as the 'modern' classical guitar. Three generations on, this tradition is continued by Hermann Hauser III and his daughter Katherin.

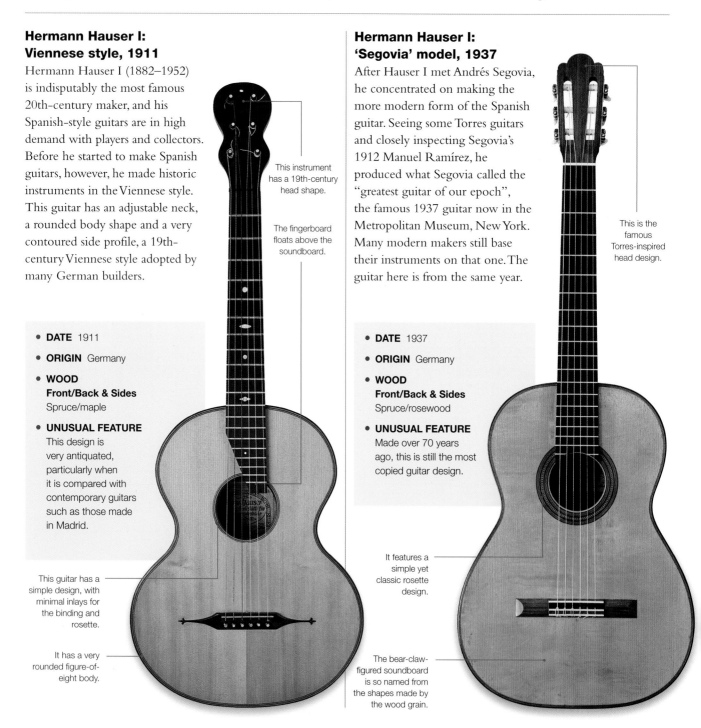

Hermann Hauser I: Viennese style, 1911

Hermann Hauser I (1882–1952) is indisputably the most famous 20th-century maker, and his Spanish-style guitars are in high demand with players and collectors. Before he started to make Spanish guitars, however, he made historic instruments in the Viennese style. This guitar has an adjustable neck, a rounded body shape and a very contoured side profile, a 19th-century Viennese style adopted by many German builders.

This instrument has a 19th-century head shape.

The fingerboard floats above the soundboard.

- **DATE** 1911
- **ORIGIN** Germany
- **WOOD**
  Front/Back & Sides
  Spruce/maple
- **UNUSUAL FEATURE**
  This design is very antiquated, particularly when it is compared with contemporary guitars such as those made in Madrid.

This guitar has a simple design, with minimal inlays for the binding and rosette.

It has a very rounded figure-of-eight body.

Hermann Hauser I: 'Segovia' model, 1937

After Hauser I met Andrés Segovia, he concentrated on making the more modern form of the Spanish guitar. Seeing some Torres guitars and closely inspecting Segovia's 1912 Manuel Ramírez, he produced what Segovia called the "greatest guitar of our epoch", the famous 1937 guitar now in the Metropolitan Museum, New York. Many modern makers still base their instruments on that one. The guitar here is from the same year.

This is the famous Torres-inspired head design.

- **DATE** 1937
- **ORIGIN** Germany
- **WOOD**
  Front/Back & Sides
  Spruce/rosewood
- **UNUSUAL FEATURE**
  Made over 70 years ago, this is still the most copied guitar design.

It features a simple yet classic rosette design.

The bear-claw-figured soundboard is so named from the shapes made by the wood grain.

Hermann Hauser II, 1958

In 1930, after a four-year apprenticeship in a Mittenwald violin-making school, Hermann Hauser II (1911–88) started working in his father's workshop, taking on the business after his father's death in 1952. He went on to make a further 500 guitars, which, rather than French-polishing them, he chose to lacquer. Over time, this results in the appearance of fine, checked lines (known as lacquer checking or crazing), a sure sign that the finish is original, and which is important to the sound. This guitar has a scale length of 646mm (25½in), which some players today prefer.

- **DATE** 1958
- **ORIGIN** Germany
- **WOOD**
  Front/Back & Sides
  Spruce/rosewood
- **UNUSUAL FEATURE**
  This guitar has a lacquer finish rather than the more typical French polish.

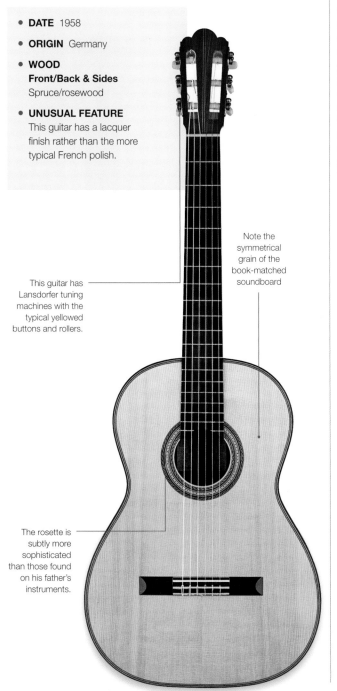

This guitar has Lansdorfer tuning machines with the typical yellowed buttons and rollers.

Note the symmetrical grain of the book-matched soundboard

The rosette is subtly more sophisticated than those found on his father's instruments.

Herman Hauser III, 1988

In 1974, Hermann Hauser III (b. 1958) started making his own guitars in the same workshop as his father. He makes his guitars in batches – and, like a farmer, certain processes are seasonal. His yearly output is usually up to 17 guitars. Besides making guitars in the style of his father and grandfather, Hauser III makes some that are based on those of Miguel Rodríguez, and also a model he dreamt up himself. Unlike his forebears, he also has the luxury of using cedar for his soundboards, as in this example.

- **DATE** 1988
- **ORIGIN** Germany
- **WOOD**
  Front/Back & Sides
  Cedar/rosewood
- **UNUSUAL FEATURE**
  This guitar has a cedar soundboard.

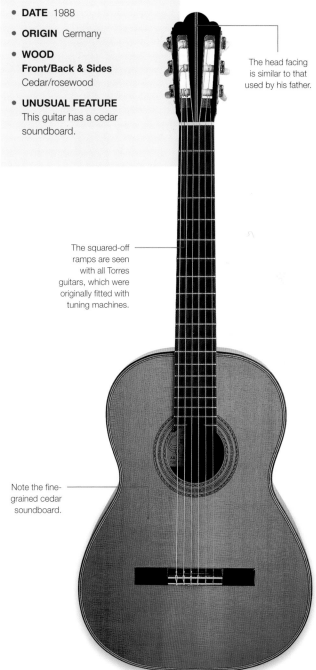

The head facing is similar to that used by his father.

The squared-off ramps are seen with all Torres guitars, which were originally fitted with tuning machines.

Note the fine-grained cedar soundboard.

Mid-20th-century classical guitars

These instruments capture the spirit of the modern Spanish guitar. Here, we see the schools of Madrid (Hernández y Aguado), Barcelona (Fleta) and, although José Romanillos worked in Britain, he now builds in the Andalucian style of Torres. During their careers, John Williams has played Fleta guitars, while Julian Bream favoured guitars by Romanillos, but they have both owned the same guitar by Hernández y Aguado.

Hernández y Aguado, 1963

In guitar making it is rare to find a partnership of two makers working together under the same label. Manuel Hernández (1895–1975) and Victoriano Aguado (1897–1982) met while working for a piano-making firm, Hernández constructing the bodies and Aguado working as a French polisher. However, Aguado was a keen guitarist, and they soon formed a partnership and began to make guitars. Their apprenticeships as piano makers means that their guitars have some unusual features, such as joining the two-piece backs without the usual dividing inlays.

- **DATE** 1963
- **ORIGIN** Madrid, Spain
- **WOOD**
  Front/Back & Sides
  Spruce/rosewood
- **UNUSUAL FEATURE**
  The back is of two halves joined without the usual central inlay.

Ignacio Fleta & Sons, 1974

Making smaller Torres-style guitars was how Ignacio Fleta (1897–1977) started his career. In the 1930s and 1940s he only made one guitar roughly every two years, because his skill in making orchestral and concert instruments was much in demand. He also made some archtop jazz guitars, which combined the traditional f-holes with a round soundhole. By the time this example was made, working with his sons Francisco and Gabriel, Fleta guitars had taken on a distinctive form, incorporating nine fanbraces under the soundboard.

- **DATE** 1974
- **ORIGIN** Barcelona, Spain
- **WOOD**
  Front/Back & Sides
  Cedar/rosewood
- **UNUSUAL FEATURE**
  The bridge has extra decorative bone inlays.

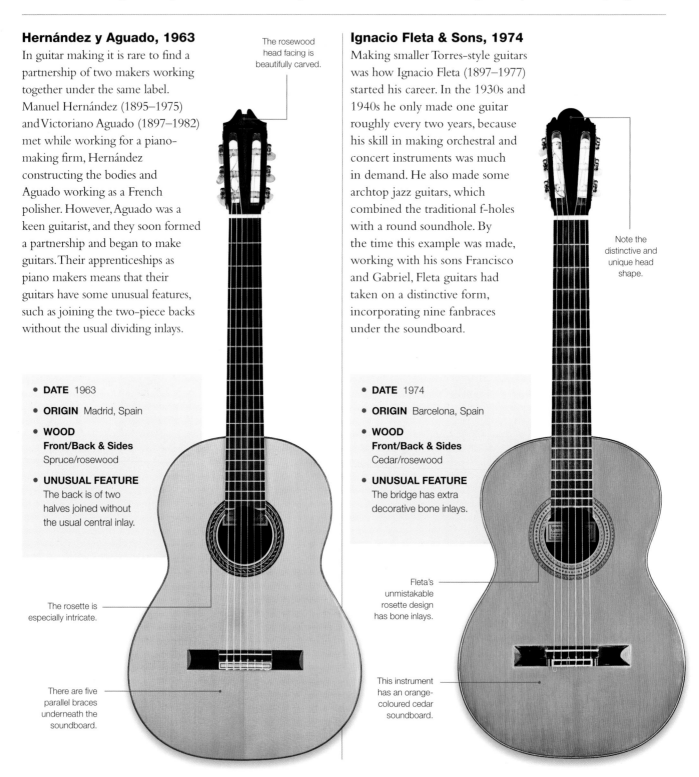

The rosewood head facing is beautifully carved.

Note the distinctive and unique head shape.

The rosette is especially intricate.

There are five parallel braces underneath the soundboard.

Fleta's unmistakable rosette design has bone inlays.

This instrument has an orange-coloured cedar soundboard.

José Romanillos, 1978

In 1967, José Romanillos (b. 1932) moved from Madrid to Britain. Julian Bream started playing his guitars, and they formed a close working relationship. On Romanillos' return to Spain, his son Liam, who had worked alongside his father since 1982, continued the business. Romanillos' legacy is not just his many truly finely crafted concert guitars but also the Spanish-guitar museum he established in Sigüenza, Spain, and the meticulously researched books on the history of musical instruments that he and his wife Marian Harris Winspear have written.

- **DATE** 1978

- **ORIGIN** Dorset, England

- **WOOD**
  Front/Back & Sides
  Spruce/rosewood

- **UNUSUAL FEATURE**
  Romanillos gave his guitars names. This one is called 'La Madreselva' (the Honeysuckle).

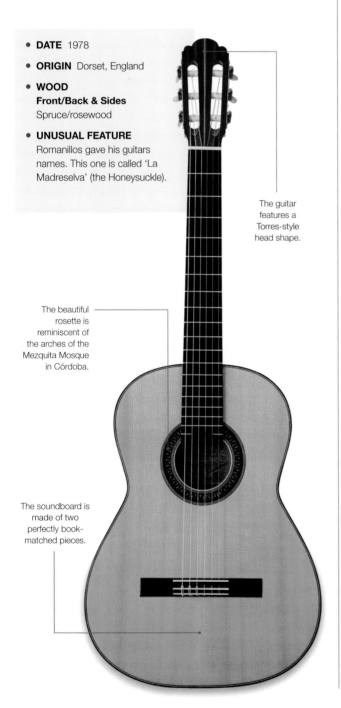

The guitar features a Torres-style head shape.

The beautiful rosette is reminiscent of the arches of the Mezquita Mosque in Córdoba.

The soundboard is made of two perfectly book-matched pieces.

Julian Bream

London-born Julian Bream, OBE (b. 1933) played on lutes and historic guitars as a youth, as well as a Maccaferri harp-guitar, and he made his professional debut at London's Wigmore Hall on a 19th-century Martin 0-28. Soon, however, he required instruments that could cope with the demands of the many compositions written for him by leading 20th-century composers, playing guitars by Edgar Mönch, Hauser, Bouchet, Hernández y Aguado, David Rubio, Romanillos and, later, Kenny Hill and Cohen and Southwell. Obtaining the 1940 Albert and Rose Augustine Hauser guitar rekindled much of his interest in body resonances, as the body resonance of the Hauer was extremely low at E♭, which produces a very profound base to the tone. For much of his later life he has been concerned with the acoustic harmony of what he calls the 'box'. This has resulted in him favouring an E♭ body resonance, even encouraging several guitar makers to construct guitars for him with this characteristic. These include guitar makers Kevin Aram, Brian Cohen and Gary Southwell.

ABOVE: *Julian Bream in concert in 1970, showing his perfect hand positions and posture. He is playing one of the first guitars made for him by José Romanillos – choosing to concertize and record on his guitars during much of the 1970s.*

Late 20th- and early 21st-century classical guitars: part one

It is notable that although Antonio de Torres 'standardized' guitar design over 150 years ago, today's makers still find ways to keep the market interesting, varied and buoyant. The guitars here show this well, offering a choice of woods, an array of soundboard struts allowing for different tones, a range of pitches, an alternative soundhole shape and even a smaller body size.

Masaru Kohno, 1974

Having been taught by Arcángel Fernández, himself a student of Marcelo Barbero, Masuro Kohno (1926–98) set up his company in Tokyo. In 1967 he won gold in the Concours National de Guitare in Belgium, where Ignacio Fleta and Robert Bouchet were on the jury. This guitar is the 'Model 15', a lower-priced Kohno model but still of exceptional quality. The scale length is a large 664mm (26⅛in) (many Japanese guitarists prefer a 645mm/25⅜in scale). The company is now called Sakurai Kohno, run by Kohno's nephew.

- **DATE** 1974
- **ORIGIN** Tokyo, Japan
- **WOOD**
  Front/Back & Sides
  Spruce/rosewood
- **UNUSUAL FEATURE**
  The 664mm (26⅛in) scale length is larger than usual.

The head outline is reminiscent of guitars by Ignacio Fleta.

The scale length of the strings is the same as the José Ramírez 'Segovia' guitars.

The isosceles-trapezium-shaped tie-block is distinctive.

Kenny Hill: FE18, 2009

As a master luthier, Kenny Hill's (b. 1948) 'Signature Series' guitars are of truly exceptional quality. However, he also operates under the name of the Hill Guitar Company, a small operation that produces the 'Performance' and 'Master' series, the latter of which comprises uncannily precise replicas of famous models. This 'Master Series' guitar is a close copy of the 1864 Torres FE18. Hill's version was initially aimed at the younger player, but, because of its tone and volume, many adults have taken it up.

- **DATE** 2009
- **ORIGIN** California, USA
- **WOOD**
  Front/Back & Sides
  Spruce/flamed maple
- **UNUSUAL FEATURE**
  This guitar for younger players compares well with many full-sized models.

The head is a classic Torres design.

The body measures just 438mm (17¼in) long.

The striking green inlays, reserved for Torres' finest models, are replicated in this instrument.

Note the diamond-shaped pearl-and-bone additions to the bridge.

David Whiteman: concert guitar, 2007

Having studied guitar making at the London College of Furniture, David Whiteman (b. 1965) built this instrument to mark his 20th year as a professional maker. The back, sides and headstock are of highly figured satinwood, which is a rare and highly prized tonewood. There are subtle mother-of-pearl embellishments in the rosette and bridge, and delicate hand-crafted purflings adorn the top and headstock. The tuners are hand-made by David Rodgers.

Rohan Lowe, 2008

Self-taught, Rohan Lowe (b. 1962) began guitar making in 1993. Coming from an artistic background, he likes to experiment with the design of the guitar, as this model testifies. To keep the air resonance down, and thus produce a good bass response, the top is well supported using two longitudinal bars, so allowing more of the sounding area than usual the opportunity to vibrate. This soundboard-bracing concept was partly inspired by the 19th-century Parisian maker Etienne Laprévotte.

The headstock is faced with satinwood.

- **DATE** 2007
- **ORIGIN** Sussex, England
- **WOOD**
  Front/Back & Sides
  Spruce/satinwood
- **UNUSUAL FEATURE**
  It is rare to see satinwood used by modern classical guitar makers.

The rosette and bridge have mother-of-pearl inlay.

The circular pearl dots on the bridge complement those in the rosette.

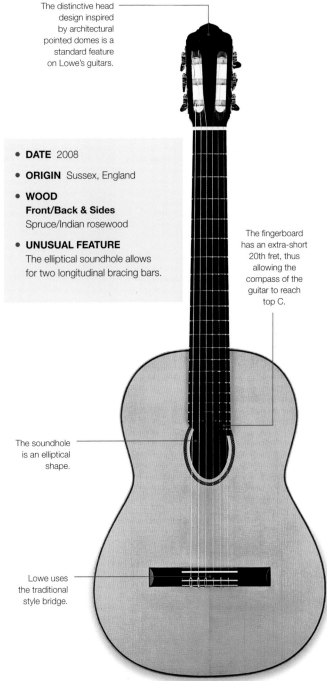

The distinctive head design inspired by architectural pointed domes is a standard feature on Lowe's guitars.

- **DATE** 2008
- **ORIGIN** Sussex, England
- **WOOD**
  Front/Back & Sides
  Spruce/Indian rosewood
- **UNUSUAL FEATURE**
  The elliptical soundhole allows for two longitudinal bracing bars.

The fingerboard has an extra-short 20th fret, thus allowing the compass of the guitar to reach top C.

The soundhole is an elliptical shape.

Lowe uses the traditional style bridge.

Late 20th- and early 21st-century classical guitars: part two

Many makers continue to strive to build the perfect guitar, often driven by the professional player. Sometimes these modifications replicate experiments tried out by earlier makers, but more often than not today's luthiers arrive at these conclusions independently. Here we see some modern guitars in the true sense of the word, including the use of new materials in their construction.

John Gilbert & Son, 1991

Originally, John Gilbert (b. 1922) moved to California to work at Hewlett-Packard, but gave that up to build guitars. His instruments are made with the utmost precision, particularly with regard to tuning – this example has tuning machines designed and made by Gilbert. Instead of a bone saddle, it is fitted with six metal pins. John's profile rose when British guitarist David Russell endorsed his instruments. Towards the end of Gilbert's career, his son Bill worked alongside him.

- **DATE** 1991
- **ORIGIN** California, USA
- **WOOD**
  Front/Back & Sides
  Spruce/rosewood
- **UNUSUAL FEATURE**
  There are six metal pins instead of a saddle.

Greg Smallman & Sons, 2002

Greg Smallman developed a balsawood-and-carbon-fibre-lattice bracing system to make his soundboards thinner and so get more volume. This guitar has a John Pearse-type arm rest to protect the paper-thin edge of the soundboard from the player's arm. The back is carved into a slight arch, providing a stronger structure without the need for back braces. Smallman's sons Damon and Kym now work alongside him.

- **DATE** 2002
- **ORIGIN** Victoria, Australia
- **WOOD**
  Front/Back & Sides
  Cedar/hardwood layers with a rosewood exterior facing
- **UNUSUAL FEATURE**
  There is a lattice soundboard bracing.

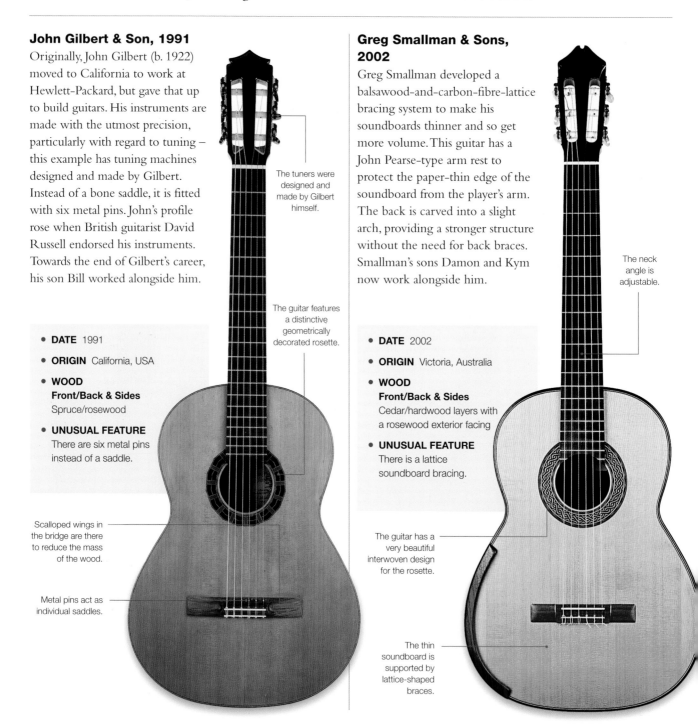

The tuners were designed and made by Gilbert himself.

The guitar features a distinctive geometrically decorated rosette.

Scalloped wings in the bridge are there to reduce the mass of the wood.

Metal pins act as individual saddles.

The neck angle is adjustable.

The guitar has a very beautiful interwoven design for the rosette.

The thin soundboard is supported by lattice-shaped braces.

Martin Woodhouse: 'Brahms' guitar, 2010

The first guitar Martin Woodhouse (b. 1981) made was under David Rubio, and one of Rubio's projects towards the end of his life was the so-called 'Brahms' guitar, which Woodhouse took on. The idea was to build an eight-string guitar – inspired by the 17th-century orpharion – to extend the range so that music by Brahms could be included in the guitarist's repertoire. This guitar has eight individual string lengths ranging between 615–650mm (24¼–25⅝in). The British guitarist Paul Galbraith is known for playing this instrument.

The head accommodates an extra two tuning pegs.

The nut, frets and saddle are all positioned at different angles.

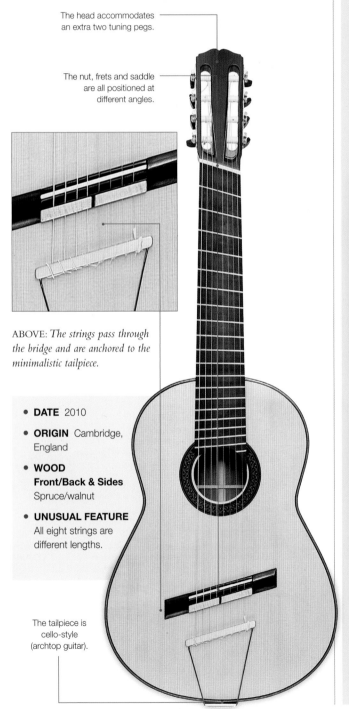

ABOVE: *The strings pass through the bridge and are anchored to the minimalistic tailpiece.*

- **DATE** 2010
- **ORIGIN** Cambridge, England
- **WOOD**
  Front/Back & Sides
  Spruce/walnut
- **UNUSUAL FEATURE**
  All eight strings are different lengths.

The tailpiece is cello-style (archtop guitar).

John Williams

The recording by John Williams (b. 1941) of "Cavatina", the haunting theme tune to *The Deer Hunter*, was a rare occasion when a classical guitarist entered the charts. Williams was first taught by his father Len, the founder of the Spanish Guitar Studios in London, but from the age of 11 he attended masterclasses with Andrés Segovia – Segovia called him 'the prince of the guitar'. He studied piano at the Royal College of Music because they had no guitar department at that time (the guitar was deemed not to be a serious instrument to study) – and by 17 he had made his first recording. Projects have included working with fellow guitarists Julian Bream and Paco Peña, and founding the 1970s classical-rock group Sky with Herbie Flowers. His Australian roots have led to a long friendship with and patronage of his fellow Australian, the guitar maker Greg Smallman. The Grammy award-winning guitarist boasts over 150 recordings credited with his name, and in 2007 he was presented with the Edison lifetime achievement award.

ABOVE: *John Williams in concert, demonstrating his perfect technique. In this photograph, taken during the 1960s, Williams is playing a more traditional-style guitar. In the early part of his career, he favoured guitars by Ignacio Fleta; he also had an instrument by Manuel Hernández and Victoriano Aguado that fellow guitarist Julian Bream had previously owned.*

20th-century flamenco guitars

Although Torres made some cypress models, it was in the 20th century that the light and low-strung flamenco guitar was really defined as a very different instrument from the classical. Some notable flamenco guitar makers were from such cities as Córdoba (Manuel Reyes) and Almería (Gerundino Fernández), but Madrid was the centre for master builders of the flamenco guitar, as seen in these examples.

Viuda de Manuel Ramírez (constructed by Santos Hernández), 1916

This guitar was built in the Manuel Ramírez workshop for his *viuda* (widow) by Santos Hernández (1874–1943) just three months after Ramírez died, and it is one of the earliest instruments that could truly be called a flamenco guitar. Segovia's famous 1912 'Manuel Ramírez' classical guitar, now on display in the Metropolitian Museum, New York, was also constructed by Hernández.

This guitar has a capo fitted, which is used to change the guitar's key to suit an individual singer's voice.

The 'Viuda de Manuel Ramírez' label has Santos Hernández's initials.

- **DATE** 1916
- **ORIGIN** Madrid, Spain
- **WOOD**
  Front/Back & Sides
  Spruce/cypress
- **UNUSUAL FEATURE**
  The *golpeador* protects the spruce soundboard from the player's nails.

This is the original ivory *golpeador*.

Domingo Esteso, 1934

Originally, Domingo Esteso (1882–1937) worked for Manuel Ramírez. After Ramírez's death he worked for Ramírez's widow until moving to his own workshop in 1919, which is still there today. Notice the Ramírez-shaped headstock and the similar use of colours in his rosette to that of the 1916 Viuda de Manuel Ramírez guitar. This guitar is very light, weighing just 1.1kg (2⅖lb), and Esteso kept the weight down further by using wooden tuning pegs as opposed to metal tuning machines.

Wooden tuning pegs are preferred by many traditional flamenco guitarists.

This is the original yellowed bone nut.

- **DATE** 1934
- **ORIGIN** Madrid, Spain
- **WOOD**
  Front/Back & Sides
  Spruce/cypress
- **UNUSUAL FEATURE**
  Unusually for a flamenco instrument, it lacks a protective *golpeador*.

The string-scale length, at 657mm (25⅞in), is a little larger than standard.

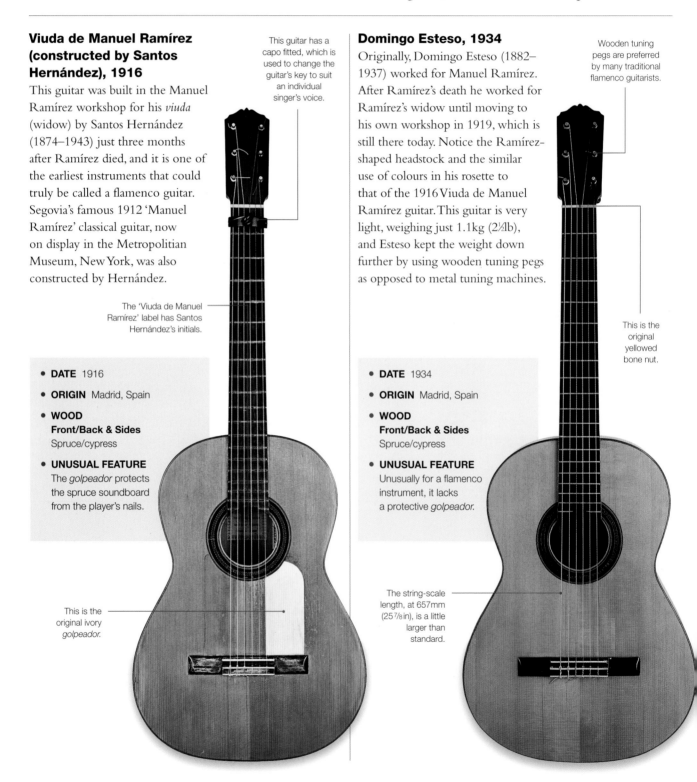

Marcelo Barbero, 1954

Before setting up his own workshop, Marcelo Barbero (1904–56) apprenticed under José Ramírez II. He also worked for a short while for Santos Hernández's widow. Barbero's early guitars have small white or black *golpeadores*, but this one, being a later model, has a double transparent one to protect the bass side of the soundboard from damage caused by the guitarist's thumbnail resting on the sixth string. On the evidence of known guitars, Barbero seems mainly to have made flamenco instruments and only a few classical ones.

Arcángel Fernández, 1958

Having learnt his craft from Marcelo Barbero, Arcángel Fernández (b. 1931) works in the Spanish tradition. Like Santos Hernández and Domingo Esteso, he worked for Barbero's widow after his master's death. In turn, Fernández taught Barbero's son, Marcelo Barbero II. This particular guitar is fitted with tuning machines and has a decorative pearl inlay to the tie-block. These are very subtle 'modern' elements that Fernández has added to the otherwise traditional instrument. This guitar has a 660mm (25⅞in) string-scale length.

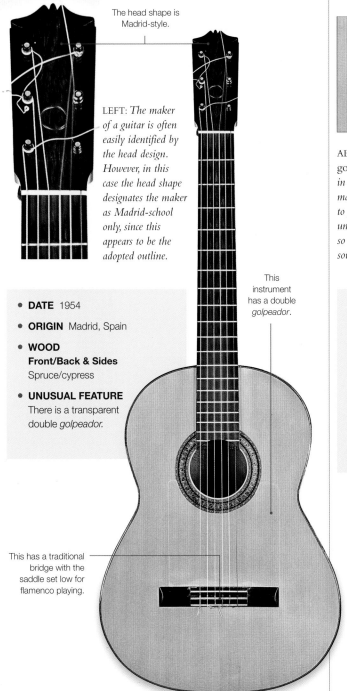

The head shape is Madrid-style.

LEFT: *The maker of a guitar is often easily identified by the head design. However, in this case the head shape designates the maker as Madrid-school only, since this appears to be the adopted outline.*

This instrument has a double *golpeador*.

- **DATE** 1954
- **ORIGIN** Madrid, Spain
- **WOOD**
  Front/Back & Sides
  Spruce/cypress
- **UNUSUAL FEATURE**
  There is a transparent double *golpeador*.

This has a traditional bridge with the saddle set low for flamenco playing.

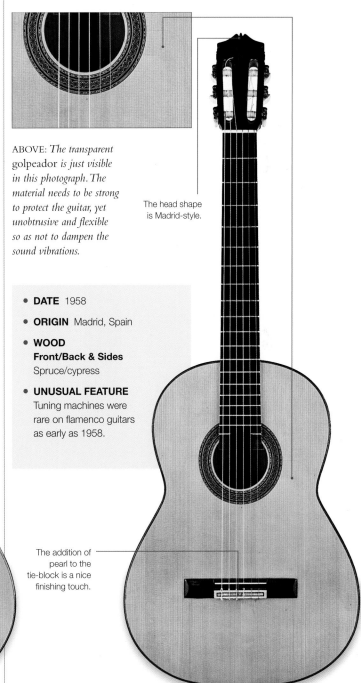

ABOVE: *The transparent golpeador is just visible in this photograph. The material needs to be strong to protect the guitar, yet unobtrusive and flexible so as not to dampen the sound vibrations.*

The head shape is Madrid-style.

- **DATE** 1958
- **ORIGIN** Madrid, Spain
- **WOOD**
  Front/Back & Sides
  Spruce/cypress
- **UNUSUAL FEATURE**
  Tuning machines were rare on flamenco guitars as early as 1958.

The addition of pearl to the tie-block is a nice finishing touch.

Late 20th- and early 21st-century flamenco guitars

Flamenco is a traditionalist art form, and what is required of the flamenco guitar has changed very little over time. Hence, guitar makers who like to add something of their own personality to the instrument usually do so in subtle ways – the unique head shapes of Manuel Reyes, Gerundino Fernández and the Conde Hermanos, for example, or Pablo Requena's pearl-inlaid rosettes.

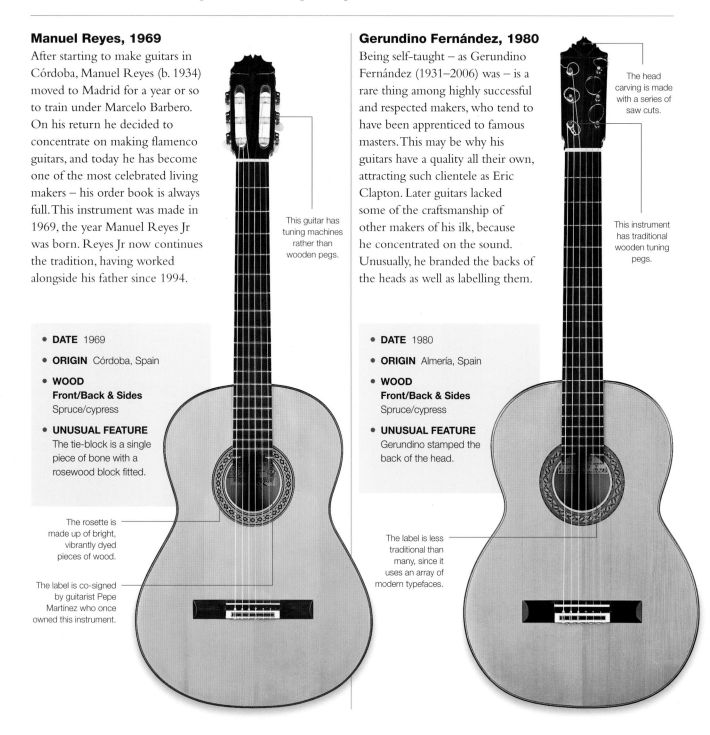

Manuel Reyes, 1969

After starting to make guitars in Córdoba, Manuel Reyes (b. 1934) moved to Madrid for a year or so to train under Marcelo Barbero. On his return he decided to concentrate on making flamenco guitars, and today he has become one of the most celebrated living makers – his order book is always full. This instrument was made in 1969, the year Manuel Reyes Jr was born. Reyes Jr now continues the tradition, having worked alongside his father since 1994.

- **DATE** 1969
- **ORIGIN** Córdoba, Spain
- **WOOD**
  Front/Back & Sides
  Spruce/cypress
- **UNUSUAL FEATURE**
  The tie-block is a single piece of bone with a rosewood block fitted.

This guitar has tuning machines rather than wooden pegs.

The rosette is made up of bright, vibrantly dyed pieces of wood.

The label is co-signed by guitarist Pepe Martínez who once owned this instrument.

Gerundino Fernández, 1980

Being self-taught – as Gerundino Fernández (1931–2006) was – is a rare thing among highly successful and respected makers, who tend to have been apprenticed to famous masters. This may be why his guitars have a quality all their own, attracting such clientele as Eric Clapton. Later guitars lacked some of the craftsmanship of other makers of his ilk, because he concentrated on the sound. Unusually, he branded the backs of the heads as well as labelling them.

- **DATE** 1980
- **ORIGIN** Almería, Spain
- **WOOD**
  Front/Back & Sides
  Spruce/cypress
- **UNUSUAL FEATURE**
  Gerundino stamped the back of the head.

The head carving is made with a series of saw cuts.

This instrument has traditional wooden tuning pegs.

The label is less traditional than many, since it uses an array of modern typefaces.

Conde Hermanos: A26, 2007

The Conde brothers were apprenticed to their uncle, Domingo Esteso, and after his death in 1937 worked for his widow under the label 'Viuda y sobrinos de Esteso' until her death in 1958. They then changed their label to 'Sobrinos de Domingo Esteso', later 'Hermanos Conde' and finally 'Conde Hermanos'. All this time they were operating from their uncle's workshop at Gravina, 7, Madrid. Today, guitars are still being sold from this address by Viuda de Faustino Conde. They are most famous for their flamenco guitars, including *negra* (rosewood) models, and they are instantly recognizable by the head shape and orange polish.

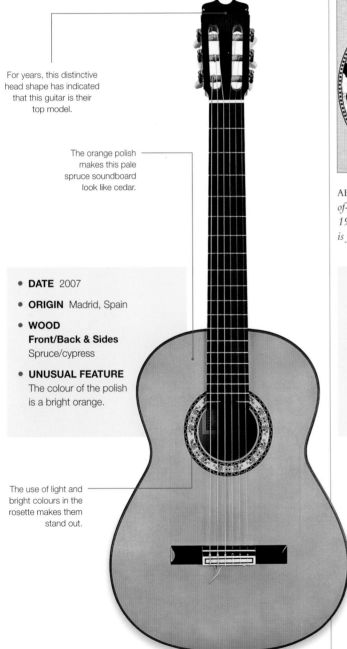

For years, this distinctive head shape has indicated that this guitar is their top model.

The orange polish makes this pale spruce soundboard look like cedar.

- **DATE** 2007
- **ORIGIN** Madrid, Spain
- **WOOD**
  Front/Back & Sides
  Spruce/cypress
- **UNUSUAL FEATURE**
  The colour of the polish is a bright orange.

The use of light and bright colours in the rosette makes them stand out.

Pablo Requena, 2004

A Spanish luthier based in England, Pablo Requena (b. 1968) builds guitars inspired by makers such as Santos Hernández and Marcelo Barbero. This example has a German spruce top and cypress back and sides – a combination of woods favoured for flamenco guitars – and is built in a traditional way, with very light bracing and timbers to produce a rich, percussive sound. Requena has made classical guitars with equal success, and players include Paul Gregory and John Mills – Island Records even ordered one of Requena's parlour guitars for singer Amy Winehouse.

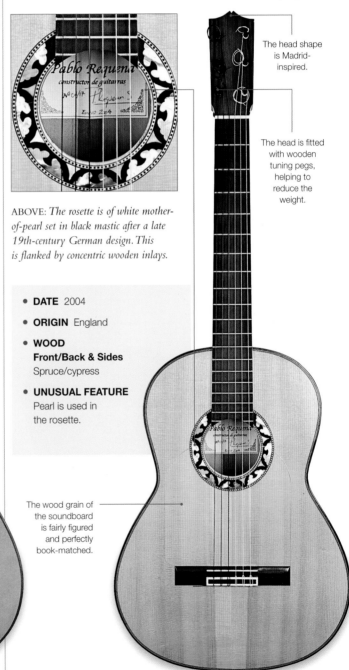

ABOVE: *The rosette is of white mother-of-pearl set in black mastic after a late 19th-century German design. This is flanked by concentric wooden inlays.*

The head shape is Madrid-inspired.

The head is fitted with wooden tuning pegs, helping to reduce the weight.

- **DATE** 2004
- **ORIGIN** England
- **WOOD**
  Front/Back & Sides
  Spruce/cypress
- **UNUSUAL FEATURE**
  Pearl is used in the rosette.

The wood grain of the soundboard is fairly figured and perfectly book-matched.

20th-century flat-top steel-string guitars: Gibson

Perhaps more famous for their superior archtop instruments, Gibson's flat-tops were not so highly regarded. However, their high-end pre-war flat-tops were very good indeed. The development of their body size can be seen in these rare examples, starting with Robert Johnson's small-bodied L-1, through the deeper-bodied 'Nick Lucas' to the larger Dreadnought type, concluding with the enormous Jumbos.

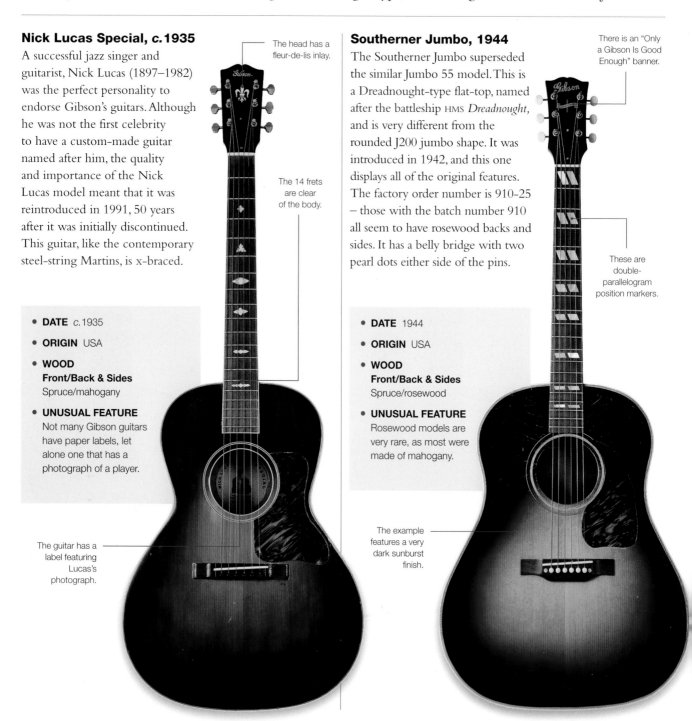

Nick Lucas Special, c.1935

A successful jazz singer and guitarist, Nick Lucas (1897–1982) was the perfect personality to endorse Gibson's guitars. Although he was not the first celebrity to have a custom-made guitar named after him, the quality and importance of the Nick Lucas model meant that it was reintroduced in 1991, 50 years after it was initially discontinued. This guitar, like the contemporary steel-string Martins, is x-braced.

The head has a fleur-de-lis inlay.

The 14 frets are clear of the body.

- **DATE** *c.*1935
- **ORIGIN** USA
- **WOOD**
  Front/Back & Sides
  Spruce/mahogany
- **UNUSUAL FEATURE**
  Not many Gibson guitars have paper labels, let alone one that has a photograph of a player.

The guitar has a label featuring Lucas's photograph.

Southerner Jumbo, 1944

The Southerner Jumbo superseded the similar Jumbo 55 model. This is a Dreadnought-type flat-top, named after the battleship HMS *Dreadnought,* and is very different from the rounded J200 jumbo shape. It was introduced in 1942, and this one displays all of the original features. The factory order number is 910-25 – those with the batch number 910 all seem to have rosewood backs and sides. It has a belly bridge with two pearl dots either side of the pins.

There is an "Only a Gibson Is Good Enough" banner.

These are double-parallelogram position markers.

- **DATE** 1944
- **ORIGIN** USA
- **WOOD**
  Front/Back & Sides
  Spruce/rosewood
- **UNUSUAL FEATURE**
  Rosewood models are very rare, as most were made of mahogany.

The example features a very dark sunburst finish.

J200, 1952

The SJ200 Super Jumbo – not to be confused with the very different Southerner Jumbo (SJ) released a few years later – was introduced late in 1937. Early models were of rosewood with a dark sunburst finish, but by the late 1940s it was a maple guitar, and this is a rare blonde-finish maple example. The J200 has a large rounded 'jumbo' body, which, with the unusual 'moustache' bridge, makes it a very distinctive guitar.

- **DATE** 1952

- **ORIGIN** USA

- **WOOD**
  Front/Back & Sides
  Spruce/maple

- **UNUSUAL FEATURE**
  Whether cows' horns or moustaches inspired the bridge design is unclear, but it is unusual either way.

The plastic buttons are tulip-shaped.

It has 'cloud' inlays.

The scratchplate has a flower motif.

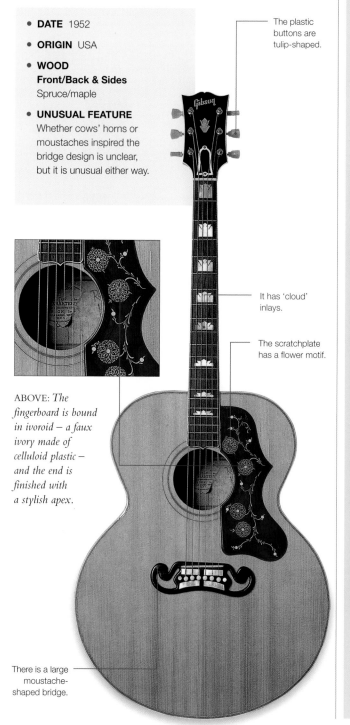

ABOVE: *The fingerboard is bound in ivoroid – a faux ivory made of celluloid plastic – and the end is finished with a stylish apex.*

There is a large moustache-shaped bridge.

Robert Johnson

The term 'legend' is over-used in many discussions of guitar players, but Robert Johnson (1911-38) is one of the figures who genuinely merits the term. The influence of his few recordings on generations of blues musicians can hardly be over-stated: Eric Clapton has called him 'the most important blues singer that ever lived'. Few real facts are known about Johnson's life beyond the most basic biographical details; his entire recorded output was captured in a total of just five days in the recording studio. He seems to have been active as a professional performer for roughly the last eight years of his short life; an unexplained sudden improvement in his guitar ability during this time may have contributed to the myth which subsequently became as powerful as his musical legacy: that he met the Devil at a crossroads at midnight and sold his soul in return for mastery of the guitar. Johnson may have knowingly encouraged the myth by writing songs such as 'Crossroad Blues' and 'Hellhound on my Trail'.

ABOVE: *Legendary American blues singer-songwriter and guitarist Robert Johnson (1911–38), left, with fellow blues musician Johnny Shines (1915–92), c.1935. This image is one of only three known photographs of Johnson which all show how long his 'guitar-playing' fingers were.*

20th-century flat-top steel-string guitars: C. F. Martin & Co., part one

Frank Henry Martin (1866–1948) was head of C. F. Martin & Co. guitar production when it really took off. During his tenure, the company made some of its finest x-braced guitars. The model numbers were in two parts: first by size, then by what Martin called the 'style'. As a general rule, the higher the number, the higher the style – but not always; for example, the 1-27 was more expensive than the 1-28.

00-42, 1902

In 1902, the 00-42 model was the most expensive guitar Martin offered and had the largest body, roughly the size of a standard classical guitar. Having abalone inlays to the soundboard, around the fingerboard and in the rosette, it was the forerunner of the famous 45, although the lack of any inlays to the back and sides marks it out from the 45. The body as well as the fingerboard binding, the bridge and the tuning pegs are all ivory. It was made as a gut-string instrument.

The tuning pegs are made of ivory.

It has 'Snowflake' abalone position markers.

- **DATE** 1902
- **ORIGIN** Pennsylvania, USA
- **WOOD**
  Front/Back & Sides
  Spruce/rosewood
- **UNUSUAL FEATURE**
  There is a lining of self-resinous lignum vitae wood inside the peg hole, which lubricates the action of the ivory friction tuning pegs.

The pyramid bridge is so called because of the shapes of the bridge extensions.

0-28, 1915

This is a classic fingerpicker's guitar. At this time, the 28 style used body trimmings of inlaid wood, imported from Germany, resembling a continuous herringbone design. All Martin guitars up to this point were made for gut strings. This guitar has a slotted headstock with mechanical tuning machines, and just a few years later they would become useful following the introduction of the steel-string Hawaiian models.

The slotted headstock has German-made tuning machines (earlier models often had French ones).

This guitar features ivory bindings, but just two years later Martin started to use celluloid.

- **DATE** 1915
- **ORIGIN** Pennsylvania, USA
- **WOOD**
  Front/Back & Sides
  Spruce/rosewood
- **UNUSUAL FEATURE**
  Martin traditionally did not use paper labels. Instead, the company chose to hot-iron-brand its guitars.

It has the famous Adirondack spruce soundboard.

OM-28, 1930

This guitar has the same style number as the 0-28, but it couldn't be more different: the neck joins the body at the 14th, not the 12th, fret like most gut-string guitars; it has an 'advanced' x-bracing capable of supporting the soundboard against the extra tension of steel strings; and it is fitted with banjo tuners. By the late 1920s, all non-Spanish-style Martin guitars were fitted with steel strings as standard. The size designation OM stood for 'Orchestra Model' and was specifically designed to compete in volume with the banjo orchestras that were popular in the 1930s.

These are banjo tuners.

- **DATE** 1930
- **ORIGIN** Pennsylvania, USA
- **WOOD**
  Front/Back & Sides
  Spruce/rosewood
- **UNUSUAL FEATURE**
  Although this guitar was made for steel strings it still has the archaic pyramid bridge.

The neck joins the body at the 14th fret.

The style 28 herringbone inlay is used on the body.

It is fitted with a fake-tortoiseshell scratchplate to protect the soft spruce soundboard from wear and tear.

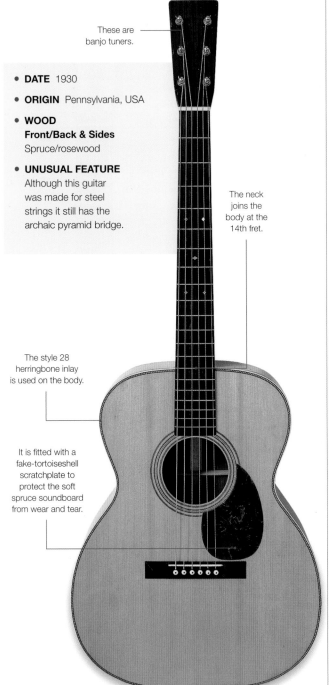

D-18: 'Elvis guitar', 1942

The D-18 was one of Martin's cheaper models, although pre-war versions are much sought after for their volume and sustain. This example was bought second-hand by the young country-music-inspired Elvis Presley – you can still see 'ELVI' on the soundboard. By now Martin's steel-string guitars had mechanical tuning machines and a wider 'belly' bridge, which was less likely to split than the older-style pyramid ones. There is much wear to the top and back caused by Presley's chunky jewellery and belt buckles.

It has metal mechanical tuners.

- **DATE** 1942
- **ORIGIN** Pennsylvania, USA
- **WOOD**
  Front/Back & Sides
  Spruce/mahogany
- **UNUSUAL FEATURE**
  Presley's name is attached to the soundboard – 'ELVI' (missing the 'S').

The large D body is named after the enormous battleship HMS *Dreadnought*, a byword for anything big.

LEFT: *The 'S' in 'ELVIS' has fallen off, probably due to some over-zealous strumming on the part of Presley.*

The belly bridge has replaced the old pyramid bridge.

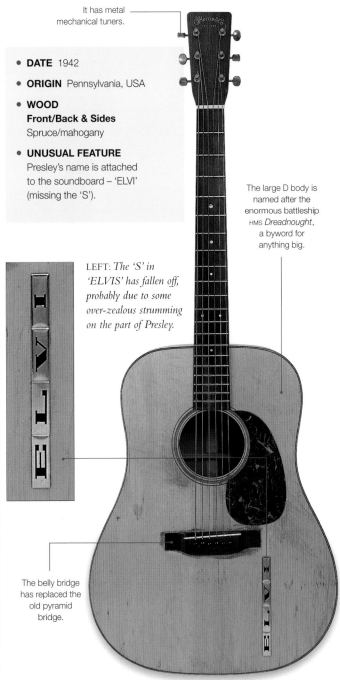

20th-century flat-top steel-string guitars: C. F. Martin & Co., part two

The Martin Guitar Company was never content with just producing best-sellers. As a successful business, it would have been so easy to sit back and just count the money. As with most artisans, the creative side often takes over, and the ultimate goal becomes to produce the perfect instrument. The examples here, however, were all produced to meet individual requirements.

'America', 1906

This guitar – basically an 0-28 with two bodies – designed by Daniel Schuyler and made by Martin, is one of only two known examples. The purpose of the second back seems to have been to stop the back vibrations being dampened by the player, thus giving the instrument more projection. This is similar in principle to the René Lacôte design for Dionisio Aguado from *c.*1830, which went one step further by putting a soundhole in the rear.

- **DATE** 1906
- **ORIGIN** Pennsylvania, USA
- **WOOD**
  Front/Back & Sides
  Spruce/rosewood
- **UNUSUAL FEATURE**
  This guitar has two bodies that are perfectly constructed.

The instrument has two backs.

This is a unique bridge.

N-20, 1968

This is the famous 'Willy Nelson' model. The N-20 was not actually made for Nelson, but he is associated with this guitar because he plays one – which is instantly identifiable because of the large hole worn through the soundboard and through which you can see one of the fanbraces. Since the advent of steel-string guitars, Martin has continued to make gut- and, later, nylon-string models but, apart from the N-20, these have been overshadowed by steel-string instruments.

- **DATE** 1968
- **ORIGIN** Pennsylvania, USA
- **WOOD**
  Front/Back & Sides
  Spruce/rosewood
- **UNUSUAL FEATURE**
  This is the most talked-about Spanish classical guitar Martin ever made.

It is equipped with steel strings.

Note the Madrid-style head shape.

There is a Spanish-style rosette.

The bridge has an unusual round-ended extension.

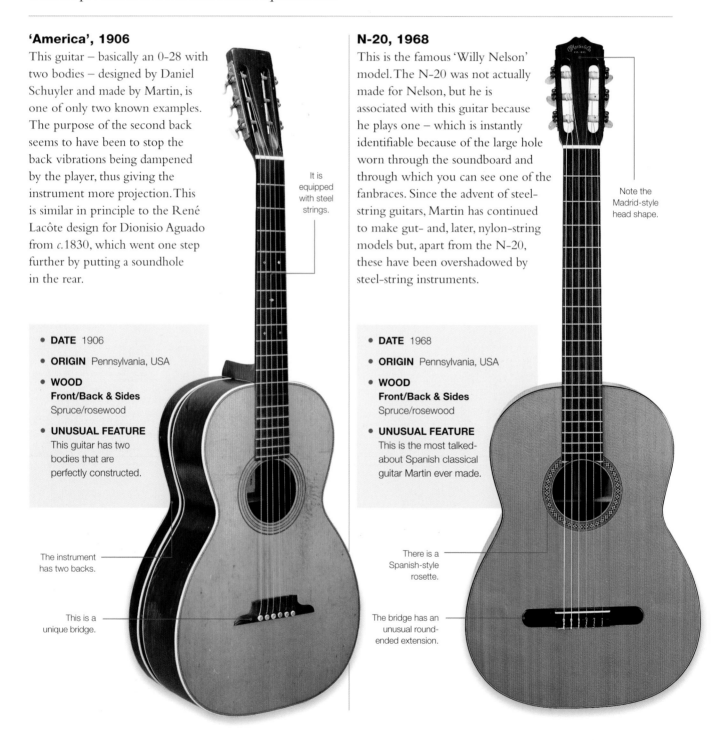

One-millionth guitar, 2004

Martin made this to commemorate its one-millionth guitar. Although the company did not use serial numbers until 1898, it had kept order books from the beginning so could estimate the number of guitars made up to that point. So, starting at number 8,000, 106 years later it reached the million. This guitar is covered with inlays, including depictions of two cherubs 'crowning' one of the earliest Martin designs and an American eagle in flight. Not to waste any potential opportunity for decoration, even the soundhole is 'closed' in a lavish design.

ABOVE: *Detail of the inlays which shows the lute-like rose. The whole guitar is garnished with 141 gemstones, including 65 diamonds, emeralds, fossilized ivory, copper, silver, and yellow and white gold.*

- **DATE** 2004

- **ORIGIN** Pennsylvania, USA

- **WOOD**
  Front/Back & Sides
  Spruce/rosewood

- **UNUSUAL FEATURE**
  The rose is a lute-type and delicately carved.

An eagle, the symbol of America, is used as decoration.

Even the rosewood body is lavishly inlaid with abalone.

A backpacker in space, 1994

As we have seen, travel guitars are nothing new. However, Martin managed to bring simplicity to its natural conclusion with this little portable instrument. To reduce the weight, there is no heavy truss-rod installed, so it comes with either low-tension steel or nylon strings. Another consideration is low cost, which enabled Martin to also sell mandolin and ukulele versions that would otherwise have been superfluous, since standard versions of these instruments are already small. It did this by outsourcing production to Mexico and not adding any of the famous Martin trimmings. Although the guitar is perfectly audible, it comes with a bridge-fitted transducer, enabling it to be amplified. Its portability has meant that it has been seen in places where carrying extra luggage is an issue – such as on an expedition to the South Pole and a mission into space.

ABOVE: *Pierre Thuot playing a c.1994 Martin Backpacker on the space shuttle Columbia. In C. F. Martin I's time it would have taken more than 90 days to travel around the world. He could never have imagined that 150 years later one of his company's guitars would be transported on the same trip in just 90 minutes.*

Among other things, the scratchplate decoration features the soundboard of a Dreadnought guitar, showing the internal bracing and an array of guitar-making tools.

It has metal bridge pins.

20th-century flat-top steel-string guitars: North American

Giving the consumer a wide choice of guitars helps keep instrument makers in business, and here we see four very different acoustic guitars: one small, one with 12 strings, one with a cutaway and one fitted with pickups and played left-handed. Although the Washburn parlour guitar dates from the 1920s, it is so popular again today that many companies are reissuing the smaller old-style instruments.

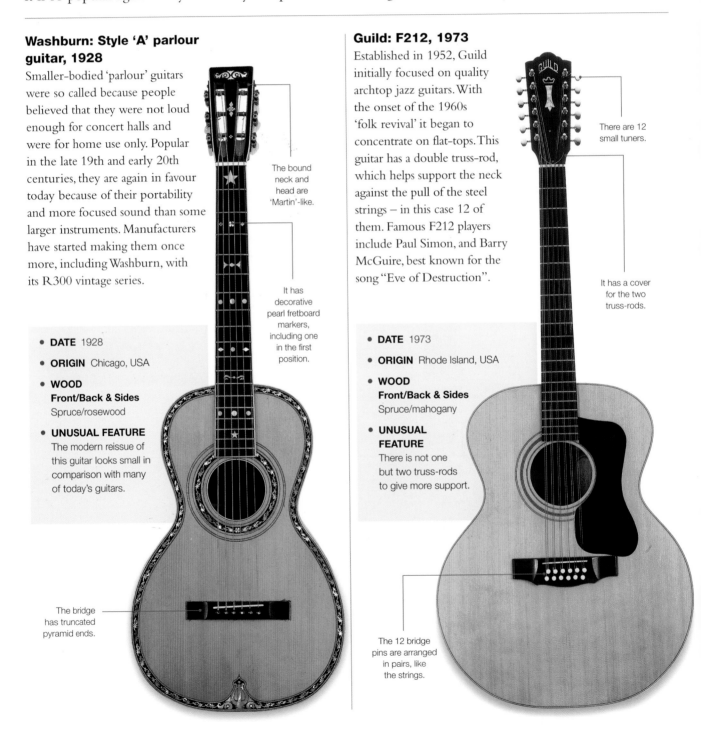

Washburn: Style 'A' parlour guitar, 1928

Smaller-bodied 'parlour' guitars were so called because people believed that they were not loud enough for concert halls and were for home use only. Popular in the late 19th and early 20th centuries, they are again in favour today because of their portability and more focused sound than some larger instruments. Manufacturers have started making them once more, including Washburn, with its R300 vintage series.

- **DATE** 1928

- **ORIGIN** Chicago, USA

- **WOOD**
  Front/Back & Sides
  Spruce/rosewood

- **UNUSUAL FEATURE**
  The modern reissue of this guitar looks small in comparison with many of today's guitars.

The bound neck and head are 'Martin'-like.

It has decorative pearl fretboard markers, including one in the first position.

The bridge has truncated pyramid ends.

Guild: F212, 1973

Established in 1952, Guild initially focused on quality archtop jazz guitars. With the onset of the 1960s 'folk revival' it began to concentrate on flat-tops. This guitar has a double truss-rod, which helps support the neck against the pull of the steel strings – in this case 12 of them. Famous F212 players include Paul Simon, and Barry McGuire, best known for the song "Eve of Destruction".

- **DATE** 1973

- **ORIGIN** Rhode Island, USA

- **WOOD**
  Front/Back & Sides
  Spruce/mahogany

- **UNUSUAL FEATURE**
  There is not one but two truss-rods to give more support.

There are 12 small tuners.

It has a cover for the two truss-rods.

The 12 bridge pins are arranged in pairs, like the strings.

Larrivée: C10, 1989

Canadian maker Jean Larrivée apprenticed under Edger Mönch, the luthier who made Julian Bream's first concert nylon-string instruments. The C10 is one of Larrivée's top models. Famous for their exquisite inlays, this one includes a seahorse to the headstock and a sequence of a bird in motion inlaid to the fingerboard. It has a Florentine cutaway, designed for easier access to the higher register, and is factory-fitted with a clear scratchplate.

- **DATE** 1989
- **ORIGIN** Vancouver, Canada
- **WOOD**
  Front/Back & Sides
  Spruce/rosewood
- **UNUSUAL FEATURE**
  The guitar has a pointed Florentine cutaway.

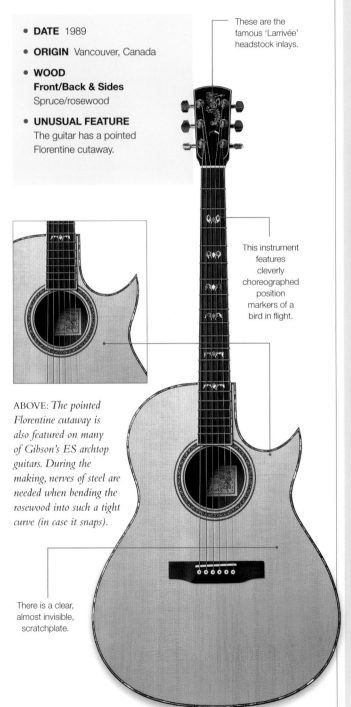

These are the famous 'Larrivée' headstock inlays.

This instrument features cleverly choreographed position markers of a bird in flight.

ABOVE: *The pointed Florentine cutaway is also featured on many of Gibson's ES archtop guitars. During the making, nerves of steel are needed when bending the rosewood into such a tight curve (in case it snaps).*

There is a clear, almost invisible, scratchplate.

Kurt Cobain

Best known as the lead singer and guitarist of the grunge band Nirvana, Kurt Cobain (1967–94) was a southpaw, but he ignored left-handed guitars and, like Jimi Hendrix, chose to play right-handed models upside down and reverse-strung – as here with this *c.*1958 Martin D-18E that he is playing on an *MTV Unplugged* show. The D-18 was the largest guitar Martin produced in the 1950s, designed to be loud. However, it was not loud enough to compete with electric instruments, so Martin released the D-18E, which came with two factory-fitted pickups. On this example, Cobain added a third pickup, bending the MTV's 'unplugged rules' by playing it through his Fender Twin Reverb amp. The guitar has three rotary controls and a pickup selector. As with all D-18 models it has a mahogany body with a spruce soundboard. The scratchplate on this guitar is an unusual shape in order to accommodate the large pickup surrounds.

ABOVE: *This photograph of Kurt Cobain is taken from Nirvana's appearance on the TV show* MTV Unplugged *which took place on 18 November 1993 in New York. A live album of material from this acoustic set was posthumously released following his suicide, which occurred just five months later. He is seen here playing a modified 'workhorse' Martin D-18E.*

20th- and 21st-century flat-top steel-string guitars: North American

Gibson, Fender and Martin are the undisputed leaders in the US acoustic-guitar business. However, Taylor, Santa Cruz, Ovation and Collings have all attracted big names, with the likes of Keith Richards, Pete Townshend, Eric Clapton, Emmylou Harris, Andy Summers, David Crosby, Joni Mitchell, Glen Campbell, Lou Reed, John Fogerty and Joan Baez all playing one of these brands at certain points in their careers.

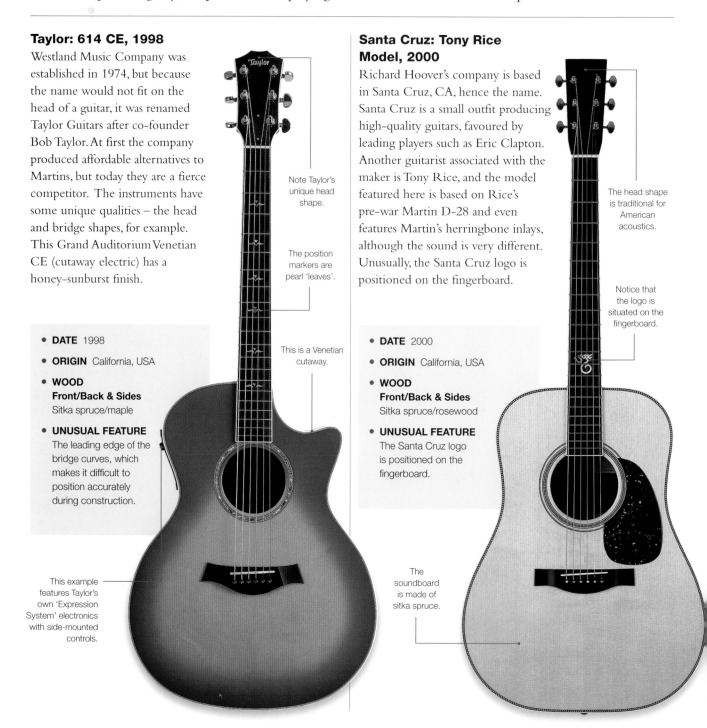

Taylor: 614 CE, 1998

Westland Music Company was established in 1974, but because the name would not fit on the head of a guitar, it was renamed Taylor Guitars after co-founder Bob Taylor. At first the company produced affordable alternatives to Martins, but today they are a fierce competitor. The instruments have some unique qualities – the head and bridge shapes, for example. This Grand Auditorium Venetian CE (cutaway electric) has a honey-sunburst finish.

Note Taylor's unique head shape.

The position markers are pearl 'leaves'.

This is a Venetian cutaway.

- **DATE** 1998
- **ORIGIN** California, USA
- **WOOD**
  Front/Back & Sides
  Sitka spruce/maple
- **UNUSUAL FEATURE**
  The leading edge of the bridge curves, which makes it difficult to position accurately during construction.

This example features Taylor's own 'Expression System' electronics with side-mounted controls.

Santa Cruz: Tony Rice Model, 2000

Richard Hoover's company is based in Santa Cruz, CA, hence the name. Santa Cruz is a small outfit producing high-quality guitars, favoured by leading players such as Eric Clapton. Another guitarist associated with the maker is Tony Rice, and the model featured here is based on Rice's pre-war Martin D-28 and even features Martin's herringbone inlays, although the sound is very different. Unusually, the Santa Cruz logo is positioned on the fingerboard.

The head shape is traditional for American acoustics.

Notice that the logo is situated on the fingerboard.

- **DATE** 2000
- **ORIGIN** California, USA
- **WOOD**
  Front/Back & Sides
  Sitka spruce/rosewood
- **UNUSUAL FEATURE**
  The Santa Cruz logo is positioned on the fingerboard.

The soundboard is made of sitka spruce.

Ovation: Custom Legend, 2006

Charles Kaman, the founder of Ovation guitars, trained as an aeronautical engineer, specializing in helicopter design. He applied his engineering background to guitars, and his first radical designs appeared in 1966. Even the materials were revolutionary – the use of fibreglass in the construction of the bowl-shaped back, for example. The Custom Legend is a high-end model, with its five-piece mahogany-and-maple neck, abalone inlays and gold-plated tuners.

Collings: D2H Koa/Koa, 2009

Bill Collings operates his guitar- and mandolin-making business in Austin, Texas. This Dreadnought model is not only designed for vocal accompaniment, but is also popular with bluegrass flatpickers who need to be heard alongside the louder banjos and fiddles. The D2H model has the decorative elements of the Martin D-28 and D-45 rolled into one, namely the herringbone trim and the abalone 'torch' inlays. This guitar has the added luxury of having not only the back and sides made of Hawaiian koa wood but also the front.

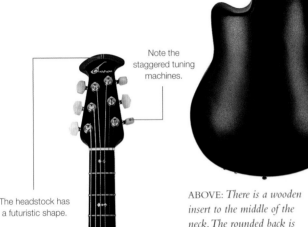

Note the staggered tuning machines.

The headstock has a futuristic shape.

The pro-studio controls are on the side.

ABOVE: *There is a wooden insert to the middle of the neck. The rounded back is very pronounced.*

- **DATE** 2006
- **ORIGIN** Connecticut, USA
- **WOOD**
  Front/Back & Sides
  Spruce/lyrachord (fibreglass)
- **UNUSUAL FEATURE**
  The back is made of a non-wooden material.

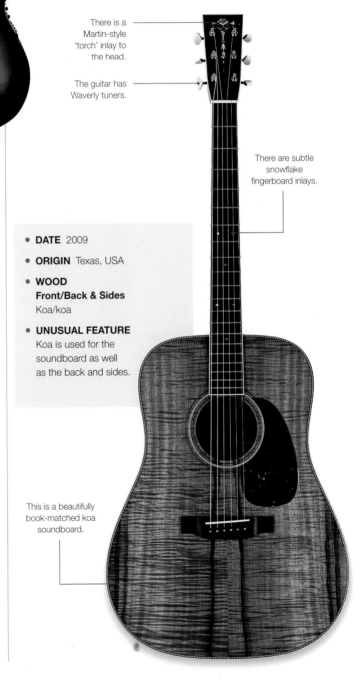

There is a Martin-style 'torch' inlay to the head.

The guitar has Waverly tuners.

There are subtle snowflake fingerboard inlays.

This is a beautifully book-matched koa soundboard.

- **DATE** 2009
- **ORIGIN** Texas, USA
- **WOOD**
  Front/Back & Sides
  Koa/koa
- **UNUSUAL FEATURE**
  Koa is used for the soundboard as well as the back and sides.

20th- and 21st-century flat-top steel-string guitars: European

Many European makers have had their share of what is often considered to be the American guitar market. Some of them have broken away from the much-copied 'jumbo' and Dreadnought designs, each developing their own bracing systems and giving their instruments their own unique sound. Often, smaller outfits will build guitars to a player's individual requirements.

Levin: Goliath, 1964

Herman Carlson Levin's (1864–1948) company existed for around 80 years – even being owned by C. F. Martin at one stage – and in that time produced over 500,000 instruments, making it the largest manufacturer in Scandinavia. The Goliath was so called because of its size and, according to the company's adverts, it was 'designed for accompanying'. There was also the Super Goliath, which was slightly more expensive because better-quality woods were used.

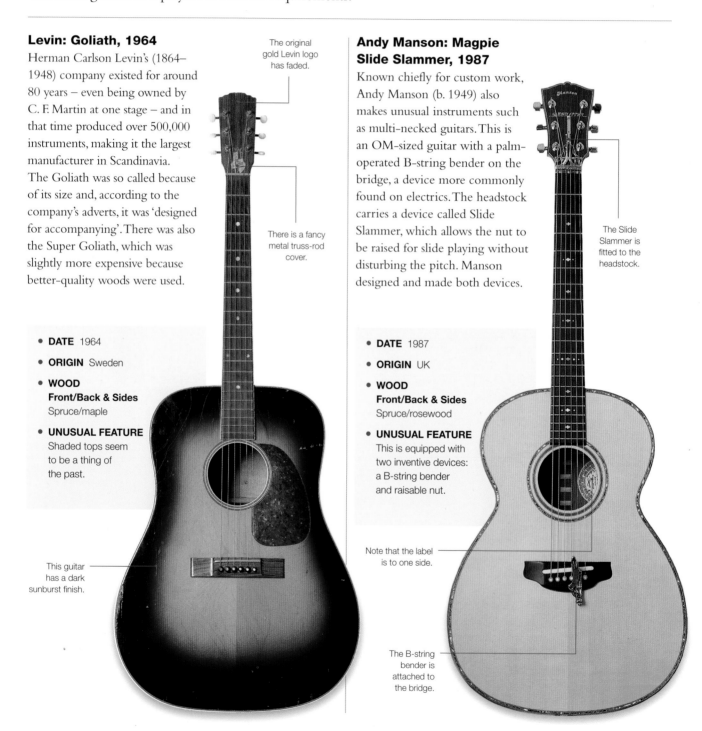

The original gold Levin logo has faded.

There is a fancy metal truss-rod cover.

This guitar has a dark sunburst finish.

- **DATE** 1964
- **ORIGIN** Sweden
- **WOOD**
  Front/Back & Sides
  Spruce/maple
- **UNUSUAL FEATURE**
  Shaded tops seem to be a thing of the past.

Andy Manson: Magpie Slide Slammer, 1987

Known chiefly for custom work, Andy Manson (b. 1949) also makes unusual instruments such as multi-necked guitars. This is an OM-sized guitar with a palm-operated B-string bender on the bridge, a device more commonly found on electrics. The headstock carries a device called Slide Slammer, which allows the nut to be raised for slide playing without disturbing the pitch. Manson designed and made both devices.

The Slide Slammer is fitted to the headstock.

Note that the label is to one side.

The B-string bender is attached to the bridge.

- **DATE** 1987
- **ORIGIN** UK
- **WOOD**
  Front/Back & Sides
  Spruce/rosewood
- **UNUSUAL FEATURE**
  This is equipped with two inventive devices: a B-string bender and raisable nut.

George Lowden: Richard Thompson Model, 2002

George Lowden (b. 1951) started making guitars professionally in 1973. Being self-taught, he did his own experimenting and came up with his famous A-frame bracing with 'dolphin'-shaped profiles. Based in Northern Ireland, his guitars have at times been mass-produced outside of the country, but are now made by a small team of people there. This guitar, one of Lowden's 'Signature Models', was designed with some input from Richard Thompson, after whom it was named. The woods chosen are beautifully figured, and the head is faced (front and back) with the same wood as the back and sides.

- **DATE** 2002
- **ORIGIN** Northern Ireland
- **WOOD**
  Front/Back & Sides
  Cedar/ziricote
- **UNUSUAL FEATURE**
  Ziricote is used on the front and back of the head as well as the back and sides of the soundbox.

The body is f-shaped and mid-sized.

The cutaway is a rounded shape.

For intonation purposes, the saddle is of two separate pieces of bone.

Fylde: Custom-built 'Harlequin', c.2003

In 1973, Fylde Guitars was founded by Roger Bucknall in Lancashire after he turned his hobby into his profession. His background in fine woodwork, music, engineering and acoustics led him to make instruments for many of the world's top musicians, including Gordon Giltrap and Davy Graham. He works mostly with hand tools, helped by a small team of assistants. He believes that the art of guitar making is a 'calling' and the maker's personality should be in every component part of the instrument.

The Harlequin head facing is of rosewood and sycamore.

ABOVE: *Bucknall gives his guitars exotic names. This one, the 'Custom-built Harlequin', built by Steve White, Roger's principal assistant at the time, gets its name from the diamonds of contrasting timber on the back.*

Notice the zero fret, a feature on all Bucknall's guitars.

- **DATE** *c.*2003
- **ORIGIN** England
- **WOOD**
  Front/Back & Sides
  Indian rosewood, sycamore and sitka spruce
- **UNUSUAL FEATURE**
  The use of a zero fret is distinctive.

20th-century archtop guitars:
American classics, part one

Here we see three of Gibson's classic archtop designs. Although the big-band era from which they come is long gone, Gibson's guitars from this period are still much in demand by players and collectors alike. Lloyd Loar was an acoustical engineer at Gibson. He had a profound influence on the company's designs in the 1920s, and all the instruments here were influenced by his innovations.

Gibson: Super 400, 1936

Launched in 1934, the Super 400 had a price tag of $400, hence the name. It was a top-of-the-range archtop and was made to impress, with its gold-plated metal parts, 457mm (18in) body, choice woods finished in 'Cremona Brown' (named after the violin-making school of Cremona), special pickguard, engraving on the tailpiece, and the open-back Grover tuners. The split-diamond headstock inlay was later used by Gibson on its Les Paul electric instruments.

- **DATE** 1936
- **ORIGIN** USA
- **WOOD**
  Front/Back & Sides
  Spruce/maple
- **UNUSUAL FEATURE**
  The pickguard has a brown, mottled-effect.

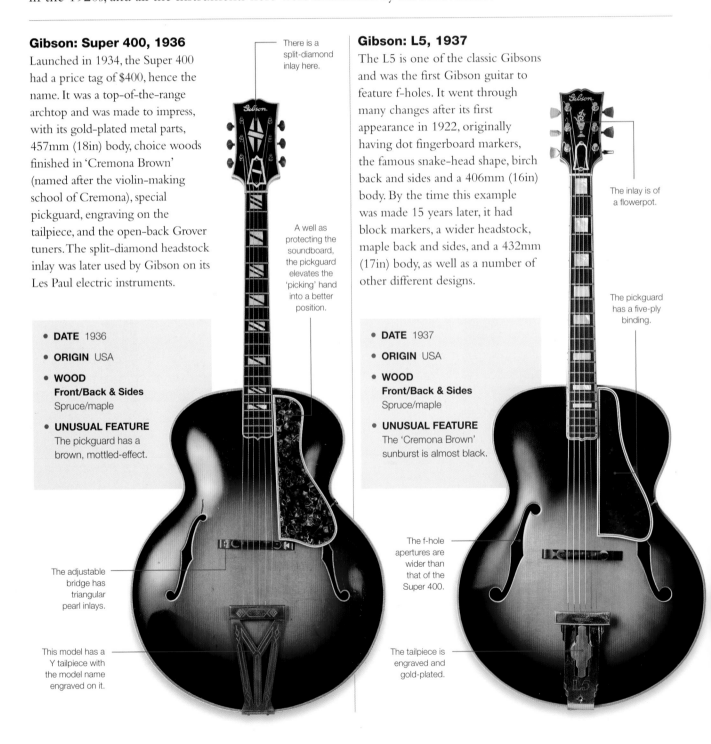

There is a split-diamond inlay here.

A well as protecting the soundboard, the pickguard elevates the 'picking' hand into a better position.

The adjustable bridge has triangular pearl inlays.

This model has a Y tailpiece with the model name engraved on it.

Gibson: L5, 1937

The L5 is one of the classic Gibsons and was the first Gibson guitar to feature f-holes. It went through many changes after its first appearance in 1922, originally having dot fingerboard markers, the famous snake-head shape, birch back and sides and a 406mm (16in) body. By the time this example was made 15 years later, it had block markers, a wider headstock, maple back and sides, and a 432mm (17in) body, as well as a number of other different designs.

- **DATE** 1937
- **ORIGIN** USA
- **WOOD**
  Front/Back & Sides
  Spruce/maple
- **UNUSUAL FEATURE**
  The 'Cremona Brown' sunburst is almost black.

The inlay is of a flowerpot.

The pickguard has a five-ply binding.

The f-hole apertures are wider than that of the Super 400.

The tailpiece is engraved and gold-plated.

Gibson: L7C, 1963

The L7 is a cheaper version of the L5; the main differences are only cosmetic. Although the L5C was introduced in 1939, the L7 didn't appear with a cutaway 'C' option until 1948. The crown head inlay was used on many Gibson models, including the Hummingbird acoustic, the SG electric and the EB bass guitar. This example has a pickup added as a later modification, so it can be used either plugged or unplugged.

The crown head inlay was used on a number of different Gibson guitars – both electric and acoustic.

ABOVE: *Gibson's serial numbers overlapped in the 1960s, and this can lead to confusion when dating the guitars. In the absence of a firm date, the different styles of 'Gibson' logos can help date the instrument.*

- **DATE** 1963

- **ORIGIN** USA

- **WOOD**
  Front/Back & Sides
  Spruce/maple

- **UNUSUAL FEATURE**
  This guitar has a single humbucker pickup with top-mounted volume and tone controls.

The cutaway is in the Venetian style.

The three-raised-parallelogram tailpiece

Lloyd Loar

When Lloyd Loar's (1886–1943) name is mentioned in connection with Gibson instruments, collectors, dealers, musicians and historians all become rather excited. However, he was neither an instrument maker nor did he work for Gibson for very long – in fact, for less than five years. But during his short time at Gibson he had a huge influence on the design and future of both the guitar and mandolin, and it is this that makes him a very special figure. By the age of 20 he was a professional musician, and he played and promoted Gibson's mandolins and mandolas, among many other instruments. In 1919, after Orville Gibson had left the company that he had founded, Loar was hired as an acoustical engineer. He worked mainly on the 'Master Model' instruments, which included the L5 archtop guitar and the F5 mandolin, and many of these instruments were signed by him.

ABOVE: *The Fisher Shipp Concert Company included Lloyd Loar on mandolin and Miss Fisher Shipp, the company manager and vocalist who later became Loar's wife (left). Here, Loar is holding a Gibson ten-string mando-viola – compared with a regular mandolin, the lower registers would have sounded better with the relatively higher-voiced female singers.*

20th-century archtop guitars:
American classics, part two

There is a long tradition of immigrant workers in America becoming successful instrument makers – C. F. Martin from Germany, Adolph Rickenbacker from Switzerland and the Greek Epaminondas Stathopoulo (Epiphone), to name but a few. This applies no more so than to the elite archtop builders: the Italian-influenced makers D'Angelico, D'Aquisto and Benedetto, and the Swedish Stromberg.

Elmer Stromberg: Master 400, 1946

Apprenticed at his father's instrument-making business, Elmer Stromberg (1895–1955) at first was known as a banjo maker, but as the banjo began to decline, his archtop-guitar making took over. This massive instrument, with its 483mm (19in) body, is very powerful, which made it extremely popular with big bands. Stromberg developed his own soundboard-bracing concepts, including, as with this guitar, the use of a single diagonal bar.

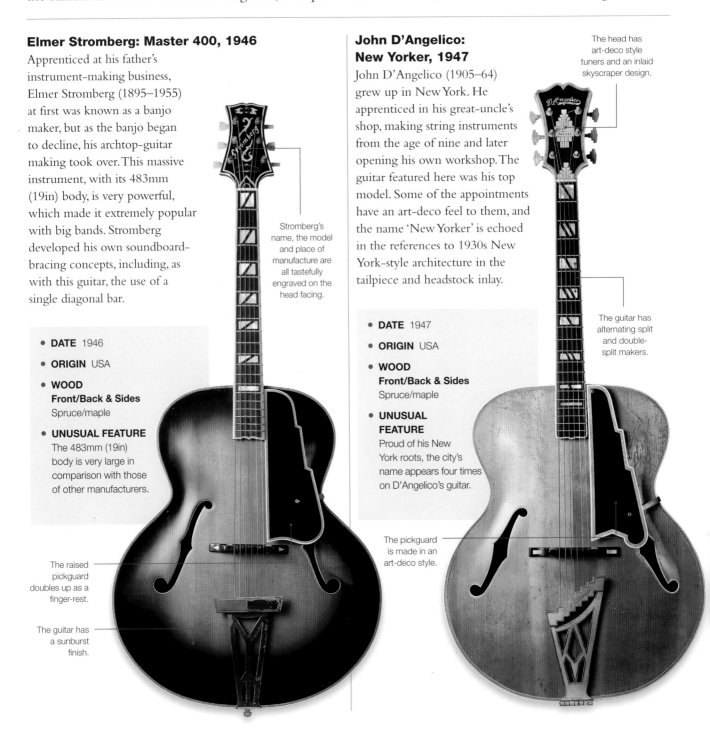

Stromberg's name, the model and place of manufacture are all tastefully engraved on the head facing.

- **DATE** 1946
- **ORIGIN** USA
- **WOOD**
  Front/Back & Sides
  Spruce/maple
- **UNUSUAL FEATURE**
  The 483mm (19in) body is very large in comparison with those of other manufacturers.

The raised pickguard doubles up as a finger-rest.

The guitar has a sunburst finish.

John D'Angelico: New Yorker, 1947

John D'Angelico (1905–64) grew up in New York. He apprenticed in his great-uncle's shop, making string instruments from the age of nine and later opening his own workshop. The guitar featured here was his top model. Some of the appointments have an art-deco feel to them, and the name 'New Yorker' is echoed in the references to 1930s New York-style architecture in the tailpiece and headstock inlay.

The head has art-deco style tuners and an inlaid skyscraper design.

- **DATE** 1947
- **ORIGIN** USA
- **WOOD**
  Front/Back & Sides
  Spruce/maple
- **UNUSUAL FEATURE**
  Proud of his New York roots, the city's name appears four times on D'Angelico's guitar.

The guitar has alternating split and double-split makers.

The pickguard is made in an art-deco style.

James D'Aquisto: Excel, 1970

Jimmy D'Aquisto (1935–95) was born in Brooklyn of second-generation immigrants from Palermo, Sicily. He was a serious guitarist and first met John D'Angelico as a client. Not long after this, he started working in D'Angelico's workshop. After the death of the master in the 1960s, he continued to work on guitars in various locations in the state of New York and eventually bought the business from the D'Angelico family. Many of his guitars were custom orders, and through this he stamped his own personality on the instruments by using features such as s-holes, wooden tailpieces and the metal-pip headstock finials.

Robert Benedetto: Cremona, 1994

In 1968, Robert Benedetto (b. 1946) started building guitars and making his own individual instruments. He has made over 800 instruments, of which more than half are archtop guitars. Benedetto is also an author, and one of his titles is the seminal *Making an Archtop Guitar*. The special custom-made guitar here was ordered by the violin maker Frank Passa. The back is made of 150-year-old curly European maple, which was probably supplied by Benedetto's customer. These instruments command a high price – in 1999, the recommended retail price of a standard Cremona was a staggering $60,000.

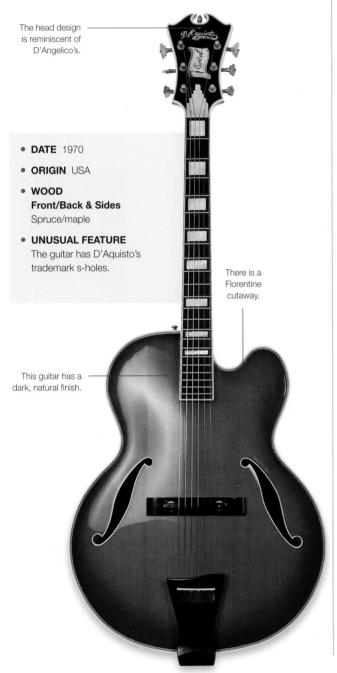

The head design is reminiscent of D'Angelico's.

- **DATE** 1970
- **ORIGIN** USA
- **WOOD**
  Front/Back & Sides
  Spruce/maple
- **UNUSUAL FEATURE**
  The guitar has D'Aquisto's trademark s-holes.

There is a Florentine cutaway.

This guitar has a dark, natural finish.

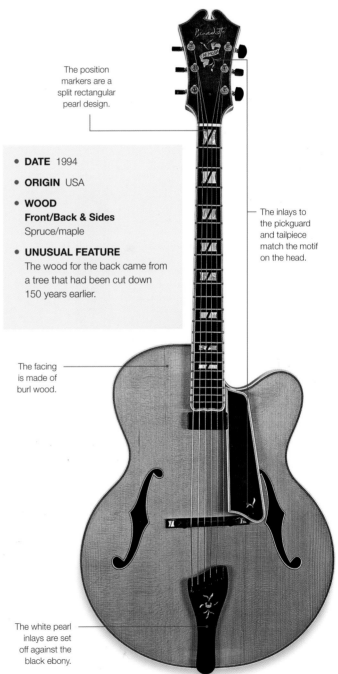

The position markers are a split rectangular pearl design.

- **DATE** 1994
- **ORIGIN** USA
- **WOOD**
  Front/Back & Sides
  Spruce/maple
- **UNUSUAL FEATURE**
  The wood for the back came from a tree that had been cut down 150 years earlier.

The inlays to the pickguard and tailpiece match the motif on the head.

The facing is made of burl wood.

The white pearl inlays are set off against the black ebony.

20th-century archtop guitars: other classics

Gibson had cornered the mainstream archtop-guitar market, while handmade ones by makers such as D'Angelico sold well to professional players and collectors. However, as these examples show, there were other companies that also had a degree of success in this field. While some are clearly Gibson-influenced instruments, others show some originality and unique features.

C. F. Martin: F-7, 1935

Martin had three ranges of archtop guitars: C, R and F. Both the F-7 and F-9 were short-lived, only being produced between 1935 and 1942. The F-9 cost $250, more than the similar-sized and similarly appointed Martin D-45 flat-top. These are very rare models, made even rarer because people have been converting them to flat-tops, in particular the F-9, being made into D-45-type instruments.

The Martin logo is vertically inlaid.

The hexagonal position markers are like those used on the D-45.

- **DATE** 1935
- **ORIGIN** Pennsylvania, USA
- **WOOD**
  Front/Back & Sides
  Spruce/rosewood
- **UNUSUAL FEATURE**
  This is a very early model, 1935 being the year Martin introduced the F range.

The sunburst finish, was called 'shaded top' by Martin when applied to its flat-tops.

Epiphone: Emperor, 1937

The Epiphone company was owned by the Stathopoulo family, originally Anastasio (1864–1915) then his son Epaminondas, or 'Epi', who gave his name to the firm. Originally a violin, lute and, later, a banjo maker, Epiphone will always be known for their beautifully made archtop guitars. These instruments were not cheap – at the time, the Emperor cost a massive $400. This example has a very dark-brown polish, which was certainly inspired by Gibson's 'Cremona' finish.

The mother-of-pearl head inlays have turned golden as the varnish has changed colour.

The mother-of-pearl block position markers have a triangular abalone inset.

- **DATE** 1937
- **ORIGIN** New York, USA
- **WOOD**
  Front/Back & Sides
  Spruce/curly maple
- **UNUSUAL FEATURE**
  The finish is very dark.

This was the new 'compensated' tailpiece.

Gretsch: Synchromatic, 1940s

Friedrich Gretsch (1856–95) formed the Gretsch Company in 1883 and at first made tambourines, soon moving into drums and guitars. When this guitar was made, Friedrich's son Fred had just about retired from being director of the company, and his grandson, also Fred, was now in charge. This Synchromatic was the company's first attempt at challenging Gibson's supremacy. The 'cat's-eye' soundholes, the stepped bridge and the harp-shaped tailpiece are all inspired by art deco.

- **DATE** 1940s
- **ORIGIN** New York, USA
- **WOOD**
  Front/Back & Sides
  Spruce/maple
- **UNUSUAL FEATURE**
  The whole design of this guitar is inspired by the styles of the art deco movement.

The tailpiece is lyre-shaped.

The scratchplate almost completely covers the treble soundhole.

The soundholes are nicknamed 'cat's eyes' because of their unusual shape.

The bridge has little steps either side of the saddle.

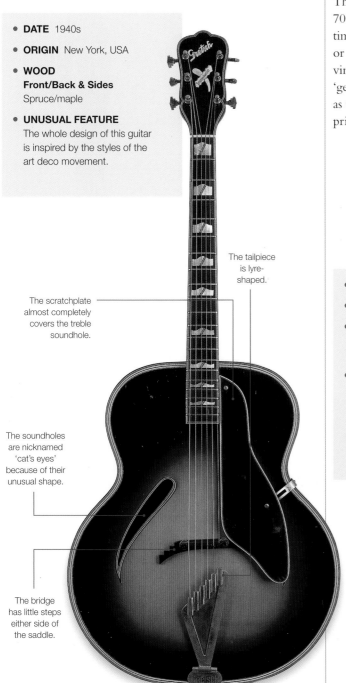

Höfner: Committee, 1957

Karl Höfner (?1864–1955) founded the Höfner company in 1887. His sons Josef and Walter joined in the 1920s. New factories, where this guitar was made, were built in 1950. Besides a rare model called the 'Golden Höfner' there were four archtops that the company offered in their catalogues. The cheapest was the Congress, then came the Senator, next was the President and the most expensive in this line was the Committee – so called because it was designed by a 'committee' of six of the UK's top guitarists. This 1957 electric version cost 70 guineas in Britain at the time, whether it had a 'Blonde' or 'Brunette' finish. The current vintage market dictates that 'gentlemen prefer blondes', as these command a higher price today.

As well as the name appearing on the head, it also occurs as a transfer on the body.

There are lavish inlays – even the truss-rod cover is inlaid with pearl.

- **DATE** 1957
- **ORIGIN** Bubenreuth, Germany
- **WOOD**
  Front/Back & Sides
  Spruce/veneered maple
- **UNUSUAL FEATURE**
  The scratchplate is made of clear celluloid, a nice feature since it is less obstructive to the eye.

This guitar is fitted with two pickups, and unlike the later thin-bodied versions, this model could be played either plugged in or acoustically.

20th-century gypsy guitars

Just like flamenco guitars, gypsy guitars are designed with one style of playing in mind – in this case, the jangly percussive sound made while vamping. Mario Maccaferri (1900–93) designed these guitars for the Parisian company Selmer. Selmer also offered four- and even seven-string versions, and those made for gut-strings. However, none is more prized than a six-string, metal-strung Selmer-Maccaferri instrument.

Selmer: Maccaferri D-hole, 1932

The Selmer-Maccaferri D-hole guitars were made only for a few years, c.1832–1934, but they have left a strong legacy. This model has a secondary soundbox with a sound reflector fitted inside, which may have been inspired by the many late 19th-century mandolins that were fitted with inner 'shelves'. Having no bone saddle or being adjustable, they came with a choice of bridges of different heights, the central part of the bridge not being fixed. This example has the full four-octave range.

- **DATE** 1932
- **ORIGIN** France
- **WOOD** Front/Back & Sides Spruce/laminated rosewood
- **UNUSUAL FEATURE** There are an internal sound chamber and reflector.

The Selmer, Paris, logo is shown here.

This guitar has a zero fret.

The soundhole is a D shape.

The interchangeable bridge gets around the fact it cannot be adjusted.

Selmer: Maccaferri Oval-hole, 1949

The oval-hole design is the one most often associated with the king of gypsy guitar, Django Reinhardt, and the soundhole shape may have been inspired by instruments made by the 19th-century Parisian luthier, Etienne Laprevotte. Green felt was often positioned under the tailpiece of these instruments, an idea borrowed from mandolin manufacturers' practice. This was designed to help protect the guitar from the metal tailpiece.

- **DATE** 1949
- **ORIGIN** France
- **WOOD** Front/Back & Sides Spruce/laminated rosewood
- **UNUSUAL FEATURE** The soundhole is an oval shape.

This guitar has Selmer enclosed tuners.

The oval soundhole – note the black spacing in the rosette, a feature usually hidden by the fingerboard in other guitars.

Green felt is used here to protect the wood.

Jacques Favino, 1975

Initially, Jacques Favino (b. 1920) worked for Bernabe Busato, later venturing out on his own. This guitar, like the original Selmers that Favino copies, features a zero fret, which helps keep the string action as low as possible above the frets and assists with the required tone. The leading edge of the bridge is hugely compensated, which is more crucial than with gut- or nylon-string guitars. These copies are close to the Selmer originals, with the main difference being a larger body size. Favino retired from building guitars in 1978, and today his son Jean-Pierre continues the business.

- **DATE** 1975
- **ORIGIN** France
- **WOOD**
  Front/Back & Sides
  Spruce/laminated rosewood
- **UNUSUAL FEATURE**
  The bridge is hugely compensated.

The tuning machines are by Salvator Billardi.

Note the extreme angled bridge; the resulting compensation improves the intonation.

The tailpiece is Maccaferri style.

Django Reinhardt

The name of Django Reinhardt (1910–53) is synonymous with gypsy jazz. He is undoubtedly one of the major figures in the whole of jazz – and indeed guitar – history. Although other musicians of his stature have had a direct, easily traceable influence on generations of players, Django's sound and style have not echoed down the years in the same way – with the exception of the large number of players who are devoted to sounding exactly like him. Reinhardt's musical vocabulary was strikingly different from that of even his closest musical collaborator, violinist Stéphane Grappelli. This difference was shaped by the well-known fact that he partly lost the use of his left hand at the age of 18 when he narrowly survived a fire in his caravan. Forced to adapt his technique to compensate for having only two usable fingers, Reinhardt nonetheless achieved an astonishing fluidity in his improvised playing. His injury may not have been immediately audible in the speed or the fluency of his playing, but it had a direct influence on his highly individual melodic choices.

ABOVE: *To add even more cool to the 1940s tweed suit and obligatory cigarette, Reinhardt is shown here playing an Epiphone Zephyr. This was the only electric jazz guitar he ever played, usually favouring his Selmer-Maccaferri instruments.*

19th- and 20th-century multi-string harp-guitars

Harp-guitars are very popular again today, especially in America, as they have been at various periods in the past – in Britain during the early 19th century, France in the mid-19th century and in America at the turn of the 19th century. There are many musicians associated with this resurgence in interest, but none more so than Gregg Miner, who has been a key figure in promoting the harp-guitar's recent popularity.

René Lacôte: Decacorde, 1826

There were many multi-stringed guitars made by René Lacôte (1785–c.1860), most with seven (heptacorde) or ten strings (decacorde). This one is slightly unusual in that it has five strings (not six) over the neck and five (not four) 'floating'. In the *Méthode Complète pour le Decacorde Nouvelle Guitare*, by Ferdinando Carulli, it states that the top five strings are tuned like a regular guitar (ADGBE), with the bass strings diatonically tuned GFEDC (descending).

In the past, the sounding length of the bass strings could be altered by moving some levers that are now missing.

The frets are for only five of the strings, since the others are not intended to be stopped.

The head accommodates ten wooden tuning pegs.

- **DATE** 1826
- **ORIGIN** Paris, France
- **WOOD**
  Front/Back & Sides
  Spruce/rosewood
- **UNUSUAL FEATURE**
  Note the unusual division of the strings (5+5 strings instead of the more usual 6+4).

Note how small the body is for such a large neck and head.

Luigi Mozzani: Nine-string Dual-arm Harp-guitar, 1910

As well as being a luthier, Luigi Mozzani (1869–1943) was a composer, teacher and concert guitarist, and he switched between concert tours and overseeing his workshops. He employed several young children, which shows in some of the workmanship, especially the hand-drawn decorations. Mozzani produced many forms of harp-guitars and regular guitars, which were inspired by earlier Viennese models, as well as violins and other instruments. This harp-guitar has two arms and a gingko-leaf pattern.

The regular tuning machines here are not very accessible.

The top two strings have a two-octave fingerboard.

The upper soundhole is part of the gingko-leaf pattern.

- **DATE** 1910
- **ORIGIN** Ferrara, Italy
- **WOOD**
  Front/Back & Sides
  Spruce/poplar
- **UNUSUAL FEATURE**
  The dual arms each have their own additional soundholes.

There are three separate saddles to the bridge.

Gibson: Style U, 1916

Unlike other harp-guitars, which are used for solo playing, the Style U was conceived as part of a family of instruments. For centuries, musical instruments had been made in different sizes for consort playing – the classic family being the violin, viola, cello and double-bass – and in photographs of mandolin orchestras from the early 20th century the Style U is often seen at the rear. The body of the large Gibson Super 400 archtop guitar measures 457mm (18in) at its widest point; the Style U, however, is a gigantic 533mm (21in). The guitar has a regular six-string neck with 12 sub-basses tuned chromatically, descending from the low E string.

John Sullivan/Jeffrey Elliot: 20-string Harp-guitar, 1986

The harp-guitarist John Doan commissioned celebrated maker Jeffrey Elliot to make him a harp-guitar. John Sullivan was called in to give his expertise on the project, and he contributed some significant elements to the basic design. At the time, Elliot had a seven-year waiting list, so they decided to let Sullivan do the making. Not wanting to create a clone of the famous Knutsen or Dyer harp-guitars, they set out to design something that was radically different. The finished result sports some 20 strings arranged with six on a standard neck, six sub-basses and eight zither-like super trebles.

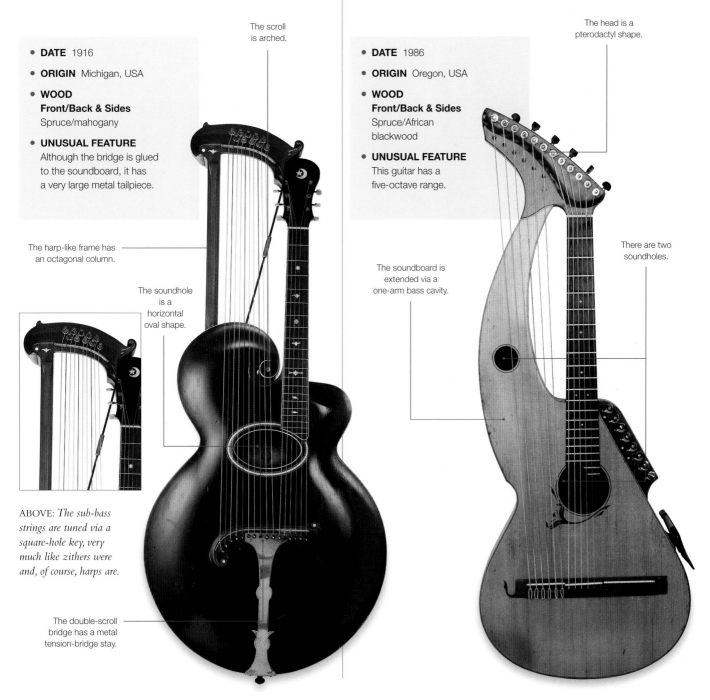

The scroll is arched.

- **DATE** 1916
- **ORIGIN** Michigan, USA
- **WOOD**
  Front/Back & Sides
  Spruce/mahogany
- **UNUSUAL FEATURE**
  Although the bridge is glued to the soundboard, it has a very large metal tailpiece.

The harp-like frame has an octagonal column.

The soundhole is a horizontal oval shape.

ABOVE: *The sub-bass strings are tuned via a square-hole key, very much like zithers were and, of course, harps are.*

The double-scroll bridge has a metal tension-bridge stay.

The head is a pterodactyl shape.

- **DATE** 1986
- **ORIGIN** Oregon, USA
- **WOOD**
  Front/Back & Sides
  Spruce/African blackwood
- **UNUSUAL FEATURE**
  This guitar has a five-octave range.

The soundboard is extended via a one-arm bass cavity.

There are two soundholes.

20th-century guitars:
unusual varieties

Innovative instrument making continued into the 20th century, and German and Austrian luthiers built many of the most interesting guitars, as the following examples show. The instruments were evidently very popular in their day, but for the most part the makers' ideas were never developed or refined; they were probably considered to be impractical, or they simply fell out of fashion.

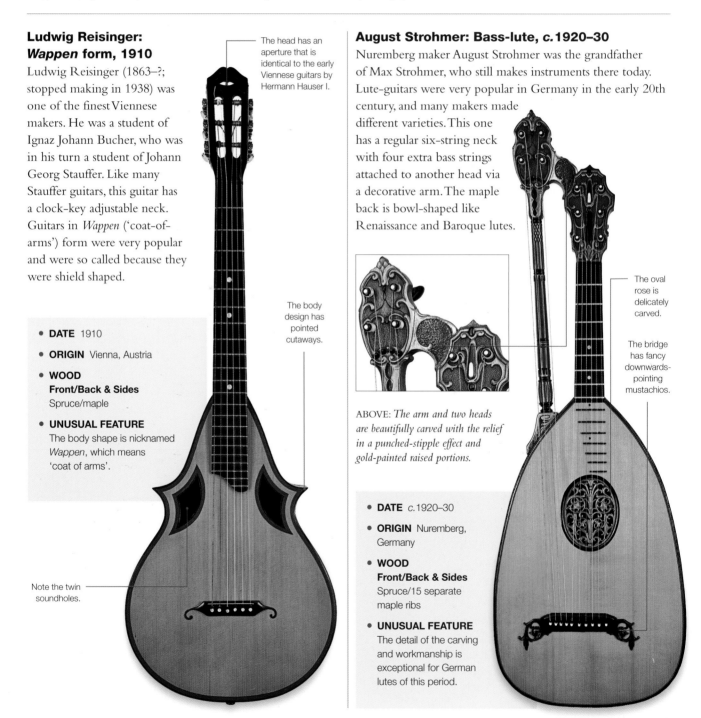

Ludwig Reisinger: *Wappen* form, 1910

Ludwig Reisinger (1863–?; stopped making in 1938) was one of the finest Viennese makers. He was a student of Ignaz Johann Bucher, who was in his turn a student of Johann Georg Stauffer. Like many Stauffer guitars, this guitar has a clock-key adjustable neck. Guitars in *Wappen* ('coat-of-arms') form were very popular and were so called because they were shield shaped.

The head has an aperture that is identical to the early Viennese guitars by Hermann Hauser I.

The body design has pointed cutaways.

- **DATE** 1910
- **ORIGIN** Vienna, Austria
- **WOOD**
  Front/Back & Sides
  Spruce/maple
- **UNUSUAL FEATURE**
  The body shape is nicknamed *Wappen*, which means 'coat of arms'.

Note the twin soundholes.

August Strohmer: Bass-lute, *c.*1920–30

Nuremberg maker August Strohmer was the grandfather of Max Strohmer, who still makes instruments there today. Lute-guitars were very popular in Germany in the early 20th century, and many makers made different varieties. This one has a regular six-string neck with four extra bass strings attached to another head via a decorative arm. The maple back is bowl-shaped like Renaissance and Baroque lutes.

ABOVE: *The arm and two heads are beautifully carved with the relief in a punched-stipple effect and gold-painted raised portions.*

The oval rose is delicately carved.

The bridge has fancy downwards-pointing mustachios.

- **DATE** *c.*1920–30
- **ORIGIN** Nuremberg, Germany
- **WOOD**
  Front/Back & Sides
  Spruce/15 separate maple ribs
- **UNUSUAL FEATURE**
  The detail of the carving and workmanship is exceptional for German lutes of this period.

Alfred Schaufuß (attributed): Archtop guitar, c. 1940–50

Alfred Schaufuß (1904–80) made this extremely fancy archtop guitar in Adorf, near the instrument-making town of Markneukirchen. After working for other local makers, he started his own business in 1924. His instruments are very richly decorated, in part because his wife worked in a pearl factory, thus making it easy for him to obtain the necessary materials for the opulent decorations. Although it is very well made, it may not be surprising to learn that this guitar was once the property of a clown.

- **DATE** c. 1940–50
- **ORIGIN** Markneukirchen, Germany
- **WOOD**
  Front/Back & Sides
  Spruce/maple
- **UNUSUAL FEATURE**
  There is a Baroque-style sunken rose.

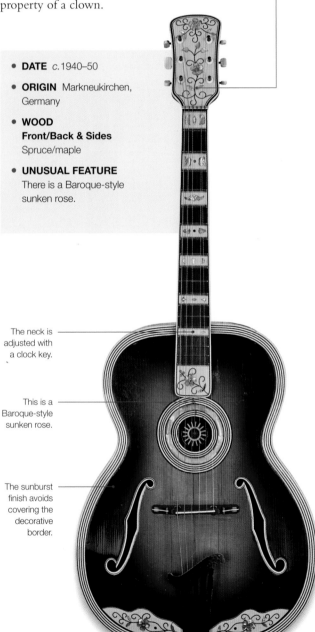

The white celluloid-and-pearl inlays extend to the head.

The neck is adjusted with a clock key.

This is a Baroque-style sunken rose.

The sunburst finish avoids covering the decorative border.

Hans Vogl slide guitar, 1914

This guitar has an inscription written on the inside of the back that translates as: "This instrument is an original invention. If it is successful, I'll never know." It has 51 metal strings, which hover over three 'scalloped' fretboards. Each set of strings is tuned differently. It is not clear whether the brass tube is a slide or a capo, or both.

RIGHT: *The brass tube is operated via the handle to the rear.*

BELOW: *The performer must have been an excellent musician to have been able to master playing 51 strings.*

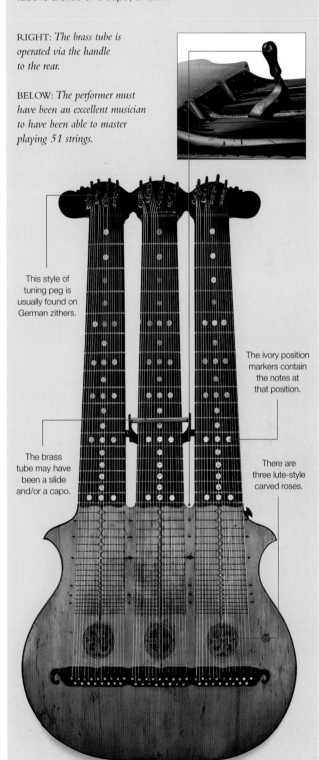

This style of tuning peg is usually found on German zithers.

The brass tube may have been a slide and/or a capo.

The ivory position markers contain the notes at that position.

There are three lute-style carved roses.

20th-century resonator guitars

Before the electric guitar, players were increasingly demanding more volume from makers. Until the 1920s, their solution was to make larger-bodied guitars, then George Beauchamp and John Dopyera had the idea of crossing a guitar with a phonograph. This, however, had already been patented by John Stroh of London, so Dopyera decided to rest the bridge on three aluminium cones, and the rest, as they say, is history.

Dobro: Style 66 Roundneck, 1929

John Dopyera and his four brothers started making instruments for the Dobro (DOpyera BROthers) company in 1928. This particular wooden-bodied resonator uses only a single cone. The body is made of magnolia, and the French-scroll pattern is achieved by sandblasting. There are two screen holes and three small open holes above the central-cone cover plate. The rectangular cutouts to the cover plate are shaped like four fans.

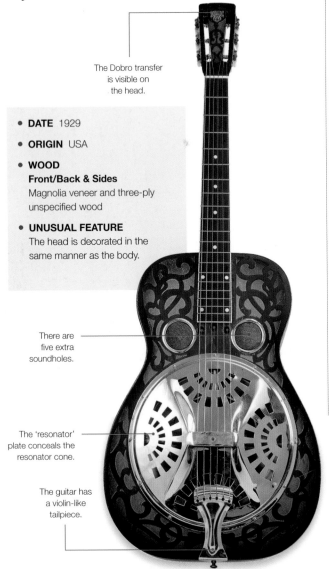

The Dobro transfer is visible on the head.

- **DATE** 1929

- **ORIGIN** USA

- **WOOD**
  Front/Back & Sides
  Magnolia veneer and three-ply unspecified wood

- **UNUSUAL FEATURE**
  The head is decorated in the same manner as the body.

There are five extra soundholes.

The 'resonator' plate conceals the resonator cone.

The guitar has a violin-like tailpiece.

National: Tricone Square-neck, 1930

John Dopyera registered the National String Instrument Corporation in 1926 (just two years before he started making instruments for his Dobro company). This is an all-metal-body tricone resonator. The lack of any engraving gives this guitar the Style-1 model designation. The Tricone, as the name suggests, has three cones, two on the bass side and one on the treble. Many square-neck resophonic guitars with wooden necks were converted to round-neck playing – probably by dealers to broaden their client base. However, this was not possible with the metal-neck ones.

There is a shield transfer.

- **DATE** 1930

- **ORIGIN** USA

- **WOOD**
  Front/Back & Sides
  All German silver metal

- **UNUSUAL FEATURE**
  Many square-neck models have their tuners reversed for lap playing, but this one still has its tuners in their original positions.

Two extra soundholes are used on this guitar.

The bridge cover and hand-rest form a T-shape.

Kerry Char: Resonator Guitar, 2000

If anyone knows what sound is required from a square-neck resophonic guitar, Hawaii-born Kerry Char (b. 1955) does. He now works in Oregon and has built a reputation for building and restoring unusual instruments. This guitar has a wooden body made completely from Hawaiian koa wood, and all the hardware is gold-plated. The square neck is specifically designed for slide and lap-steel playing.

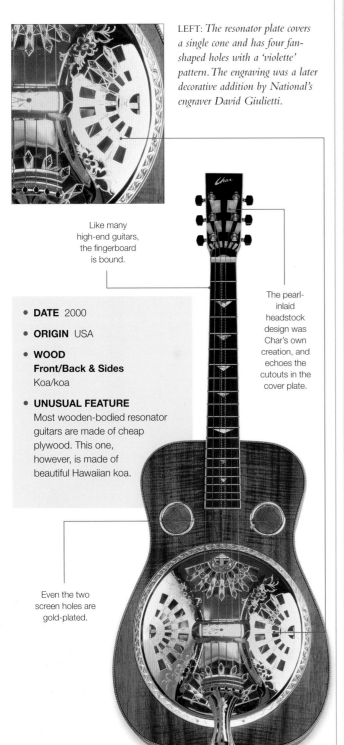

LEFT: *The resonator plate covers a single cone and has four fan-shaped holes with a 'violette' pattern. The engraving was a later decorative addition by National's engraver David Giulietti.*

Like many high-end guitars, the fingerboard is bound.

The pearl-inlaid headstock design was Char's own creation, and echoes the cutouts in the cover plate.

- **DATE** 2000
- **ORIGIN** USA
- **WOOD**
  Front/Back & Sides
  Koa/koa
- **UNUSUAL FEATURE**
  Most wooden-bodied resonator guitars are made of cheap plywood. This one, however, is made of beautiful Hawaiian koa.

Even the two screen holes are gold-plated.

Resonator mandolins

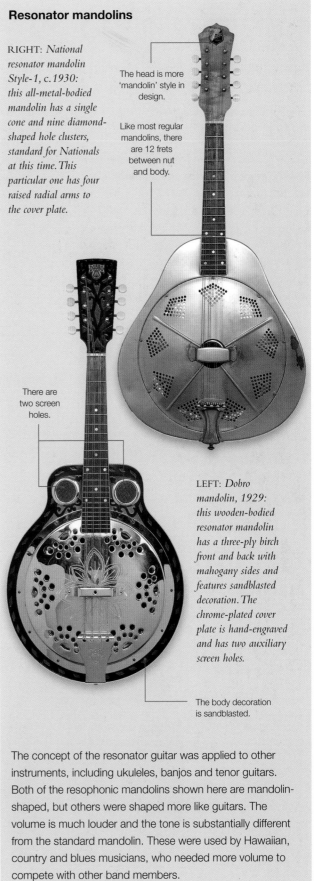

RIGHT: *National resonator mandolin Style-1, c.1930: this all-metal-bodied mandolin has a single cone and nine diamond-shaped hole clusters, standard for Nationals at this time. This particular one has four raised radial arms to the cover plate.*

The head is more 'mandolin' style in design.

Like most regular mandolins, there are 12 frets between nut and body.

There are two screen holes.

LEFT: *Dobro mandolin, 1929: this wooden-bodied resonator mandolin has a three-ply birch front and back with mahogany sides and features sandblasted decoration. The chrome-plated cover plate is hand-engraved and has two auxiliary screen holes.*

The body decoration is sandblasted.

The concept of the resonator guitar was applied to other instruments, including ukuleles, banjos and tenor guitars. Both of the resophonic mandolins shown here are mandolin-shaped, but others were shaped more like guitars. The volume is much louder and the tone is substantially different from the standard mandolin. These were used by Hawaiian, country and blues musicians, who needed more volume to compete with other band members.

20th-century acoustic bass guitars

Before the advent of the electric pickup, acoustic basses, by virtue of the slow-moving, low frequencies of the long, thick strings, had to be large in size. They were designed to be played in groups with other instruments spanning the whole possible acoustical range – in some cases these were 60-piece orchestras. Some were related to the mandolin and others to the guitar, and each was tuned accordingly.

Jean Rowies (attributed): Gelas Mando-bass, 1924–29

This mando-bass, attributed to Jean Rowies, is one of a quartet of Gelas-designed instruments. It is about 1.8m (6ft) tall and one of the most unusual designs imaginable: the bridge is fixed to the true, or inner, soundboard, which is cranked at approximately a 20-degree angle to the fingerboard. The upper soundboard is largely conventional, but the inner soundboard runs beneath it, so it has no need for any bracing.

Notice the metal rollers or barrels instead of ivory or bone used for gut-strung instruments.

- **DATE** 1924–29
- **ORIGIN** France
- **WOOD**
  Front/Back & Sides
  Spruce/maple
- **UNUSUAL FEATURE**
  It has two soundboards. The strings pass through a fixed bridge and are anchored to a tailpiece.

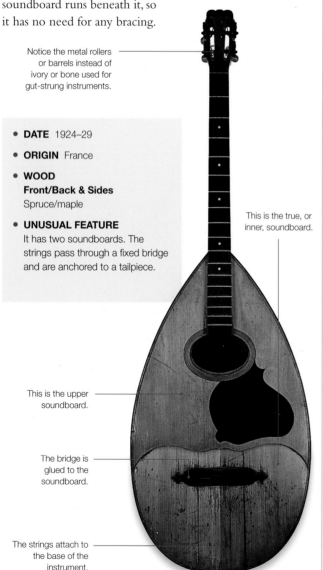

This is the true, or inner, soundboard.

This is the upper soundboard.

The bridge is glued to the soundboard.

The strings attach to the base of the instrument.

Gibson: Mando-bass, 1929

The Gibson mando-bass has a place in history all of its own. If the violin (which is tuned the same as a mandolin) could be a part of a wider family (viola, cello and double-bass), then why, asked Gibson, couldn't the mandolin? So the company created the mandola, mando-cello and the mando-bass, and mandolin orchestras swept the USA. Unlike the Neapolitan mandolin, however, the oval-shaped Gibson flat-backed mandolin family had an arched rather than a flat soundboard. This one is a 'black face', named after its black finish.

The Gibson logo is located here.

- **DATE** 1929
- **ORIGIN** USA
- **WOOD**
  Front/Back & Sides
  Spruce/maple
- **UNUSUAL FEATURE**
  This has a so-called 'black-face' finish, but many were made in red-mahogany sunburst, brown or plain orange.

Note the black finish.

The guitar has a carved archtop soundboard.

Prairie State Bass, *c.*1930

Made by the Larson Brothers under the name Prairie State, this whopping acoustic bass, although officially classed as a flat-top guitar, has a slight arch to the soundboard. It has a movable bridge and a cello-like spike at the bottom. To help support the large surface area and the pull of the hefty bass strings there is an internal supporting rod running from the lower to the upper block.

Mexican Six-string Bass, 1960

The mariachi band can include violins, guitars, trumpets and vihuelas (five-string), all of which are underpinned by the acoustic basses. The mariachi tradition goes back to the 19th century, but here we have an example of an instrument from the 1960s. The idea is thought to have been introduced by the Spanish, and this instrument is reminiscent of the 1759 Sanguino guitar (see '18th- and early 19th-century transitional guitars, part one') with its deep body and comparatively short neck.

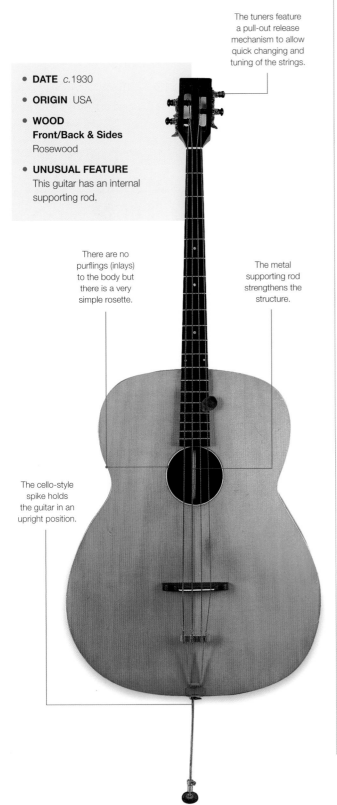

The tuners feature a pull-out release mechanism to allow quick changing and tuning of the strings.

- **DATE** *c.*1930
- **ORIGIN** USA
- **WOOD**
  Front/Back & Sides
  Rosewood
- **UNUSUAL FEATURE**
  This guitar has an internal supporting rod.

There are no purflings (inlays) to the body but there is a very simple rosette.

The metal supporting rod strengthens the structure.

The cello-style spike holds the guitar in an upright position.

- **DATE** 1960
- **ORIGIN** Mexico
- **WOOD**
  Front/Back & Sides
  Cedrela/mahogany
- **UNUSUAL FEATURE**
  Traditionally bass guitars have four strings. This one, however, has six.

The six tuning machines have paddle-shaped heads.

The neck here is tapered.

The unusual choice of woods make it even more exotic-looking.

ABOVE: *Many arched guitar backs are carved by skilled craftsmen. However, this guitar has a particularly pronounced bent back which, because of the severity of the arching, was probably done in a hot press.*

20th- and 21st-century acoustic bass guitars

With each passing decade, guitars were getting louder – then came a lull. Under the influence of TV programmes such as *MTV Unplugged*, as well as Neil Young's annual Bridge Benefit concerts, the idea of playing acoustically while retaining a band atmosphere became popular. Acoustic bass guitars often feature in these sessions, with a sound somewhere between an electric bass and a double bass.

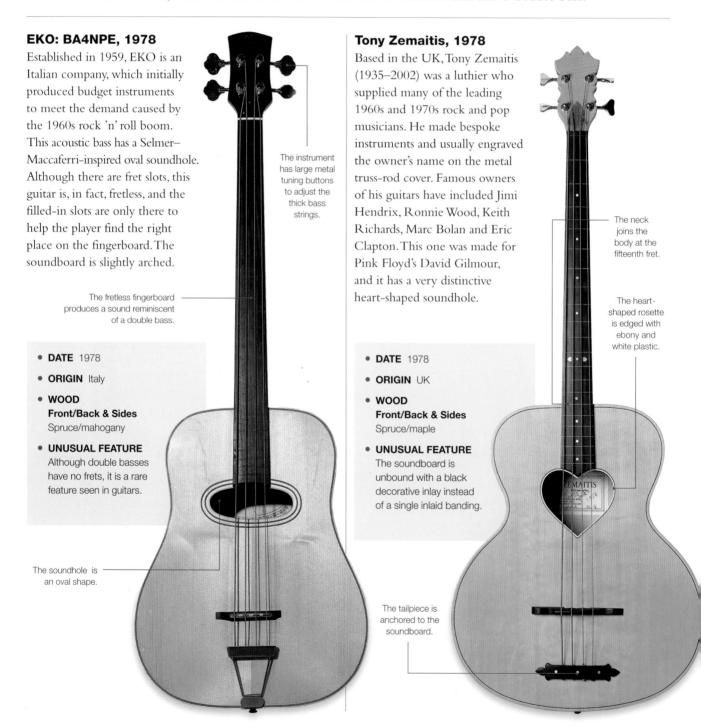

EKO: BA4NPE, 1978

Established in 1959, EKO is an Italian company, which initially produced budget instruments to meet the demand caused by the 1960s rock 'n' roll boom. This acoustic bass has a Selmer–Maccaferri-inspired oval soundhole. Although there are fret slots, this guitar is, in fact, fretless, and the filled-in slots are only there to help the player find the right place on the fingerboard. The soundboard is slightly arched.

The instrument has large metal tuning buttons to adjust the thick bass strings.

The fretless fingerboard produces a sound reminiscent of a double bass.

- **DATE** 1978
- **ORIGIN** Italy
- **WOOD**
  Front/Back & Sides
  Spruce/mahogany
- **UNUSUAL FEATURE**
  Although double basses have no frets, it is a rare feature seen in guitars.

The soundhole is an oval shape.

Tony Zemaitis, 1978

Based in the UK, Tony Zemaitis (1935–2002) was a luthier who supplied many of the leading 1960s and 1970s rock and pop musicians. He made bespoke instruments and usually engraved the owner's name on the metal truss-rod cover. Famous owners of his guitars have included Jimi Hendrix, Ronnie Wood, Keith Richards, Marc Bolan and Eric Clapton. This one was made for Pink Floyd's David Gilmour, and it has a very distinctive heart-shaped soundhole.

The neck joins the body at the fifteenth fret.

The heart-shaped rosette is edged with ebony and white plastic.

- **DATE** 1978
- **ORIGIN** UK
- **WOOD**
  Front/Back & Sides
  Spruce/maple
- **UNUSUAL FEATURE**
  The soundboard is unbound with a black decorative inlay instead of a single inlaid banding.

The tailpiece is anchored to the soundboard.

C. F. Martin: B-65, 1990

The B-65 was designed by Dick Boak, now Martin's archivist and the Director of their Artists Relations. This is essentially a Martin jumbo-sized acoustic bass guitar with a factory-fitted Fishman pickup with pre-amp. The volume and tone knobs are located on the bass-side of the upper bout, and it has an imitation tortoiseshell scratchplate. Four-string guitars are not a new thing for Martin, as the company has been making tenor guitars since the 1920s.

Fender: Kingman SCE, 2010

Leo Fender (1909–91) formed the Fender Electric Instrument Co. in 1946, mainly making electric lap-steels and amplifiers. However, in the 1950s he became famous for producing electric guitars, notably the Telecaster and the Stratocaster. This guitar has a classic Fender neck with a C-shaped (oval) profile and Gibson-style block position markers. It also has a Fishman pre-amp with a guitar tuner. It is of a Dreadnought size, but with a cutaway to the treble side.

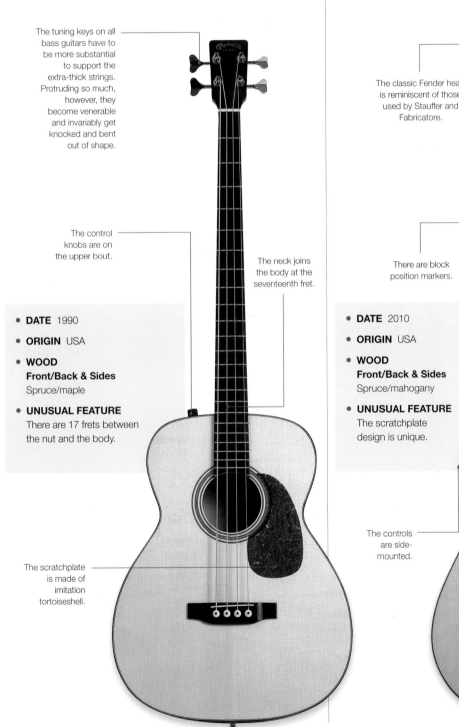

The tuning keys on all bass guitars have to be more substantial to support the extra-thick strings. Protruding so much, however, they become venerable and invariably get knocked and bent out of shape.

The control knobs are on the upper bout.

The neck joins the body at the seventeenth fret.

- **DATE** 1990
- **ORIGIN** USA
- **WOOD**
  Front/Back & Sides
  Spruce/maple
- **UNUSUAL FEATURE**
  There are 17 frets between the nut and the body.

The scratchplate is made of imitation tortoiseshell.

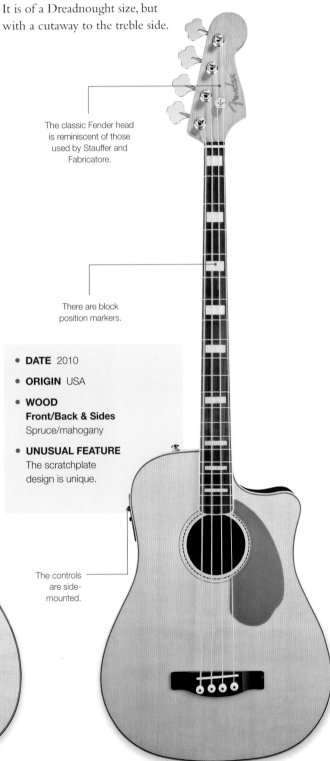

The classic Fender head is reminiscent of those used by Stauffer and Fabricatore.

There are block position markers.

- **DATE** 2010
- **ORIGIN** USA
- **WOOD**
  Front/Back & Sides
  Spruce/mahogany
- **UNUSUAL FEATURE**
  The scratchplate design is unique.

The controls are side-mounted.

Glossary

alfabeto system
An early development of guitar tablature notation.

altered tension chords
Dominant-seventh chords with extensions (extra notes) drawn from outside the parent major scale.

altered tuning
Ways of tuning the guitar other than 'standard tuning'.

arpeggio
Chord notes played in succession, upwards or downwards.

artificial harmonic
A harmonic formed on a shortened string that is fretted by the left hand.

bambino
A small guitar popular in the 19th century.

barre chord
A chord shape in which one finger, usually but not always the index finger, is pressed across the fretboard to fret several strings at the same time.

bend
A change of pitch which is achieved by moving (pushing or releasing) a vibrating string sideways.

blues scale
A scale including 'blue notes': notes that give the characteristic blues feel to the music. There isn't one definitive form of blues scale, but it will typically include the minor third from the root, the flattened fifth (as well as the perfect fifth) and the minor seventh.

book-matched
Wood that has been sliced open with the grain arranged symmetrically.

RIGHT: *This is a fretless acoustic bass, made by Italian firm EKO in 1978.*

bossa nova
A Brazilian style, which was very popular in the 1960s, drawn from samba and with a strong jazz flavour.

bridge
The bridge is attached to the top (soundboard) of the guitar, and carries the saddle and the bridge-pins or tie-block that secure the strings at that end.

cant
When the soundboard is bent at the bridge, it is 'cant'.

capo (Cejilla)
A device which is fixed across the strings to raise the pitch.

catgut strings
Gut (from animals but not from cats; the origin of the term 'catgut' is uncertain) preceded nylon as the material for classical guitar strings, and is still preferred by some players.

chitarra battente
A particular type of Italian, wire-strung Baroque guitar.

chord
Two or more notes sounded together or in quick succession.

chordophone
The technical term used to describe any stringed instrument.

chromatic scale
A succession of notes formed entirely of semitone steps.

cistre, cittern or English guitar
A wire-stringed instrument that was popular in the late 18th century.

cleats
Small pieces of added wood (usually to assist a repair).

country picking
A style used especially in country music, typically with root and fifth alternating on the bottom strings and busy fingerwork on the top strings.

course
A pair of strings set close together and treated as one note.

cutaway
The term describes the shape of guitar body that gives the left hand the ability to access the highest frets on the fingerboard.

DADGAD
An alternative guitar tuning popular in folk and folk-rock.

damping
Touching a string to stop it vibrating.

diatonic
Involving only notes proper to the prevailing key without chromatic alteration.

diminished chord
A chord containing the root note, minor third and diminished fifth.

dissonance
A combination of two or more notes that 'clash', i.e. that do not harmonize together comfortably.

dominant seventh
A chord formed from a major triad plus the minor seventh from the root, tending to resolve to a triad with the root a perfect fourth higher. In the major-minor key system, the dominant seventh chord is constructed from the fifth step of the scale (the dominant) and resolves to the tonic chord (which is constructed on the first step of the scale).

Dorian mode
A scale formed by playing the white notes of the piano from D to D (or starting from the second step of any other major scale).

double stopping
Playing two strings at the same time.

drop-D
A type of altered tuning, which involves retuning the bottom E string down to D.

extended chord
General term for ninth, 11th or 13th chords – chords that build on seventh chords by adding further thirds on top.

falsetas
Instrumental (guitar) phrases in flamenco music.

fan bracing
A typical pattern formed by the reinforcing wooden strips on the inside of a guitar body.

fifth (1/5) comma meantone temperament
The technical term for a type of tuning, different from 'equal temperament' (in which there are 12 equal semitones in each octave). In meantone tuning, fifths are tuned slightly narrow, in order to achieve a better tuning of thirds. The 'comma' is a mathematical proportion, fractions of which define different varieties of meantone tuning.

fingerboard
Another name for the fretboard.

fingerstyle technique
Using the individual right-hand fingers to play different strings, as opposed to strumming across several strings.

fingertapping
Tapping on the fretboard to produce various notes, especially by using the right hand.

finial
A decorative terminal feature, usually an extension of the head.

floating bridge
A bridge that is not attached to the soundboard but which the strings pass over; it is attached towards the base of the guitar.

floating fretboard
A fretboard that is not attached to the soundboard.

fret dressing
Repairing the wear and tear on frets.

LEFT: *This cittern is inlaid with over a thousand pieces of hand-cut mother-of-pearl.*

frets
Raised ridges on the fretboard. The left hand presses just behind a fret to shorten the vibrating length of the string and thereby alter (raise) the pitch.

gauge
The gauge refers to the thickness of a guitar string.

golpeador
The Spanish word for a scratchplate, applied especially in flamenco.

guide finger
Keeping a finger in contact with a string to help locate the next playing position for the left hand.

hammer-on
Sounding a new note, not by plucking it with the right hand but by changing the pitch of an already-sounding string with a hammer-like motion.

harmonic
A note sounded not by fully pressing the string on to the fretboard but by lightly touching it at a 'node', a point that allows it to vibrate around the touching finger. Harmonics have a distinctive, pure sound.

headstock
Positioned at the end of the guitar neck, the headstock holds the strings and their tuning mechanism.

interval
The distance from one note to another.

lick
A characteristic phrase, usually melodic. For instance, a blues lick is a typical blues figure.

luthier
Stringed instrument maker.

major scale
A succession of notes with the following sequence of intervals: tone, tone, semitone, tone, tone, tone, semitone. This sequence is formed when playing the white notes on a piano from C to C.

minor scale
There are several forms of minor scale, but all crucially vary from the major in that the third of the scale is flattened, so that a C minor scale starts: C D E♭ F G.

mode
A series of diatonic notes within an octave.

montuno
A type of repeating bass pattern much used in salsa and other Latin styles.

movable chord
A left-hand chord shape that can be moved up or down the fretboard.

mustachios
A decorative extension to the bridge.

natural tension chords
Extended dominant chords (ninth, 11th and 13th chords): broadly speaking, these are the ones which keep to the notes of the parent major scale, as opposed to those with chromatic alterations.

RIGHT:
The Levin Goliath was so called because of its large size.

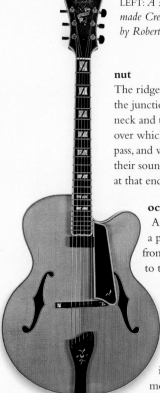

LEFT: *A special custom-made Cremona guitar by Robert Benedetto.*

nut
The ridge that forms the junction between the neck and the headstock, over which the strings pass, and whichdefines their sounding length at that end.

octave
An interval of a perfect eighth, from one note to the next note (up or down) with the same note-name.

open chord
Chords which include one or more open strings.

open tuning
A type of altered tuning, in which the open strings are tuned to a chord.

palm muting
A right-hand technique, allowing the palm (or the edge of the palm, from below the little finger to the heel of the palm) to rest lightly on the strings just beside the bridge, damping the strings slightly.

passing notes
Notes in a melody that do not belong to the underlying chords, which enable the linking of different chord notes to create melodic phrases.

pedal
In music theory, this term refers to a note that is held while the harmonies go through several changes. Most pedal notes are in the bass.

peg box
The part of the headstock that houses the tuning pegs. Applies to classical instruments/slotted headstock only.

pentatonic scale
A five-note scale. One common pentatonic scale has a pattern of major seconds (tones) and minor thirds such as G A C D E (G), but other pentatonic scales are also possible.

Phrygian mode
A scale that is formed by playing the white notes of the piano from E to E (or starting from the second step of any other major scale).

pickguard
A thin plastic plate attached to the top face of the guitar, positioned to prevent damage by scratching from fingernails or a plectrum.

pickup
An electrical device to capture and amplify the guitar's sound.

pickup bar
When a piece starts on an upbeat (or anacrusis), this is notated as an incomplete bar or 'pickup bar' before bar 1.

pin bridge
A type of bridge in which the strings are fixed with the aid of a pin.

pitch
How high or low a note sounds (as we perceive it), which is determined by its fundamental frequency.

plantilla
The outline of the body.

plectrum
A small plastic disc held in the right hand, usually between thumb and forefinger, to pluck or strum the strings.

power chord
A chord containing only the root and fifth (plus any octave doublings).

progression
The change from one chord to another.

pull-off
Sounding a new note not by plucking it with the right hand but by using a left-hand finger which was previously fretting a note, pulling the string and releasing it to make a lower note than it was previously sounding.

purflings
Decorative inlaid strips that are added on the edges of a guitar.

re-entrant tuning
Any tuning which in which the strings are not ordered from the lowest pitch to the highest.

relative tuning
The method of tuning the strings by successively tuning pairs of strings against each other. Typically, this will start by tuning the open A string against the low E string fretted at the fifth fret.

repertoire
A general term meaning a collection or list of pieces. Often used to define the list of pieces played by a performer.

rest stroke
A right-hand technique in which the finger presses the string downwards and, after releasing, then rests on the next string. On the last string, however, the player controls the finger rather than resting it.

riff
A repeated harmonic and/or melodic pattern forming the basis of a song.

roller holes
The holes in the side of the headstock in which the machine heads are fitted.

root note
In a scale or chord, the root is the defining, 'home' note.

rose
A two- or three-dimensional decoration covering the soundhole.

rosette
The decorative inlay which surrounds the soundhole.

saddle
Resting point on the bridge, from which the string length starts.

scratchplate
The thin plastic plate positioned to protect the top face of the guitar from scratches.

semitone
On a guitar, the smallest interval between adjacent notes in Western harmony; on any given string, the interval from one fret to the next.

seventh chord
A four-note chord formed by taking a triad (formed of root, third, fifth) and adding a seventh.

shuffle
A swung rhythm with a comfortable, easy feel and a repeated pattern such as the 'sixth shuffle'.

slide
Moving smoothly from one pitch to another by sliding the fretting finger up or down the string. Also refers to the metal or glass device used to create a particular sound.

slotted (bar) frets
Rectangular-shaped strips (see frets).

slur
In notation, a curved line drawn from one note to a different note, indicating that the second should be played without separately enunciating it, for instance (in guitar music) by using a left-hand hammer-on or pull-off.

soundboard
On an acoustic guitar, the resonating top part of the body.

soundport
A hole in the side of the guitar, designed to enhance the sound, especially for the player's benefit.

spread chord
A chord where the notes are not sounded simultaneously but one after another, and then allowed to ring so that the whole chord is heard.

square neck
A guitar neck which has been left square (not rounded) at the back.

standard tuning
From bottom to top: low E, A, D, G, B, high E.

stave
The five lines that are used for conventional music notation.

suspended chord
A chord including a suspended note: one which 'wants' to resolve downwards or upwards to form a triad.

sympathetic strings
Strings which resonate independently of the main ones.

syncopation
A rhythm that cuts across the beat.

T-frets
T-shaped strips that are inserted into the fretboard (see frets).

tablature
Guitar notation in which horizontal lines represent the strings, and numbers indicate the fret to be played.

tailpiece
A device in which the strings are anchored to the end of the guitar body.

Terz guitar
A six-string guitar with a smaller string length (commonly 543–563mm, 21⅜–22¼in) tuned a minor third higher than a standard guitar.

theorbo
A long-necked lute with extra bass strings, used mainly in Baroque music.

three-chord trick
Chords I, IV and V: the chords most commonly used in any key, and sufficient for many songs, including the basic form of 12-bar blues.

thumb chord
A chord in which the left-hand thumb reaches round the fretboard to fret the lowest string, or occasionally even the lowest two strings.

tie-block
The component of the bridge just behind the saddle, to which the strings are tied.

timbre
The character or quality of a musical sound, sometimes described as the 'tone colour'.

time signature
The underlying metre of the music.

In notation, the time signature appears as a pair of numbers on the stave at the beginning of the piece: the upper number indicates how many beats in each bar, the lower number indicates what note value each beat has.

tonic chord
If a piece of music is 'in C major', C is the tonic note and C major is the tonic chord. The tonic is the home note, or keynote.

transverse brace
A wooden bar that is used to support the soundboard, running from one rib to another.

triad
A three-note chord. In Western harmony, this is usually constructed using the root note, and notes a third and a fifth above this.

truss-rod
An adjustable steel rod within the neck of a guitar, designed to control the angle of the neck against the tension of the strings, and the pull that they exert on the neck.

tuning pegs
These are housed in the headstock and are turned in order to tune the strings.

voicings
The way the notes of a chord are arranged. A chord may be voiced in different ways, by using combinations of different strings or frets.

volute
A strengthening enlargement to the neck where it joins the headstock.

x-bracing
A pattern of bracing used for the tops of many classical and acoustic guitars.

RIGHT:
A square-necked resonator guitar, built by Kerry Char in 2000.

Index

BELOW: *Made by Ramírez in 1902, this is one of their more expensive models.*

LEFT: *This guitar is shaped like an early 17th-century viola da gamba.*

BELOW: *This wooden-bodied resonator was made by the Dobro company.*

Gilbert, John: classical guitar
    212
Gilberto, João 114
Giron, Claude: guitar 186
Gläsel, Mortz: guitar 192
glissando 101
golpeador 116, 167
Graham, Davey 60
Grappelli, Stéphane 112
Gray, David 33
green issues 171
"Greensleeves" 75
Gregory, Paul 217
Gretsch: Synchromatic 235
Guild: F212 224
guitarra latina 156

guitarra moresca 156
gypsy guitars 236–7
gypsy-jazz style 112–13

H

half-open chords 96–7
    chord diagrams 146–7
hammer-ons 68
hand positions 21
harmonic minor scale 112, 113
harmonics 100
harp-guitars 238–9
harp-lutes 190
Hauser, Hermann I 165
    Segovia model 206
    Viennese style guitar 206
Hauser, Hermann II: classical
    guitar 207
Hauser, Hermann III: classical
    guitar 207
Haynes, John: Tilton model
    guitar 195
Hernández, Santos 165, 166
    guitar 214
Hernández y Aguado: classical
    guitar 208
Hill, Kenny: FE18 210
Höfner: Committee 235
holding a guitar 20–1
Hopkins, Lightnin' 55
Hot Club Quintet 112
Humphrey, Thomas 170

I

improvisation 98–9
intervals 62

J

Jansch, Bert 97
jazz
    12-bar blues in 90–1
    chords 86–9
    classic licks 92–3
    dominant seventh voicings 138–9
    major seventh voicings 142–3
    minor seventh voicings 140–1
Jobim, Antonio Carlos 114
Johnson, Robert 219

K

Kaman, Charles 227
Keaggy, Phil 82
key changes *see* transposition
keys 60–1
Kohno, Masaru: classical guitar 210

L

Lacôte, René 162
    Decacorde 238
    six-string guitar 189
Lagoya, Alexandre 204

Lang, Eddie 98
Laprévotte, Etienne 211
Larrivée: C10 225
Larson Brothers 245
Latin jazz 114–15
lazy barres 96
Leadbelly 119
least movement principle 31
left-hand
    basic technique 22–3
    first position 44
Legnani, Luigi 163, 192, 193
Levin: Goliath 228
Light, Edward: dital-harp 190
Llobet, Miguel 164
Loar, Lloyd 168, 231
Lorca, Antonio de 162
Lowden, George: Richard
    Thompson Model 229
Lowe, Rohan: classical guitar 211
Lucas, Nick 218
Lucia, Paco de 167
lutes 156, 175
Lyon and Healy 169
lyre-guitar 184

M

m⁷♭⁵ chords 136–7
Maccaferri, Mauro 204
McCartney, Paul 41
McGhee, Brownie 52
major chords: chord diagrams 124–5
major seventh chords: chord
    diagrams 132–3
major seventh jazz voicings 142–3
mando-basses 244
mando-lyre 179
mandolins 178, 179
    resonator mandolins 243
Manson, Andy: Magpie Slide
    Slammer 228
Martin, C. F. & Co. 163, 168, 191
    0-28 220
    00-42 220
    2½-40 194
    "America" 222
    B-65 247
    Backpacker 223
    D-18 "Elvis guitar" 221
    Dreadnought 168, 170
    F-7 234
    OM-28 221
    N-20 222
    one-millionth guitar 223
    Stauffer model 194
Martín, Juan 167
Mauchant Frères: archtop guitar 196
melodies, integrating 74–5
Metheny, Pat 42
metronomes 21
Mills, John 217

minims 32
minor chords: chord diagrams
    126–7
minor seventh chords: chord
    diagrams 130–1
minor seventh jazz voicings 140–1
Mitchell, Joni 76
Molino, Ferdinando 184
Montoya, Carlos 167
Montoya, Ramón 167
montuno 115
Moretti, Federico 157, 161, 184
Morlaye, Guillaume 157
    Le Premier Livre 181
Mozzani, Luigi: harp-guitar 238
Mudarra, Alonso: *Tres Libros de
    Música en Cifra para Vihuela* 181
muting strings 84, 87

N

National: Tricone Square-neck 242
notation
    chord boxes/diagrams 23, 122
    chord slashes 57
    dots 45
    standard notation 32, 123
    tablature (tab) 33, 123
    ties 45
notes, finding 32, 64–5

O

octave relationships 64
"Ode to Joy" 43
offbeats 27
open D, essential chords in 150–1
open G, essential chords in 148–9
open tunings 80–3
ouds 156, 174
Ovation: Custom Legend 227

P

Pagés, Joséf 161, 162
    six-course guitar 185
Pagés, Juan: six-course guitar 185
pandura 156
Panormo, George Lewis:
    Bambina guitar (attrib.) 197
Panormo, Louis: guitars 162,
    163, 191
passing notes 38
Peña, Paco 167, 213
pickup bars 45
plectrums 21
position playing 42
practice 46
Prairie State Bass 245
Pratten, Madame Sidney 191, 197
Presti, Ida 204
Preston, John: cittern 177
Pujol, Emilio 164
pull-offs 69

ABOVE: *This Spanish guitar, with its beautifully carved head, was made by Francisco Simplicio in 1929.*

RIGHT: *The L5 is one of the classic Gibsons and was the first one to feature f-holes.*

BELOW: *This guitar was made by Antonio de Torres in 1864.*

ACKNOWLEDGEMENTS

The publisher would like to thank the following for their kind permission to reproduce photographs in this book. Abbreviations key: T = top, C = centre, B = bottom, R = right, L = left. All photography by Laurie Evans except the following: **AKG** 181R, Album / Oronoz / 6BL. **Alamy** Pictorial Press Ltd 145BR, The Art Archive 156BL, 157TL. **The Art Archive** Tate Gallery London / Eileen Tweedy 159BL. **Jeff Babicz** 155BL, 171TL. **Bruce Banister / fineandrareguitars.com** 204R, 206R, 209L. **Bibleoteca de Catalunya, Barcelona** 155TL, 158BL. **Bridgeman Art Library** Cincinnati Art Museum, Ohio, USA / Bequest of Mary M. Emery 160BL, Prado, Madrid, Spain / Index 160BR, Russell-Cotes Art Gallery and Museum, Bournemouth, UK 161C, Christie's Images 2C, 163TR, Isabella Stewart Gardner Museum, Boston, MA, USA 166TR, British Library, London, UK / British Library Board 175TR. **Rudi Bults** The Fellowship of Acoustics 179R. **C. F. Martin Archives** 168TC, 169TL, 171BR, 220L, 220R, 223L, 223R. **François Charle** 236L, 236R, 237L. **Chris Andrada** 222L. **Collection Musée de la Musique / Jean-Marc Anglès** 183R. **John Doan** 239R.

Fender Musical Instruments Corporation 246R. **Fotolia** Philippe Devanne 15CR. **Getty** 48BR, 92BR, 95TR, 166BL, 168BL, 209R, 219R, AFP 31TL, Buyenlarge 155TL, Cover 74CR, FilmMagic 33TL, Frank Driggs 98BR, Hulton Archive 225R, 97BR, 119CR, Michael Ochs Archives 135BR, 151BR, 114BL, Michael Ochs Archives/Stringer 25BR, 52BL, 55CR, 71TR, 73CR, Redferns 7TR, 41TR, 55TL, 60BR, 76BR, 133BR, 149BR, 165TL, 213R, 237R, 112BR, Rolls Press/Popperfoto 34BR, Stockbyte 157BR, Tom Copi 114BR, WireImage 42BL. **Guild of American Luthiers, www.luth.org** 196L. **Guitar Salon International** 205R. **Heritage Auctions** 224R, 231L, 235L. **Hill Guitar Company** Larry Darnell 210R. **Horniman Museum** 182R. **iStockphoto** grynold 120L. **Lebrecht Music and Arts** 164BL, 167TL. **London Guitar Studio** 217L. **Malcolm Maxwell** 33TR, 159TR, 163TL, 165CR, 167BR, 184R, 185TL, 185BL, 185R, 186L, 186C, 188R, 189L, 190L, 191L, 191C, 191R, 192L, 192R, 193TR, 196R, 197L, 197R, 198L, 198R, 199L, 199R, 200L, 201R, 201T, 206L, 211L, 214L, 217R, 233R, 238L, 240L, 240R, 241L, 241R. **Museu de la Música de Barcelona** 184L. **NASA Archives** 223R. **David E. Nelson** 5BR, 170BL, 213L. **Outline Press Ltd** 121BR, 182L, 195L, 195R, 207R, 210L, 214R, 219L, 221L, 221R, 222R, 224L, 225L, 226L, 226R, 228L, 228R, 229L, 234L, 234R, 235R, 245L, 246L, 246R, 247L. **Philkeaggy.com** 82BR. **Amalia Ramirez** 200R, 201L, 202L, 202R, 203L, 203R, 203TC, 204L. **Adrián Rius** 164TR. **Topfoto** Topham/Fotomas 162TC. **University of Iowa** Redpath Chautauqua Collection, University of Iowa Libraries, Iowa City 231R. **Victoria and Albert Museum** 187L, Manuel Terrero 189C, 189R. **Ulrich Wedemeier** 174R, 177L.

ABOVE: *This is a converted five-course guitar made c. 1770.*

With very special thanks to the following for allowing their guitars to be photographed: The National Music Museum in South Dakota, Gregg Miner, Jim Forderer, Taro Takeuchi, Miles Roberts at Kent Guitar Classics, David Crozier at Guitar Junction Ltd and Old School Guitars, Rainer Krause, Stefan Schwenteck, Malcolm Weller, Esteban Antonio, Rohan Lowe, Pablo Requena, Michael Shellim, Juan Teijerio at London Guitar Studio and James Westbrook.